Involving Children in Sunday Worship

Based on the Revised Common Lectionary, Year B

Forbid
Them
Not

Carolyn C. Brown

Abingdon Press
Nashville

FORBID THEM NOT:
INVOLVING CHILDREN IN SUNDAY WORSHIP
Based on the Revised Common Lectionary, Year B

00 01 02 03 04 05 06 07 08 — 15 14 13 12 11 10 9 8 7 6

This book is printed on recycled, acid-free paper.

Library of Congress Cataloging-in-Publication Data

(Revised for vol. 2)
Brown, Carolyn C. (Carolyn Carter), 1947–
  Forbid them not.
  Includes indexes.
    Contents: Year A— Year B —Year C.
    1. Children in public worship. 2. Common lectionary.
  3. Worship (Religious education) I. Title.
BV26.2.B76   1991   264'.0083   90-45012
ISBN 0-687-13256-8

Quotations from the Good News Bible—Old Testament—Copyright © American Bible Society
1976; New Testament—Copyright © American Bible Society 1966, 1971, 1976 are used by permission.
  Quotations from the New Revised Standard Version Bible, Copyright 1989 by the Division
of Christian Education of the National Council of the Churches of Christ in the USA are used
by permission.
  All readings taken from the *Revised Common Lectionary* © 1992 by the Consultation on Common
Texts are used by permission.

MANUFACTURED IN THE UNITED STATES OF AMERICA

CONTENTS

*This is one volume in a three-volume series. Each volume contains worship material for lectionary cycle A, B, or C. Since the lections for a few special days do not change from one lectionary cycle to another, material for each of these days appears in only one of the three volumes. Apropriate cross references in the table of contents lead the reader to material in other volumes of the series.

WHAT IS IN THIS BOOK, AND HOW CAN I USE IT ?

There seem to be two opposing camps when it comes to children's participation in congregational worship. On one side are those who say that worship is really for adults—that children should be taught to behave until they appreciate what is going on, or that they (and their parents) should be relieved by the provision of a children's church or other activity during the worship hour. On the other side are those who say that the congregation's worship should be reworked entirely, to make it appealing to children. Proponents of this side claim that once adults loosen up and begin to worship as children worship, they will not miss the staid old adult-oriented forms.

This series carves out a middle ground, based on the convictions that

• children *do* belong in the sanctuary, worshiping with God's people; that

• worship planners are responsible for creating worship experiences that are meaningful to all who come to the sanctuary, including children, youths, and adults (this does not require that all worshipers find all parts of worship equally meaningful, but that each worshiper has some appreciation for the whole, and special appreciation for certain parts within the whole); and that

• children can worship meaningfully, using traditional forms, *if* they are learning the meaning of those forms, and *if* the forms include content that reflects *their* lives and concerns as well as those of adults.

This book is written for worship leaders who share these views and want to be responsive to the elementary-school-aged children in worship, but who are uncertain about how to do this effectively and do not have large amounts of time to develop their skills in this area. It is written for those whose consciousness has been raised by books which advocate the inclusion of children in congregational worship, but who are at a loss for "what to do this Sunday."

This series offers specific suggestions for prayers, litanies, sermon illustrations, and ways to present Scripture that will include children without offending adults. Although it is based on the texts of the Revised Common Lectionary, those who do not follow that lectionary can use the index to locate suggestions related to any Scripture passages.

This series could be used by the pastor who plans worship alone, by a staff team, by a liturgical team which includes both clergy and laity, or by a worship committee. It is a reference to be used with commentaries and liturgical resources in preparing a service for each Sunday. As you gain confidence and insight into what is meaningful for children in your congregation, the ideas here should become springboards to other ideas and to home-grown prayers, litanies, and so on.

Materials for each Sunday include:

From a Child's Point of View, a commentary on each of the readings for the day. The main ideas of each passage are expressed in children's terms and connected to children's concerns. On Sundays when there is a reading that is best for children, that reading is presented first. When there is no central theme or focal reading, the texts are presented in lectionary order.

Watch Words offers vocabulary helps, warning against words that are beyond the understanding of elementary children or that are easily misunderstood by them; it suggests words that speak clearly to worshipers of all ages.

Let the Children Sing suggests several hymns (chosen from church hymnals) that are related to the Scripture themes, and which children can sing—at least in part. The assumption here is not that every hymn sung in worship ought to be child-accessible, but that one or two each week could be. These hymns have been chosen because they have concrete language, themes to which children respond, or tunes that are easily sung. Some have been included because of the repetition of a word, phrase, or chorus which even a nonreader can sing each time it appears—for instance, the Alleluias in "Christ the Lord is Risen Today."

The Liturgical Child outlines a variety of ways to use the passages in worship to bring them alive for children (and adults). Specific directions for dramatic readings, litanies, and congregational readings are given for some passages. Children's prayer concerns related to the theme or time of year are listed for inclusion in the congregation's prayers. And possibilities are raised for relating other parts of the worship service to the day's theme for children. No worship planner will use every idea offered for every week, but can select several that will fit the worship experience planned for the congregation.

Sermon Resources are offered in the belief that children do listen to at least parts of sermons and can learn from those parts. These resources are offered to be included in the "real" sermon rather than in a segregated children's sermon. The assumption is that if we communicate to children that the sermon is for them too, they will learn to listen to more and more of it as their attention span for verbal messages grows. So this section includes potential sermon illustrations and stories that will catch the attention of children and also will speak to adults, based on their childhood experience. Occasional sermon-related assignments for children to do during the sermon will be found here as well.

Finally, for each week there will be a one-page **Worship Worksheet**—a sheet of games, puzzles, or questions related to the day's passages. Just as children often work on projects (even homework) while they watch TV, they are often more apt to listen to the sermon if they have something to do with their hands.

When the minister expresses interest in their worksheets as the children leave the sanctuary, posts the sheets on a bulletin board in the narthex, or refers to them during the sermon, children can see that this activity is one way they can participate in worship. Both parents and children will realize that the Worship Worksheets are not just a clever attempt to keep children quiet so that the adults can worship.

The purchase of this book gives you permission to reproduce these Worship Worksheets for your children each week. Look carefully at each worksheet before reproducing it. Some, especially those for Propers in which the readings do not share one central theme, offer two half-page activities, each related to a separate theme. Choose the one that goes with your worship theme and enlarge it to full-page size on a copy machine. Then reproduce that page for the children. Unless they are enlarged, the half-page activities may not provide enough space for children to work.

The Worship Worksheets can be distributed by ushers as children enter the sanctuary, left in a designated place for the children or parents to pick up, or they can be placed in a Worship Kit.

A Worship Kit could be a large paper envelope or sealable plastic bag containing the Sunday bulletin, the Worship Worksheet, a small pencil, and bookmarks for marking the hymns and readings for the morning. Bookmarks can be made of strips of poster board decorated with appropriate stickers. To emphasize the church year, poster board of liturgically correct colors could be used. An older children's class, a group of teenagers, or an adult may be willing to prepare such bookmarks as a contribution to the congregation's worship life. Children can be asked to leave the bookmarks and pencil in the envelope, and the envelopes can be placed on their seats, to be picked up for use the next week.

Note: In some congregations the Worship Worksheets may be difficult to reproduce. Worship leaders in such congregations may focus their efforts on other suggestions.

FIRST SUNDAY OF ADVENT

From a Child's Point of View

Old Testament: Isaiah 64:1-9. The abstract theological language and poetic imagery of this passage are hard for children to understand. But its thought pattern is familiar: The writer begins to lash out at others, wishing that God would come in a dramatic display of power and set things right. But when he remembers that God has always come only to the righteous, he honestly admits that God has no reason to defend him and his people. Finally, he prays that God will love and protect them in spite of their failings.

Many angry children and adults go through the same process in praying about their frustrations with unjust people and situations.

Psalm: 80:1-7, 17-19. For children, the format of this psalm is more significant than its content—it is filled with poetic imagery and requires knowledge of the sweep of Old Testament history. In verses 1-2 and 4-6, a problem is described. The repeated response in verses 3 and 7 identifies God as the only one who can solve the problems. The format invites us to join the psalmist in describing the impossible situations we face and asking God to set them right. Some problems children describe include endless fighting in their family, addictions to drugs and alcohol, worries about having enough money for food and clothes, concern for the environment, and fears about war on the playground and in the world.

The response in verses 3, 7, and 19 needs to be paraphrased for young children: Rescue us, O God! Only you can lead us to peace and safety.

Gospel: Mark 13:24-37. Because children hear apocalyptic language literally, the dark sun, falling stars, and powerful quakes are frightening. When these vivid images are combined with the mini-parables, both of which need to be explained to children, young worshipers are overwhelmed by the diverse details. For them, the double message of the text is simply the promise that God will come (does come) and the warning to "stay awake!" This message may be best explored without direct reference to the specifics of the text or by focusing on only one subsection.

In its Advent context, the message is a reminder that God surprised people with Jesus and that God still surprises us by working among us today. We remember that God cares about the problems of the world and works to solve them. And we stay awake and on the job for God.

Epistle: I Corinthians 1:3-9. Paul greets the Corinthians, and all Christians who watch for God, with promises of God's presence and gifts. He warns children with long Christmas wish-lists not to overlook the gifts that God has already given them. Paul's abstract list needs to be translated into specific, recognizable gifts. "Knowledge and utterances" refers to all we know and do because we are part of a church. "Spiritual gifts" include our abilities that help us to do God's work—patience with younger children, ability to sing in the choir, and so on. God's strength is not so much to give us the power to do amazing feats as to give us the power to keep trying when we are discouraged. Paul insists that God has given each of us exactly what we need to "watch for God" and "work for God" effectively.

Watch Words

Advent means *coming*. During Advent we remember how people watched and waited for God to come in Jesus, and we watch and wait for God to come and work in our world and lives.

Several of today's texts speak of God's *anger*. Describe that anger as God's response to unfair, mean deeds. Differentiate between that and the violent anger some children experience at the hands of adults or older children.

Avoid *iniquity, unclean,* and *transgressions,* in favor of more common words such as *sin* and *wrongs.* When possible, speak of specific sins rather than *sin* in general.

Let the Children Sing

Though children have trouble following the meaning of the words of "Watchman Tell Us of the Night," they catch the sense of watching when they join in singing it responsively. One half of the congregation could sing the traveler's lines, with the other half singing the watchman's responses. Or the congregation could sing the traveler's lines to the choir or to a soloist taking the part of the watchman.

The imagery and vocabulary of "Hail to the Lord's Anointed" fit today's texts but are hard for children. To help children learn this traditional hymn, read the words of verse 2, put them into your own words, and relate them to today's theme before the hymn is sung. Children, who might otherwise give up on the whole hymn, can then focus on this one verse.

"Open My Eyes That I May See," though filled with abstract language, is a good prayer for people who watch for signs of God at work during Advent. Encourage younger children to sing at least the first phrase of each verse.

The Liturgical Child

1. Light the first candle of the Advent wreath, saying:

> We light the first candle of the Advent wreath to remind ourselves to stay awake and watch for signs of God at work in our world. Mary and Joseph were ready to be parents to God's Son.

The shepherds left their sheep to see the baby the angels told them about. The wise men took a long trip, following the star, to find Jesus. So stay awake! Keep on the job! God is at work today! Do not miss out!

2. With your voice, indicate the change from self-righteousness to honest reflection in verses 4-5 of Isaiah 64. Read verses 1-4 loudly, proudly calling down God's anger on those who deserve it. End verse 4 abruptly, caught by what you have said. Pause briefly, then read the phrases of verses 5-7 with thoughtful self-inspection. Pause again before the "Yet" of verse 8 to draw attention to the new prayer that grows from this reflection. The brief phrases of The New Jerusalem Bible emphasize the thought-progression in verses 5-7.

3. Base a prayer of petitions on the format of Psalm 80. A leader offers a series of prayers about current situations that need God's attention in families, communities, and the world. After each prayer, the congregation responds with Psalm 80:3, or a paraphrase of it. (Children and adults see many of the same problems in the world. Describing those problems in specific, concrete terms rather than long, abstract generalities enables children to share the prayers—e.g., name the fears of the soldiers in two armies lined up against each other and pray for their leaders, rather than praying about "powers confronting each other with violence in the world.")

Sermon Resources

1. Begin by describing situations which you think only God could rectify. Include some that involve children. Then invite children to draw pictures, on the backs of bulletins or on other paper, of situations they wish God would fix. As children leave the sanctuary, speak to them briefly about what they have drawn. Consider posting their work.

2. To paraphrase Jesus' story about the servants left at work by the traveling master, tell about a child who was hired by neighbors to care for their cat while they were on vacation for two weeks. When the family returned earlier than planned, they found the cat's litter dirty, the food and water dishes empty, and several crushed drink cans that had been taken from the refrigerator. The hired child, who had not expected them to return so soon, was very embarrassed.

ADVENT

begins today. During Advent we remember how people watched and waited for Jesus. We also watch for signs of God at work today.

Signs are put along highways to warn drivers about what is ahead. Draw some signs for Advent about God's work.

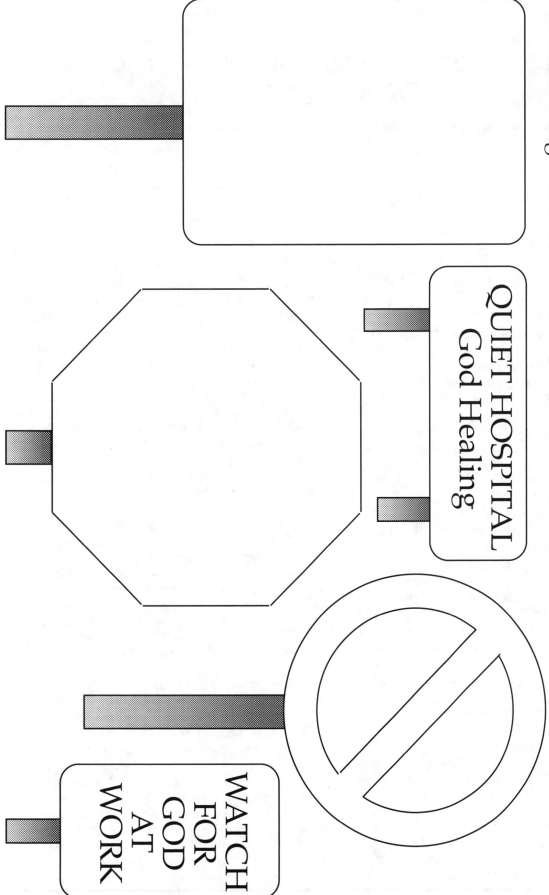

QUIET HOSPITAL
God Healing

WATCH
FOR
GOD
AT
WORK

SECOND SUNDAY OF ADVENT

From a Child's Point of View

Old Testament: Isaiah 40:1-11. Children are confused by the profusion of poetic images in this familiar Advent prophecy and generally tune out before the end of the reading. They are more likely to hear and remember one or two phrases that are repeated in the liturgy than to recall the message of the passage.

The first two verses must be read in historical context and speak mainly to adults who have enough life experience to appreciate the promise of relief. Some older children find in the phrase, " 'Comfort, O comfort my people,' says your God" reassurance that God cares for us.

The action called for in verses 3-5 sounds like a massive construction project to literal thinkers. They immediately picture bulldozers and cranes they have seen along the roads. So they depend on the preacher to give everyday examples of ways we are to build a highway for God.

The message of verses 6-11, especially verses 6-8, is beyond children's experience and understanding. (Consider omitting them to focus on verses 1-5.) The image of God as a caring shepherd in verse 11, however, assures older children that they can depend on God's love and care.

Psalm: 85:1-2, 8-13. The poetic images of this passage strike children as strange. They tend to giggle at their mental pictures of two human forms named Righteousness and Peace kissing each other, and one named Faithfulness exploding up out of the ground. Explaining all this is more trouble than it is worth to either preachers or children. So read this for adults and trust that children will hear and appreciate it later in their lives.

Epistle: II Peter 3:8-15a. The adults in the early church were concerned about why Jesus had not yet returned in glory. Children, however, live very much in the present. The future return of Christ is significant to them only because of what it says about the present world. If that return is presented as a fearful judgment, children view the world as a dangerous place, under the control of a threatening God. If the return is presented by recalling that God was here in the beginning and that God also will be at the end of the world, children view the world as a safe place, under the care of a loving, powerful God. The difference is critical to their feelings about the world and their place in it.

As the year 2000 approaches, more and more end-of-the-world talk is likely. Children are particularly frightened by groups that set specific dates and make vivid claims about what will happen on that date. They need to be told to ignore all such claims. When specific claims are being touted in the community, children need to be assured that those claims are false. The Bible repeatedly insists that Jesus' return will surprise everyone.

Gospel: Mark 1:1-8. Children in congregations which practice mainly infant baptism need help in understanding the purpose of John's "baptism of repentance for the forgiveness of sins." Explain that it was a ceremony people carried out to show that they were going to make some changes in the way they lived. Underlying that baptism was, and is, the belief that we can change. Children often believe just the opposite. They feel trapped by what is demanded of them at home and school. They sense that both adults and peers expect them to behave in certain ways and would be suspicious of any changes, even for the better. They feel powerless to change their behavior or to resolve difficult situations that confront their families and friends.

In this passage, John insists that we can make changes. He baptized with water to call his listeners (and us) to make needed changes. He promised that "the One who comes" would give the people the power of Holy Spirit, so that they could make even greater changes. Help the children celebrate this power that has been given to them.

Watch Words

Repent may be a new word. Use *change* as it's synonym, to build understanding and familiarity with it. John wanted people to *change* their ways.

Avoid theological abstractions about *confession* and *repentance*. Speak instead about *making changes* in our lives, to live more like God's people.

Let the Children Sing

"Lord, I Want to Be a Christian" is the most child-accessible hymn about making changes. Focus on what "more" we can be. Consider creating new verses to match the changes suggested in today's sermon.

Sing about God's dependable care, with the hymn version of Psalm 23 that is most familiar. (Children understand paraphrases of the psalm more readily than the shepherd hymns filled with theological language about its meaning.)

The Liturgical Child

1. Open worship with John's call to prepare the way of the Lord. Begin with a trumpet fanfare from the back of the sanctuary. Then have Isaiah 40:3-5 either sung or read by a strong male voice, also from the back of the sanctuary. Worship leaders and choirs then process on a hymn such as "Come Christians, Join to Sing" (even nonreaders can join in on the Alleluias), or a musical setting of John's call (the musical "Godspell" offers a very effective one).

2. Light the first two candles of the Advent wreath, saying:

Last week we lighted a candle to remind ourselves to watch for places where God is at work in the world. Because God is at work, we can light a candle this week for change. God calls us to make changes. God calls each of us to make some changes in what we do and say at home, at school, at work, and with our friends. And God calls us all to work together to change our world to make it more fair for everyone. Advent is a time for making changes for God.

3. If you sing the Gloria Patri regularly, feature "As it was in the beginning, is now, and ever shall be" today. Either,

A. point out the phrase, put it into your own words, and note that when we sing it, we, like Isaiah and the psalmist, say that God was God in the beginning and always will be God. Or,

B. use the phrase as a congregational response to a litany praising God, who creates and takes loving care of the world in the past, the present, and the future.

4. Have each section of the Isaiah lection read by a different reader, perhaps including readers of different ages. For example, an older adult reads verses 1-2, an older child reads verses 3-5, a mid-adult reads verses 6-8, and a teenager reads verses 9-11. All need to be standing near a microphone so that they can step up to it to read in quick succession.

Sermon Resources

1. One symbol for God's presence from the beginning through the end of history is the combined Alpha and Omega. Explain the meaning of the letters and point out any Alpha and Omega symbols among your Chrismons, on paraments, or carved or painted in your sanctuary. (Use a flashlight to highlight those that are out of reach.)

2. Recall children's questions about God:
   If God made the world, who made God?
   What was there before there was God?
   What will God do after the world is over?
In responding to them, describe the attributes of God upon which we can depend.

3. Build the entire sermon around a comparison of the construction of a highway and "preparing the way of the Lord." Discuss deciding where to build the road, clearing the land, grading the road bed, paving for heavy traffic, and landscaping.

Use the Key to decode these Advent phrases: Draw a star ★ by each one every time you hear it in worship today.

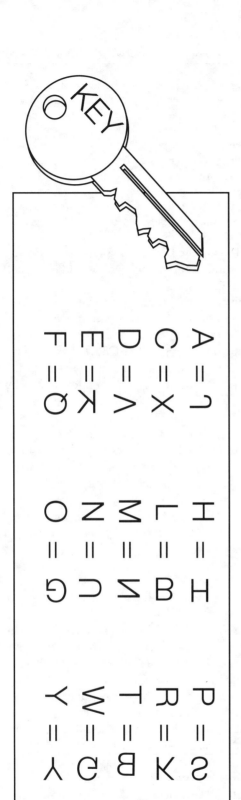

KEY

A = ꟼ	H = H	L = B	P = S
C = X		R = K	
D = Λ	M = И	T = B	
E = Ƶ	N = U	W = Ɡ	
F = Ꝺ	O = O	Y = ʎ	
	G = Ꞡ		

Advent Phrases: Prepare the way of the Lord! Repent! Comfort, O comfort my people!

Second Sunday of Advent | © 1993 by Abingdon Press.

THIRD SUNDAY OF ADVENT

From a Child's Point of View

Today's theme is joy. To children, it seems that Christmas joy is based on the parties, presents, decorations, and family visits. It will take work to help them identify and respond to the reasons for Christmas joy found in today's texts.

Old Testament: Isaiah 61:1-4, 8-11. The changes in speakers and poetic imagery make this passage difficult for children to follow. Older children will catch occasional phrases and, if the passage is read with joy, will hear its joyful feeling. However, all children will depend on the preacher to point out the source of Isaiah's joy.

Isaiah cites three reasons for our Christmas joy. First, God is on the side of the underdog (verses 1-4). This is happy news for children in a world controlled by older people. It is happier news to children who feel they are not as smart or athletic or popular as their peers. It is the happiest news to children who feel they are undervalued because of their race, economic standing, and so on.

Second, God loves justice—or in children's words, fairness or fair play (vs. 8). Elementary children are extremely interested in fair rules for clubs and games, and they value adults whom they feel treat children fairly. Because even privileged children often feel that they are not fairly treated, knowing that God wants fairness is a cause for joy among children.

Third, God has saved us (verse 10). During Advent, that saving is illustrated by telling the story of God coming to live among us.

Psalm: 126 or Luke 1:47-55. (The psalm is preferred for this day. See the fourth Sunday of Advent for notes and ideas for Luke 1:47-55,

which is preferred for that day.) Especially if it is read with feeling from The Good News Bible, children hear the joy in this psalm. Without knowing the historical context or unraveling the verses about planting and harvesting, they can understand that the psalmist's happiness is a response to something God has done. Children gain more by using verses 1-3 as their own response to what God did at Christmas, and what God does for us today, than by hearing explanations of the historical context and references.

Epistle: I Thessalonians 5:16-24. Verses 16 through 18 are the easiest for children to understand and offer most for them to think about during the final days before Christmas. During a week that often includes participation in Christmas programs and parties at school and in organizations, it is easy for children to be swept up in selfish wants, and fears that they are being slighted. It is also easy to become tired and crabby. Paul urges children (and the rest of us) to remember what we are celebrating and to be thankful and happy. On this third Sunday of Advent, verses 23-24, especially as translated in the Good News Bible, may then invite the preacher to outline specific ways we can celebrate Christmas faultlessly and completely—with spirit, soul, and body.

Gospel: John 1:6-8, 19-28. The key word for children in this text is *witness*. John responded to what God was doing through Jesus by becoming a witness. He talked to everyone who would listen. We are called to follow John's example and share the joy of God's Christmas activity with others. We can be joyful witnesses.

Watch Words

Do not call children to *rejoice* or speak about *Christmas joy* without citing specific reasons for such activities and feelings.

Children use the word *fair* before they use either *just* or *justice*. Point out that the words mean the same thing. Then use them interchangeably to help children learn the connection.

Witness means to see and tell what happened. At Christmas we are to *witness* to what God has done and is doing.

Let the Children Sing

Young readers can join in on the repeated "rejoices" in the chorus of "Rejoice, Ye Pure in Heart."

The words of "There's a Song in the Air," while not familiar, are simple enough for older children to read as they sing this carol about the spread of Christmas joy.

Both "Joy to the World" and "O Come, All Ye Faithful" are filled with joy, but are also filled with long, difficult words. Children respond more to the music than to the words of these carols, so if you sing these, have the organist pull out all the stops and set an upbeat tempo.

Sing about witnessing Christmas joy with "Go Tell It on the Mountain."

The Liturgical Child

1. Light the first three candles of the Advent wreath, saying:

We lighted the first candle of the Advent wreath to remind ourselves to watch for God at work in our world. We lighted the second candle to remember the changes God wants us to make. And today, we happily light the third candle of the Advent wreath for joy. We light this candle because God loves us and takes care of us. We light it because God pays special attention to the people others ignore and overlook. We light it because God came to live among us as a tiny baby, who grew into a man who loved and taught and healed and died to save us. This is the candle of Christmas joy.

2. Invite older children or youths to pantomime

the Gospel text as it is read. As verses 6-8 are read, "John" takes his place at the center of the chancel. The questioners enter on verse 19 and use their bodies and hands to emphasize their questions. John responds with his hands and body. All leave on verse 28. Simple costumes add a lot. One good practice session is essential.

3. Create a litany that expresses Christmas joy. The worship leader describes the joy of someone involved in the birth of Jesus (Mary, Elizabeth, the shepherds, wise men, and so forth) and the joy of people today. The congregation responds with the psalmist's words, "How we laughed, how we sang for joy!" For example:

Leader: Elizabeth was very old when she became pregnant with her son, John the Baptist. Mary was a poor girl living in a small town in an unimportant country when she was chosen by God to be Jesus' mother. Mary went to stay with Elizabeth while they waited for their sons to be born.

People: How we laughed, how we sang for joy!

4. Use I Thessalonians 5:16-18 as the Charge and I Thessalonians 5:23-24 as the Benediction. Read or recite from The Good News Bible.

Sermon Resources

1. *How the Grinch Stole Christmas*, by Dr. Suess, is a book that has been turned into a yearly TV special. Like Ebeneezer Scrooge in Dickens' *Christmas Carol*, the Grinch is disgusted by Christmas. After attempting to stop it by stealing the presents and food on Christmas Eve, the Grinch discovers that Christmas joy is based on more than presents and parties.

2. Straighten out children's misconceptions about how several Christmas customs express our joy. Adult comments often lead children to conclude that we participate in such activities as caroling in nursing homes and gathering food and gifts for the poor in order to remind ourselves of our own security and health, and therefore to become more joyful. Children also get the idea that we give gifts to show how much we like and love one another, rather than to share our joy. The Christian gives a gift to say, "I am so happy about what God has done and is doing that I want to share that happiness. So here is a gift which I hope will give you happiness."

Collect the **Christmas Joy** words
we use in worship today.
Write each one you hear in the
space below.

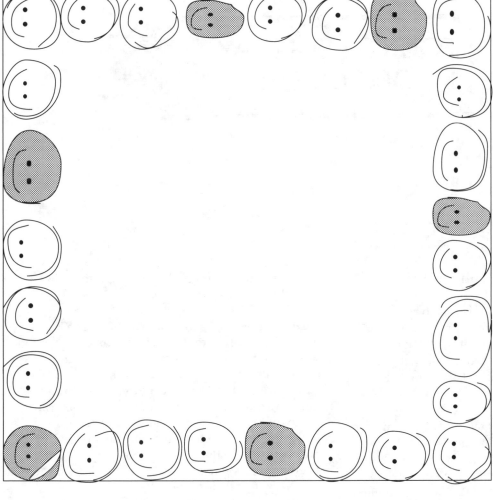

Some words to listen for:
Alleluia, **Happy**, REJOICE!

Make a Christmas card about
Christmas Joy. Draw a picture
and write some words about what
makes you joyful at Christmas.

Third Sunday of Advent | © 1993 by Abingdon Press.

FOURTH SUNDAY
OF ADVENT

From a Child's Point of View

Today's texts focus on two of God's promises. David is given a promise which is kept when Mary is told about the birth of Jesus. Mary is given a promise that she will be the mother of God's Messiah. That promise is also kept.

Old Testament: II Samuel 7:1-11, 16. Children enjoy this story, but cannot follow it as it is read from the Bible. They depend on the preacher to retell it, eliminating the overwhelming details to focus on the key events: David offered to build a house (a temple) for God. God replied that God did not need a house, but would give a dynasty (a different kind of house) to David. Because they like riddles and jokes based on word plays, children enjoy God's humorous word play on "house" when it is pointed out.

Gospel: Luke 1:26-38. The story of the Annunciation may not be familiar to all children. If they are hearing the story for the first time, the conception vocabulary can be a major obstacle to understanding. To bypass this obstacle, simply say that Mary would become pregnant even though she was not yet married. Older children and soap opera-wise children will add the details using their own vocabulary. (The Good News Bible offers the best translation of these terms but may not be the best choice today because it does not use the "house of David" terms which connect this story to the Old Testament reading.)

All children accept the story literally and take it at face value. Questions about the meaning of the doctrine of the Virgin birth are beyond their mental ability.

Luke 1:47-55 or Psalm 89:1-4, 19-26. (The Magnificat is the preferred reading for this Sunday.) The Magnificat is Mary's response to the Annunciation. Psalm 89 is the psalmist's response to God's promise to David. Children need to hear the stories behind these poems before they can make any sense of the poems. Even then, they will respond more to the feelings expressed by the poets than to the content of the poetic images. Therefore, it is important that the readers of the poems express their confident joy.

David, the shepherd boy chosen to be king of a struggling nation which became strong under his leadership, could also have sung the Magnificat. Older children enjoy identifying people today who either long to sing or can sing this song. They also enjoy naming times in their own lives that make them want to sing Mary's song.

Epistle: Romans 16:25-27. This doxology is the least child-accessible of today's texts. No translation makes it meaningful to children. So read this for the adults.

Watch Words

Do not use *Annunciation* without identifying the story to which it is connected, and do not use *Magnificat* without explaining its Latin base.

Do not expect children to catch the play on *house* in II Samuel. Explain what kind of *house* David intended to build for God and what kind of *house* God promised to David.

18

Let the Children Sing

"To a Maid Engaged to Joseph" tells the Annunciation story in words older children can read with understanding. Its simple melody is easy to sing the first time.

"My Soul Gives Glory to My God" ("Song of Mary" in some hymnals) by Miriam Therese Winter invites us to sing along with Mary. Older children can read the words. Younger children will follow the first two verses before getting lost in difficult words.

"There's a Song in the Air," "Gentle Mary Laid Her Child," and "What Child Is This?" are carols that focus on Mother and Child in fairly simple, concrete language.

The Liturgical Child

1. Light all four candles of the Advent wreath, saying:

> We light the fourth candle of the Advent wreath for the promises God made and kept. Today we especially remember God's promise to David that his family would be rulers forever, and God's promise to Mary that she would have a son who would be a Savior and ruler of the world. As we light this candle, we know that God kept those promises when Jesus was born, lived, taught us, died for us, and rose again. God keeps promises!

2. Introduce the Old Testament and Gospel lessons as stories that belong together. With a few comments about promises made and kept, read the lessons one after the other.

3. Ask a teenage girl to present the Magnificat as a dramatic reading or recitation. She may read at a lectern or stand in costume at the center of the chancel. Practice with her for a strong reading.

4. Children's Christmas excitement is at fever pitch this week. In the church's prayer, remember their excitement about visiting grandparents and cousins, parties, and hoped-for presents. Also pray about selfishness and tired crabbiness that can get in the way this week.

5. Create a litany about the promises God has made and kept. Briefly describe God's promise to Abraham and Sarah, the rainbow promise to Noah, the promise to the slaves in the desert that "I will be your God and you will be my people,"

and so forth. Begin each description with "God promised . . . " and conclude each with, "And God did." The congregation's response to each promise is, "We can count on God to keep the promises!"

Sermon Resources

1. Knock-knock jokes are one way children celebrate and explore the humorous possibilities in word plays. Tell a knock-knock joke to prepare listeners to catch and enjoy God's play on the word *house*. For example:

Knock! Knock!
Who's there?
Apple (repeat first three lines several times)
Knock! Knock!
Who's there?
Orange
Orange who?
Aren't ya (sounds like "orange") glad I didn't say "apple" again?

2. Talk about our promises. Children are allowed to go out if they promise to be back at a set time. Parents coax hesitant young swimmers to jump into the pool with the promise, "I'll catch you!" Scouts recite and are urged to keep the Scout promise. Children make promises to each other to meet at the park, to write from camp, to keep their secret, and so forth. "But you PROMISED!" is the anguished response when any of these promises is broken. Adults have learned to place different values on different promises and to accept that promises can be broken. For children, a promise is a promise and should be completely dependable. God keeps promises on children's terms.

3. Consider a dialog sermon in which Mary and David (in costume) compare and contrast their experiences with God's promises. Some points to discuss:

• Both were poor nobodies who were chosen by God;
• both were given a promise and a task; and
• both were promised that God would bring blessings through them.

4. As they leave the sanctuary, speak briefly with children about the pictures they drew and the Magnificats they wrote using the worship worksheet.

Listen as **Luke 1 : 26 - 38** is read.
Draw a picture of what happened.

MAGNIFICAT means " I praise."

Listen when Mary's MAGNIFICAT
is read from **Luke 1 : 47 - 55.**
What did Mary praise God for?

I praise God for . . .

I praise God for _____

Now write your own MAGNIFICAT.
What do you praise God for on this
Sunday before Christmas?

_____'s MAGNIFICAT

I praise God for _____

CHRISTMAS EVE/DAY
(THIRD PROPER)

Note: The lectionary offers three sets of readings for Christmas Eve/Day. The readings are identical in each of the three cycles. In this series, Year A offers the second Christmas Proper (texts from the Roman Shepherd's Mass held at dawn on Christmas Day); Year B offers the third Christmas Proper (texts for later in the day or on the Sunday following Christmas); Year C offers the first Christmas Proper (the traditional texts for Christmas Eve). Any of the three is appropriate for use at any Christmas Eve or Day worship service.

The lessons of the Third Proper include no telling of the Christmas story, but only theological statements about its significance. While they are not the first choice for congregations which include large numbers of children, neither are they totally inaccessible to children. Children, though unable to appreciate the intellectual points of these texts, do respond to their awe in the face of God with us. Carefully planned liturgical presentation of the texts offers more to children than does the sermon. Review Years A and C for additional ideas for Christmas Eve/Day.

From a Child's Point of View

Gospel: John 1:1-14. Older children are interested in the fact that while Matthew and Luke begin their good news about Jesus with stories about his birth, Mark starts with Jesus as a man, and John introduces us to Jesus with a poem about who Jesus is. With this information, they are ready to listen for what John tells us about Jesus.

To understand what they hear, they need to be told that "the Word" was sort of a code word for Jesus. Everything the Word was or did, John said that Jesus was or did. Thus prepared, children can learn from the poem that Jesus was with God at Creation, that Jesus is the source of all life, that Jesus was not accepted by many people he met, and that Jesus makes us God's children. The most intriguing of these statements is that Jesus and God are one and that Jesus was at the beginning and will be at the end. On Christmas, children need to hear that no one understands how these things can be. They are mysteries—truths that we know but cannot explain. The New Revised Standard Version offers the best translation of the Prologue for children.

Epistle: Hebrews 1:1-4 (5-12). Verses 1-4 answer the question, "Why is Jesus important?" by stating that God spoke to us through Jesus. The writer notes that this was not the only time God had spoken and mentions prophets and angels as examples of God's other efforts. Children recognize that God speaks to us also through the Bible, through the beauty of the natural world, and through other people (often teachers). When they hear some of the things described that God told us through Jesus, they agree that God spoke to us most clearly in Jesus.

The comparison of Jesus to the angels is rather peripheral for Christmas Eve. But children are curious about angels, and if the optional verses are read dramatically, with pauses between the related quotes and careful inflection within the quotes, children grasp the writer's point. The Good News Bible is the easiest translation for children to understand.

Psalm: 98. Children will catch occasional phrases in this praise psalm. Particularly, they will hear the opening call to sing to God, who has done marvelous things; the familiar call to make a joyful noise (verse 4) with songs and instruments (verses 4-6); and the call for seas and hills to join in the praise (verses 7-8). These concrete praises are easy for children to own as their response to the events of Christmas.

Old Testament: Isaiah 52:7-10. This text is too complicated for children, especially on Christmas. Its images baffle concrete thinkers and require knowledge of the Exile and Return. This one is for the grown-ups.

Watch Words

For children, *Word* is simply a code word for Jesus. Christmas Eve or Day is not the time to use or introduce *Logos*.

Let the Children Sing

"Joy to the World!" (based on Psalm 98), "O Come, All Ye Faithful," and "Hark, the Herald Angels Sing" express the triumph of Christ come to earth that is found in the texts. All three carols are, however, filled with long words—*exultation*—and strange phrases—"Veiled in flesh the Godhead see." Because children generally learn Christmas carols by hearing them rather than by reading them, there are often misconceptions. Children respond more to the feel of the music than to the meaning of the words. So if you sing them, keep the tempo and sound bright and strong.

Even nonreaders can join in on the repeated lines of "Good Christian Friends, Rejoice."

The Liturgical Child

1. Since these lessons assume knowledge of the Christmas story, present the story in tableau before the service begins. Invite worshipers to arrive early enough to stop by a live nativity scene outside or to get a close look at a tableau in the chancel. If this is done in the sanctuary, replace the prelude with carol singing. Sing the first verse of story-telling carols that are familiar to children. Something to do while waiting for worship to begin is appreciated both by children, fueled with Christmas sugar and excitement, and by the adults who sit with them.

2. To set the mood of quiet wonder, begin with a soloist walking slowly down the center aisle (perhaps carrying a candle), singing "I Wonder as I Wander" or "What Child Is This?"

3. Light the four Advent candles and the Christ candle, saying:

> Tonight we light the four candles of Advent waiting. We light one for the people who waited for hundreds of years for God's Messiah. We light one for Mary and Joseph waiting for Jesus to be born. We light one for all the waiting we have done getting ready for this night. We light one for all the people who are still waiting tonight for God's love and justice and peace. But tonight, we can finally light the Christ Candle. Jesus is born! The Messiah has *come!* So let us all say, "Merry Christmas!"

4. If you celebrate Holy Communion, introduce it as the feast table of King Jesus. Describe what people are wearing as they gather tonight in different climates. Name some of the different languages they are using to sing and pray. Then point out that all of them are worshiping the same King Jesus, who is Lord of the whole world. Identify the words of institution as words addressed to all these different people who love Jesus and are loved by Jesus.

5. Read Psalm 98 in the New Revised Standard Version as the Charge and Benediction. Conclude with, "Merry Christmas! Indeed!" or "Let all the people say,'Merry Christmas! Amen.'"

Sermon Resources

Remember that on Christmas Eve or Day, few children follow any sermon. They participate more fully in liturgy that is planned with their excitement and concerns in mind.

1. With several Chrismons, illustrate the nature of Christ as outlined in these texts. Point them out in their places on the tree with a flashlight beam. Alpha and Omega stand for Jesus' presence at both the beginning and the end of time. The stars stand for the light Jesus brought to the world. The crowns stand for Jesus' rule of the world. Crosses remind us that Jesus' rule is based on his forgiving love and death.

There is no Worship Worksheet for this service. The mood and stories of Christmas worship should be so dramatic that papers and pencil would get in the way.

FIRST SUNDAY AFTER CHRISTMAS

From a Child's Point of View

Gospel: Luke 2:22-40. Because children are interested in babies, they are interested in what happened during this Temple rite. Comparing the purposes of those rites to today's baptism or dedication of infants is helpful. Both are ways of saying that this baby is one of God's people.

The stories of Simeon and Anna will be unfamiliar to most children. But during a week that may include visits with grandparents, children will be interested in these two older people. Again, Luke tells of God's singling out two unimportant people to recognize the Christ Child. Both Anna and Simeon were very old and, as far as we know, did nothing noteworthy during their long lives. They simply lived day to day, worshiping God and loving people around them. The implication is that God approved of their dedicated lives and that people who live as Anna and Simeon did will also be able to recognize God at work.

Epistle: Galatians 4:4-7. Children recognize and follow the opening summary of Jesus' birth, then quickly get lost in the maze of references to the Law, to adoption, and to sonship. Paul's complex point is beyond them. Children may, however, hear from the preacher an invitation to be God's children, calling upon God as Jesus did.

Psalm: 148. Today this is a response to God's love as expressed in the birth of Jesus and in the joy and happiness the worshipers have experienced while celebrating this Christmas. Younger children enjoy the calls to specific animals, weather, and other parts of creation to praise God. They quickly add their own calls to other parts of the universe to join the praise. Older children realize that animals and inanimate objects cannot praise God in the same way humans can. They are more comfortable in addressing new calls for praise to different groups of people. Its simple words and familiar vocabulary make this a psalm that middle-elementary students can read with the congregation.

Old Testament: Isaiah 61:10-62:3. The profusion of poetic images make this the least child-accessible of today's texts. If the clothing images of verse 10 and the garden images of verse 11 are illustrated in concrete detail, and the meaning of the verses is presented in paraphrase, as below, children will begin to get the prophet's point.

> I will rejoice in the Lord!
> My whole being will praise my God!
> God has dressed me with saving love
>   and covered me up with righteousness
> In God's clothes, I am as well dressed as
>   a bridegroom and bride wearing their very
>   best clothes, jewels, and flowers.
> Just as the earth makes plants grow,
> God makes justice and praise grow for all to
>   see.

Watch Words

Dedication is used a little differently in the texts today from the way we generally use it in church. Today it is a specific ritual for first-born Jewish sons. They were "set aside for" or *dedicated* for God. Parents then reclaimed their sons by paying a small ransom to the priest in charge. The Bible tells us that some special sons, such as Samuel, and perhaps Jesus, were not paid for and thus

23

remained set aside for God. Point out signs that identify items or buildings at your church that are *dedicated* to God.

Let the Children Sing

"All Creatures of Our God and King" parallels the praises of Psalm 148 and is filled with Alleluias that even nonreaders can join in on.

Before singing "Angels from the Realms of Glory," point out the clue words with which the verses begin. These words tell us who we will be singing about in that verse. If the last verse in your hymnal begins with the line "Saints before the altar bending," suggest that Simeon and Anna are two such saints, bending before the altar in Jerusalem. Younger children will simply join in on the repeated chorus.

"Good Christian Friends, Rejoice," with its repeated phrases, is another good choice for young readers.

The Liturgical Child

1. Light the four Advent candles and the Christ candle, saying:

> Today we light the four candles of Advent waiting. But we also light the Christmas candle, the Christ candle. We light it because Jesus was born in Bethlehem in a barn. We light it because Jesus showed us how much God loves us. We light it because Jesus died and rose again to forgive us. We light it because Jesus is our Lord!

2. See The Liturgical Child #1 in Year A of this series for a responsive congregational reading of Psalm 148.

3. Keep the Christmas pageant going. Ask a couple with a young infant to play Mary, Joseph, and Jesus. Ask two older members of the congregation to take the roles of Simeon and Anna. These costumed actors pantomime the story as it is read. Simeon takes the baby in his arms, raises his head to address the "Nunc Dimittis" to God, then turns to speak to the parents before returning the baby to them. Anna then comes close to see the baby. With happy face, she turns to God, her arms outstretched in the classical position of praise. You may want one reader or two, with a man reading Simeon's story and a woman reading Anna's. The Good News Bible offers the easiest translation for children.

4. Choose a musical version of "Nunc Dimittis" for the benediction. Many new hymnals include several versions. In "The Song of Simeon," Simeon's request to depart in peace (having seen God's Son) can be shared by worshipers who are departing from worship in peace after celebrating the birth of that Son. The words of this version are simple enough for children to understand. The tune is a lilting folk melody.

5. Remember children's week-after-Christmas concerns in the church's prayers. After weeks of parties and anticipated gifts, there is little left to look forward to. Some children probably were disappointed; others may have received the gifts they wanted but found them less satisfying than they expected. And the winter weather may have everyone cooped up in the house.

Sermon Resources

1. Compare the experiences of Mary, Joseph, and Jesus during the days after Christmas with our experiences during the days after Christmas. Describe the hassles of return trips: Their trip with a newborn baby and our trips back home after enjoyable but tiring Christmas trips. Tell about the dedication in the Temple with Simeon's greeting and warning, and about settling down as a family in Nazareth. Point out that God continued to work in the everyday events of their lives. Then point out that God is still at work and needs our help in the dreary days after Christmas as much as during the exciting days before Christmas.

2. As the children leave the sanctuary, remember to speak with them about the pictures and poems they created on the Worship Worksheet.

Listen to **Psalm 148**. If the poet said to you, "Praise God!" what would you say? Think about Christmas and write 4 praises for God.

Praise God _____

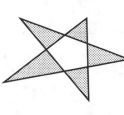

Praise God _____

Praise God _____

Praise God _____

Use the decorated-ball code to find what Luke said about the boy Jesus.

"He ___ ___ ___ and became ___ ___ ___ ___ ___ ___, filled with ___ ___ ___ ___ ___ ___; and the favor of was upon him." (Luke 2 : 40)

⊕=D	⊕=M	⊗=G	⊕=I
⊘=E	⊙=W	☺=S	⊘=R
⊚=O	⊕=T	●=N

First Sunday After Christmas | © *1993 by Abingdon Press.*

NEW YEAR'S EVE/DAY

From a Child's Point of View

The beginning of the new year is a good time to look at our world and our place in it. Ecclesiastes outlines the patterns in that world. The psalmist praises God's work in creation and ponders our place in the world God created. Jesus reminds us that we are called to make a difference in the world; then he tells us how to do that. And John promises that, even when it seems least so, God is in control.

Old Testament: Ecclesiastes 3:1-13. Children hear paraphrases of this passage regularly, even from Bible-illiterate parents, as they try to teach children that they cannot always do what they wish, but must live within established patterns— "There is a time for playing and a time for doing your homework." Children both love and hate those patterns. They find security in following daily schedules at home and school. Just try to shorten the bedtime ritual in order to leave for a meeting and hear the howl of protest. And even the most rebellious child will admit that when bedtime is ignored too many nights in a row, trouble follows.

But like Qoheleth, children very much want to do what they want to do when they want to do it. They protest leaving a neighborhood basketball game just because it is dinnertime. They feel put upon when called to take care of a younger sibling instead of being allowed to play with their friends. Learning to live comfortably with patterns of daily life is a task for childhood and also a tension with which we live as adults. Those who view this passage pessimistically overlook the value of the patterns and the possibility that many of those patterns are part of God's good plan.

Children both understand and appreciate verses 1-8 as they are read, especially when read from the New Revised Standard Version. But they depend on the preacher to put the message of verses 9-13 into simpler words.

Psalm: 8. Like the psalmist, children often sense God's presence when observing the natural world. The power of the wind and water at the beach, the size of the world when viewed from a mountaintop or an airplane window, the delicate smallness of insects and flowers—all lead them to ponder the vastness of the world and their place in it.

The Good News Bible presents the psalmist's response in language most children understand, but it speaks of humanity in exclusively male terms. The New Revised Standard Version, on the other hand, speaks of people in the third person plural. In worship, it is often effective to use the first person plural, so that worshipers can speak with the psalmist.

Gospel: Matthew 25:31-46. Children quickly understand Jesus' point that we are called to make a difference in this world (and in the new year). Though they hear that the crucial question is whether one has responded to the needs of "the least of these my brothers," many children will need help in identifying modern examples of "the least of these" in their homes, schools, and community.

Epistle: Revelation 21:1-6a. This picture of the new Jerusalem ("new place" or "promised land") toward which God is leading the whole world is filled with symbolic pictures too complex for children. But if the children are told that the voice that speaks is God's, and if they are directed to listen carefully to what the voice says, they can find the two chief messages: (verses 3b-4) God will be with us and will care for us; and (verses 5b-6a) just as God was at the beginning of the world, so God will be at its end. (Comparing alpha and omega to A and Z helps to clarify the second point.)

Watch Words

Speak about *God's world*, rather than *creation* or *the natural order*.

Speak about *people*, instead of *humanity, mortals*, or *man*. Talk specifically about what God calls men and women and boys and girls to do.

Let the Children Sing

Sing about God's world, using "All Things Bright and Beautiful," "I Sing the Mighty Power of God," "This Is My Father's World" (only if children already know it), or "For the Beauty of the Earth."

"Lord, I Want to Be a Christian" is a good commitment hymn for a new year. Consider making up a verse or two tailored to the worship theme. If it is familiar to your children, "Be Thou My Vision" is another way to enter the new year.

If you celebrate communion, sing "I Come with Joy." The tune is simple and catchy. Children understand many of the phrases the first time they sing them, then learn others with a few repetitions. This is a good communion hymn to add to the congregation's repertory.

The Liturgical Child

1. Line out Psalm 8, urging worshipers to match your tone and feeling as they repeat each phrase (emphasize the italicized words). For example:

O Lord,
Our Lord. (with great conviction)
Your greatness is seen in all the earth. (joyfully)
Your praise reaches up to the heavens. (loudly)
It is sung by children and babies. (softly)

2. When reading the Gospel lesson, take the role of Jesus. With your hands, direct the sheep to one side and the goats to the other. Then turn toward the sheep as you read the verses about them and toward the goats as you read the verses about them. Read with great expression, letting your voice show the surprise and fear of both the sheep and the goats when they hear Jesus' judgment of them.

3. Pray for the new year, identifying hopes and dreams for the year and asking for the help that will be needed. For example:

Lord God of the Universe, we stand on the edge of a new year. We are full of hopes and dreams. We dream of peace among friends and among countries. We dream of enough food and a comfortable home for everyone. Hear each of our dreams for the world in the new year. (PAUSE)

God, our Father and Mother, all of us have our own personal hopes for the year ahead. We dream of learning new things, meeting new friends, going to wonderful places, and doing new interesting and fun things. Hear each of our dreams for the new year. (PAUSE)

Sermon Resources

1. Offer a version of Qoheleth's "times" that fits your congregation. Include some that ring true for children:

There's a time to play with your friends and a time to play with younger brother and sister.
There's a time to go to bed and a time to get up.
There's a time to play games and a time to help with chores.

2. Turn the sermon into a State of God's World speech. Introduce it by referring to the President's State of the Union address later this month. Then proceed to describe either the state of God's larger world or the state of your congregation. Identify specific ways in which the concerns of today's texts affect the coming year. Offer challenges. Be sure to include your hopes and dreams for activities in which children participate, and challenge children to undertake specific missions (especially to "the least of these") during the coming year.

Draw a picture of God's world.

Draw yourself in God's world.

"O Lord, our Lord, your greatness is seen in all the earth!" (Psalm 8 : 1)

"Yet you have made _____ your name ruler over everything you made."

Finish the sentences below to make a New Year's prayer.

A Prayer for 19 ___ ___

God, I hope that _____

God , please help me _____

God, others who need your help this year are _____

In Jesus' name.   Amen

| January | February | March | April | May | June |
| July | August | September | October | November | December |

FIRST SUNDAY AFTER THE EPIPHANY/ BAPTISM OF THE LORD

The title this Sunday could be, "Oh, what a difference the Holy Spirit makes"—to Jesus at his baptism, to the Ephesian disciples at theirs, and to creation.

From a Child's Point of View

Gospel: Mark 1:4-11. Children need help to understand the difference between John's baptism of the people, and the baptism of Jesus. The people who came to be baptized by John were repenting—that is, they were admitting that they were not living the way God had taught them to live and were promising that they would work hard to do better. John warned that if they did not make the needed changes, God would punish them. John was like a stern teacher or coach. The people were like errant students, promising to work harder. It was up to the people to make the promised changes.

But when Jesus was baptized, something very different happened. Jesus did not make promises about what he was going to do. Instead, he turned himself over to God. In response, God called Jesus "My Son" and sent the Holy Spirit to work through Jesus. Jesus was like a boat owner who turns over command of his boat to a new captain, to be used however the captain wants.

Epistle: Acts 19:1-7. The disciples Paul met, like the disciples of John the Baptist, were trying to live better lives. But after they turned their lives over to God through Jesus, they found new power. They were surprised by what God could do through them that they could not do on their own.

Literal-thinking children wonder why they cannot speak in tongues, as those Christians did. The answer is that God's power works through different people in different ways. Some people become great teachers, some build hospitals, and so forth. These Ephesian disciples were able to speak in tongues. But no matter how God chooses to work through us, we are often surprised by what God can do.

Old Testament: Genesis 1:1-5. The story of creation offers a familiar example of God's power. Few children, however, will have noticed the presence of the Holy Spirit in the opening verses of the creation story, and they will not notice it today unless it is pointed out. But once it is pointed out, children are awed by the fact that God wants to put the power that created the world to work through them. Older children, who tend to be very ecologically aware, find meaning in hearing their efforts to clean up the world described as one of the ways God's Holy Spirit works through them.

Psalm: 29. This celebration of the power of God, displayed in a thunderstorm coming in from the sea, across the mountains, and out into the desert is meant to be enjoyed rather than analyzed. The frightened child in each of us is comforted by the fact that the power of the storm is God's power. The psalm can challenge worshipers of all ages to let this immense power be unleashed in their lives.

Watch Words

Identify *Holy Spirit* as God's power at work in the world and God's presence with us. If you use *Holy Ghost*, explain that it is not a good Halloween-type spook or God's ghost (God is not dead), but another name for *Holy Spirit*. You might also want to speak of *God's Spirit*.

Review the terms you use in talking about *baptism* and in your baptismal rite. Take time to explain terms that may be foreign to children.

Let the Children Sing

Hymns about Jesus' baptism are filled with difficult words and concepts. "Christ, When for Us You Were Baptized" can be sung by older children after the worship leader reads through the verses and explains their meaning. (This is also good preparation for adults who may be singing this for the first time.)

Celebrate God's great power with the concrete creation language of "I Sing the Mighty Power of God."

Even beginning readers quickly learn the chorus of "The Lone Wild Bird." Before singing it, explain that the bird you are singing about is the dove and that this is a song about and to the Holy Spirit.

Promise submission to the Spirit with "I'm Goin' to Sing When the Spirit Says Sing." Consider making up verses that coincide with the points of the day's sermon.

The Liturgical Child

1. This prayer of confession should be read by a worship leader (it is too hard for children to read):

God, you have baptized us with the Holy Spirit. You have filled us with your power, but we are afraid to use it. You have told us we can do great things in your name, but we say, "I've never done that before!" or "We couldn't do that!" You have promised that you will tell us what to say, but we are shy about speaking for you, even among our friends. You have given us eyes to see problems and minds to solve them, but we look away and say, "What a problem! That's too big for me to figure out!" Forgive us for ignoring the power you promise us. Forgive us for not trusting your power. Forgive us for not really wanting to try. Amen.

Assurance of Pardon: God understands. God knows our fears and forgives them. God sticks with us and urges us on. God's power gives us

the courage to try scary new ministries, to speak up when we know we should, and to say, "Let's try this." Thanks be to God.

2. If there are to be baptisms today, invite the children to come to the font or pool just before the baptism. Explain the ritual, paying special attention to the ways it reminds us that we are God's sons and daughters, and also to the role of the Holy Spirit. Allow the children to stay where they can see easily.

3. Remind worshipers of their own baptisms with water: Worship leaders could walk up and down the aisles, dipping a hand or evergreen branch into bowls of water, flinging the drops over the congregation, and saying such phrases as, "Remember, you are God's sons and daughters!" or "The power of God is with you and works through you!" Keep the phrases simple so that children understand them as they feel the water spray over them.

4. For this Sunday in Year C of this series, directions are included for Psalm 29 to be read with stormy sound effects, provided by worshipers or by a children's class or choir.

Sermon Resources

1. Introduce *dove* as a Christian code word. Recall other dove stories in the Bible and instruct listeners to expect stories of God's power wherever doves appear. Point out any dove symbols in your sanctuary.

2. Tell stories about the surprising power of God's Holy Spirit. For example, Robert Coles interviewed black children during the early 1960s when the schools in the South were being integrated. He was astounded by their courage in the face of daily threats from angry mobs. One eight-year-old girl from North Carolina told of a time when she was "all alone, and those [segregationist] people were screaming, and suddenly I saw God smiling, and I smiled. . . . A woman was standing there [near the school door], and she shouted at me, 'Hey, you little nigger, what you smiling at?' I looked right at her face, and I said, 'at God.' Then she looked up at the sky, and then she looked at me, and she didn't call me any more names" (*The Spiritual Life of Children* [Houghton Mifflin, 1990], pp. 19-20).

Listen carefully when **Mark 1:4-11** is read. Draw a picture of what happened.

What did John the Baptist look like? What did Jesus see?

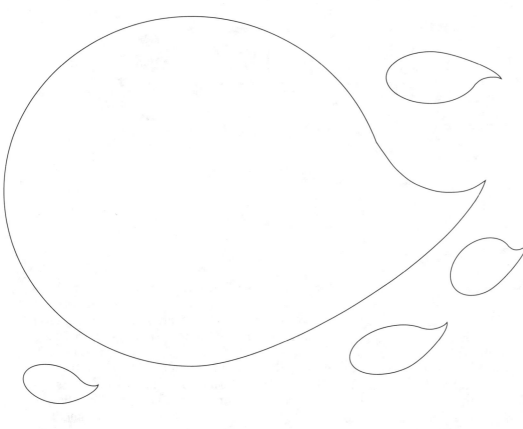

Fill in the spaces that have dots to find a two word name.

Listen to what is said about this name. Then write a definition for it on this dictionary page.

_____'s Dictionary   12

H

- H -

_____ :

SECOND SUNDAY AFTER THE EPIPHANY

From a Child's Point of View

Gospel: John 1:43-51. Philip and Nathanael are among the least known of the twelve disciples. Nathanael is mentioned in the Bible only in this text and in the lists of "the twelve," in which he is sometimes called Nathanael and sometimes Bartholomew. Children whose parents tend to call them by a brother's or sister's name, or those who tend to feel lost in the crowd in classes and on teams, can empathize with Nathanael's "nobody" status. They also appreciate the fact that Jesus noticed Nathanael and recognized him as a worthwhile person. The unstated promise is that God, who noticed and sought out Nathanael, will not overlook the least among us.

When he met Jesus, Nathanael was surprised that the Messiah knew him and wanted his help. He was also surprised that God's Messiah was from Galilee. Nathanael did not think much of Galilee and did not expect God to speak to him through a Galilean. The warning here is that God also may come to us in surprising ways and through surprising people.

Old Testament: I Samuel 3:1-10 (11-20). The story of God's call to Samuel is proof that God seeks out children as well as grown-ups. In this situation, God wanted Samuel to deliver a very unpleasant message. He was to tell Eli that God was punishing Eli's whole family severely. Samuel bravely did the job. The story ends by noting that God continued to speak to Samuel and that, while growing up—not when he was grown—Samuel became known and respected as a person to whom God spoke and who did God's will.

The story also provides a lesson on how to respond when God seeks us out. Like Samuel, we are to say, "Speak, Lord, your servant listens," and then pay close attention and obey. Literal thinkers will need other examples of how God speaks to us, besides through a voice in the night. Examples children recognize include a sense deep inside that God wants them to do something for a person in need or to stop an activity they know is wrong; a sense that God is telling them something through a Bible story they read or hear; or a feeling during a crisis, or when in sight of natural beauty, that God loves them and takes care of them.

(This text and the psalm appear again in Proper 4 of this year. Consult that section for additional resources.)

Psalm: 139:1-6, 13-18. The psalmist ponders a point that children (and Nathanaels of all ages) appreciate. God is always aware of us and looking out for us. Though some of the poetic images are hard for younger children, and older children will giggle knowingly at the womb references, most children can follow the psalmist's thoughts as the poem is read. The Good News Bible offers the easiest translation for children to understand.

Epistle: I Corinthians 6:12-20. Because most children experience themselves as spiritual and physical wholes, Paul's point that we are to respond to God's call with body, as well as with soul, has little meaning. To relate this text to the others for the day, simply point to verse 19 and describe ways we can keep our bodies pure temples for God. Needless to say, the sexual relationships Paul describes as an example are best replaced with calls to avoid drugs and alcohol (often available to older-elementary children), eat foods that are good for us, and get exercise.

Watch Words

If you speak of God's presence in everyday terms and celebrate the truth that God seeks out each one of us, vocabulary offers few barriers.

Let the Children Sing

The chorus of "Here I Am, Lord" recalls Samuel's response to God. Older children can follow the words of the verses, but all children can learn the chorus. Consider singing the verses and chorus responsively; as an anthem, an adult choir could sing the verses, with a children's choir singing the chorus; as a hymn, the congregation could sing the verses, with a children's choir or class singing the chorus. If the hymn is new to the congregation, ask that the chorus be introduced to the children during their choir practice.

The Liturgical Child

1. To bring the psalm to life, imagine yourself as the poet talking to God, rather like Tevye talked with God in *Fiddler on the Roof.* Use your hands to emphasize references to "me" and "you." Especially in verses 13-18, read whole sentences rather than phrases.

2. Present the stories of Samuel and/or Nathanael as readers' theater. The worship leader takes the part of the narrator. Other children, youths, and adults take the other parts. (For Samuel, select a fourth- or fifth-grade boy. For Eli, choose one of the older men in the congregation. God's voice may be heard-off stage or read by a visible man, woman, or child.) Practice together until all know their parts well enough to keep the reading moving smoothly. Work on how different lines are expressed. For instance, how did Samuel say, "Speak, Lord, your servant listens"? Was there hesitant fear in his voice, or was he enthusiastically excited? And how did Nathanael's statements sound?

3. Affirm your faith with responsive statements describing the ways God calls us. The congregational response is that of Samuel: "Speak, Lord, your servant listens."

God, you reach out to us in so many ways. Keep us alert. Help us to pay attention.

When you spread your beautiful world out for us to see; when we feel your power in the power of the ocean waves; when we see tiny bugs and huge elephants and know you made them both; when we see your rainbow, may we say . . . (CONGREGATIONAL RESPONSE)

When we are tempted to do what is wrong, but remember what you have told us through our leaders; when everyone else is doing it, but we hear your voice deep inside us saying, "Don't!"; when we want something enough to steal it, but know your rule against stealing, may we say . . . (CONGREGATIONAL RESPONSE)

When we see problems and feel you urging us to help solve them; when we see your world littered with garbage and dirtied by pollution, and know there is even one thing we could do to help; when we see people ignored and teased by others and know they need our friendship, may we say . . . (CONGREGATIONAL RESPONSE)

When we are sad and lonely, and feel your loving care surrounding us; when friends call to ask how we're doing; when people smile that they understand and say, "How can I help?" may we say . . . (CONGREGATIONAL RESPONSE)

When we open our Bibles to read stories, and psalms, and letters to the churches, may we say . . . (CONGREGATIONAL RESPONSE)

God, you reach out to us in so many ways. Keep us alert. Help us to pay attention. And may we say . . . (CONGREGATIONAL RESPONSE)

Sermon Resources

1. Tell other biblical stories of God's call. God did not call Abraham and Sarah until they were quite old, but David was called when he was young. God called Moses through a burning bush. Through Moses, God called Joshua to lead the people into the Promised Land. Isaiah was called to be a prophet while he was worshiping in the Temple. God spoke in a dream to Solomon.

2. Tell about your call to the preaching ministry. When did it happen? How did God "speak" to you? How did you respond?

God seeks us.

We
sometimes
put
up road
blocks.

God keeps
trying
until a way is
found.

Find the way
to
this listening
servant.

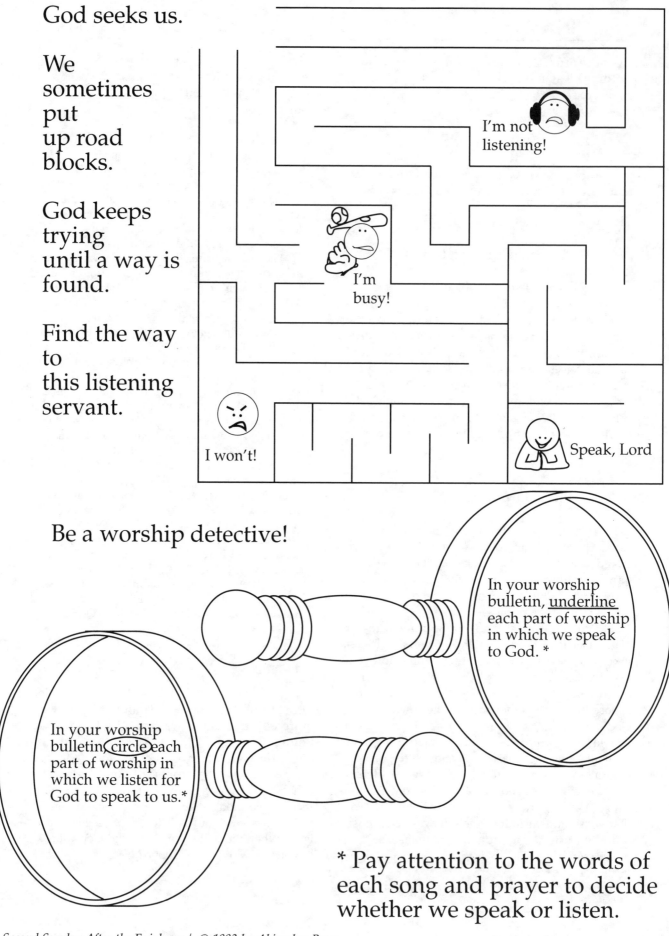

I'm not
listening!

I'm
busy!

I won't!

Speak, Lord

Be a worship detective!

In your worship
bulletin, <u>underline</u>
each part of worship
in which we speak
to God. *

In your worship
bulletin, circle each
part of worship in
which we listen for
God to speak to us.*

* Pay attention to the words of
each song and prayer to decide
whether we speak or listen.

THIRD SUNDAY AFTER THE EPIPHANY

Today's texts have one message for both children and adults: You must do something! The Ninevites had to do something in response to Jonah's message. The fishermen had to either follow Jesus or keep working. And Paul told Christians how to act.

From a Child's Point of View

Old Testament: Jonah 3:1-5, 10. Many children know the story of Jonah's encounter with the fish. If that story is briefly summarized with attention to how much Jonah hated the Ninevites, they will be primed to hear today's reading as the less familiar next chapter in the saga.

The focus here is on the Ninevites who heard God's warning and acted in response. The Ninevites might have responded in other ways—they might have laughed at Jonah, beat him up for saying such awful things, or ignored him, hoping he was wrong. Children would be the first to say that it would have been fair for God to destroy the Ninevites, had they responded in such ways. "God did warn them. They knew what would happen." The Ninevites, however, took Jonah's message seriously and took action. We, like the Ninevites, are to pay attention to God and do what God asks.

Children also need to be reassured that God does not look for people to destroy. Instead of destroying Jonah for his disobedience, God sent a storm and a fish to help him rethink what he was doing. (It was like putting him in a "time-out" chair.) Instead of simply destroying Nineveh, God gave the people a forty-day warning. When they used those forty days to change their ways, God happily changed the plan. God loves us.

Gospel: Mark 1:14-20. The call of the four fishing disciples is also familiar. Children, like adults, are caught by the suddenness of Jesus' demand for a decision and response. Though commentators suggest that this was probably not the fishermen's first encounter with Jesus, the point is that on the day Jesus asked the four to leave everything and follow him, they had to make a decision and act immediately. They could not put it off. They either followed or they did not. And what they chose to do affected the rest of their lives. Children, as well as adults, make decisions every day. Sometimes their decisions do not have huge impact (refusing to join in teasing an unpopular classmate), but sometimes they do (refusing drugs or alcohol). We are to act like disciples everyday.

Epistle: I Corinthians 7:29-31. Paul has instructions for Christian disciples in action. We are to remember that being a disciple is more important than anything else in life. It is more important than what we wear, what we own, who we marry, what we get to do and don't get to do at school and home, and so forth. Children will not hear this when the passage is read, but will depend on the preacher to restate Paul's point.

Psalm: 62:5-12. A strong, confident reading of this psalm by one reader does most to communicate its message to children. Rather than follow complete sentences, they will hear the psalmist's tone and the single words that describe God's power (*refuge, rock, honor*). The weighing of the rich and the poor in verse 9 and the comments about riches and robbery in verse 10 require more explaining than their message here merits.

Watch Words

Before using *repent* to describe what the Ninevites did, recall its use by John the Baptist in the Advent texts. Remind worshipers that *repent* describes actions, rather than feelings.

Today, a *disciple* is someone who does what God asks.

Let the Children Sing

"I Sing a Song of the Saints of God" and "Lord, I Want to Be a Christian" are probably the best discipleship hymns for children.

"Take My Life and Let It Be Consecrated," with its references to serving with different parts of the body, is a good choice if children know the word *consecrated*.

If you introduced "Here I Am, Lord" last Sunday and worshipers enjoyed it, sing it again this week to build familiarity.

The Liturgical Child

1. In honor of the four fishermen who became disciples, decorate with fish netting. Drape it around the pulpit and lectern, and loop it over the arms of a large cross to remind worshipers of our call to be disciples.

2. Create a responsive prayer of petition. The congregation's response to each prayer: "God, help us to do something." For example:

> We call you our Father and our Mother. We claim to be your children. We say that all people are members of your family. So when we see people who are hungry or need clothes, people who are homeless, people who are sick, with no medical help nearby . . . (CONGREGATIONAL RESPONSE)
>
> Creator God, you made the heavens and the earth. We believe that you call us to be stewards of the earth. So when we see litter along the roads, rivers that are polluted, garbage dumps overflowing . . . (CONGREGATIONAL RESPONSE)

3. *Charge and Benediction:* Jesus said to Peter, Andrew, James, and John, and he says to us today, "Follow me." So I charge you to follow him. At home, at work, at school, and at play, do any needed disciple's work every day. Treat everyone kindly. Forgive people who hurt you. Share your lunch, your friendship, and your time with those who need you. Make friends with the lonely, the outsiders, even the enemies. And as you do, remember that Jesus also said, "I will be with you always, even til the end of the world." Amen.

Sermon Resources

1. Confronted with calls for action from God, parents, teachers, bosses, and so on, people of all ages offer similar excuses:
- "I didn't hear you."
- "I didn't understand what you wanted."
- "That's too hard!"
- "You do not understand what you are asking!"

Use these excuses in telling several versions of stories: a ten-year-old boy asked to baby-sit his little brother after school on a pretty day; Jonah trying to avoid God's assignment; the Ninevites trying to avoid repenting. Then point out the real reasons behind these excuses:
- "I don't want to!"
- "I'm afraid to!"

2. Describe situations in which action is required. The refrain after each situation is "Do something!" Include such things as:

Jackie watched the Olympic gymnasts with wonder. She thought they were beautiful and could almost feel what it would be like to do those flips . . . .

Chris just moved in down the street from Lee. Lee watched him move in, saw the bike come off the truck, even saw Chris exploring the new yard . . . .

Sandy's friends delighted in _____ (the ethnic group most put down in your area) jokes. They told them continually and laughed loudly. The jokes made Sandy uncomfortable . . . .

Draw a picture of
or
write about
something you do to follow Jesus.

Disciple at Work

_____
(Your name)

In his prayer, the writer of
Psalm 62 called God

MY
FORTRESS

and

MY REFUGE

Pick the one you like best.
Use it to write your own prayer.

God, you are _____

_____

Thank you for _____

_____

Help me _____

_____

_____

Amen

FOURTH SUNDAY AFTER THE EPIPHANY

From a Child's Point of View

Old Testament: Deuteronomy 18:15-20. Setting the scene is an important part of presenting this passage. Children need to know before the reading that Moses is talking about how God does and does not communicate with us.

Moses' warning against expecting God to speak through the "magic" practices that would be encountered in the Promised Land interests children because they are fascinated by magic. They need to hear the difference between the slight-of-hand magic tricks done to entertain, and the attempts to contact the spirit world or the dead to learn secret messages.

Older children are curious about how such things as auguring and divination are done and what they aim to accomplish (an encyclopedia can provide details). While their curiosity needs to be satisfied, children also need to hear clearly Moses' warning that God does not speak through such means and that therefore they are to be avoided. This is good preparation for encounters during early adolescence with New Age channelers, and even dabblers in witchcraft.

Moses then insists that God will speak to them instead through prophets, and especially through one unique prophet (Jesus). Because children's curriculum devotes less time to prophets than to other biblical characters, most children will need to hear examples of biblical and modern prophets to understand the "job description." Jonah, who was highlighted last week, is one of the most familiar and usable examples.

Gospel: Mark 1:21-28. Though older children can understand the difference between the scribes, who based all their teachings on what this

or that expert had said, and Jesus, who simply spoke what he knew to be God's word, the difference is of little significance to them. They are more interested in the healing story.

The bottom line of that story is that Jesus has power over all the evil powers that disrupt and corrupt life. In children's words, Jesus/God can beat out any other power in the universe. So we are safe. We can trust God's power.

The most, but not completely, satisfactory explanation of the demons is that they are "used-to-thinks." "Used-to-thinks" are ideas people used to believe but which now have been proved wrong—that is, people used to think that the earth was flat; they used to think that the sun traveled across the sky each day. Similarly, people used to think that our problems and illnesses were caused by little invisible demons that went around causing trouble. Today we think that our medical problems are caused by germs and body disorders, and our other problems are caused by uncontrolled evil wishes and desires—selfishness and cruelty. But no matter how you describe evil, Mark insists that Jesus can overpower it.

Psalm: 111. This is an acrostic, an alphabet psalm, praising God for powerful deeds. It fits well with either the Old Testament or the Gospel lesson. Unfortunately, most of the praises are general and use abstract words. Older children will catch a line here and there. Most children will appreciate the format more than the content.

Epistle: I Corinthians 8:1-13. The Corinthian argument about eating meat sacrificed to idols is not an issue today. Furthermore, there are no obvious parallels. Though adults can identify the principle behind Paul's answer and apply it to a variety of other situations, such thinking is beyond the mental abilities of children. About all they can glean from this text is that being considerate of the needs of others is a very high priority among Christians.

Watch Words

A biblical *prophet* is not a person who predicts the future, but a person who speaks God's message to others. To many children, an *unclean spirit* sounds like a dirty ghost. Remember that when you speak of *demons* and *exorcism*, children will take everything you say very literally. Even older children still see monsters and demons in the dark. Children also tend to tune in and out of such discussions, and therefore often misunderstand what is said.

Let the Children Sing

Praise Christ, who overcomes all evil, by singing "Come, Christians, Join to Sing." Invite nonreaders to join in on, maybe counting, the Alleluias. Nonreaders also can join in on the phrase "may Jesus Christ be praised" which is repeated twice in each short verse of "When Morning Gilds the Skies."

If the focus is on God speaking, sing, or ask a children's class to sing, the familiar camp song, "Kum-Ba-Ya." Consider creating some verses especially for this service.

"This Is My Father's World," known by many older children, recalls several ways God communicates with us.

The Liturgical Child

1. Have the reader of the Deuteronomy lection assume the role of Moses. After setting the scene, the worship leader may step to the center of the chancel, Bible in hand, to read the text dramatically, using the free hand for rhetorical gestures. Or, after the worship leader sets the scene, a costumed Moses may come to the chancel to present the memorized text dramatically. In either case,

consider adding verse 14, to explain the reason for Moses' warning.

2. Following a sermon about God speaking to us through other people, include among the church's prayers opportunities (perhaps times of silence) for worshipers to thank God for the people who have been prophets to them.

3. Create a litany prayer calling on Jesus to overpower the demons that trouble our lives. The congregation's response: "Lord Jesus, defeat the demons that trouble us." For example:

God of giving love, we must fight the demon of selfishness every day. There are so many things we think we need, and even more that we want. We want the right clothes, the latest car, and all the toys we see on television. (CONGREGATIONAL RESPONSE)

Forgiving God, the demon of war seems to be stronger than ever. No matter how hard we try to solve our problems peacefully, we find ourselves fighting at school, fighting at work, even fighting at home and with our friends. It is not surprising that so many countries are at war. (CONGREGATIONAL RESPONSE)

Sermon Resources

1. The Sundays after Epiphany are good days to celebrate the ways God is revealed to us. Today, focus on the way God speaks to us through people. Tell stories of biblical prophets and people you consider prophetic today. Describe people who speak to us publicly and those who speak to individuals. Tell about people through whom God has spoken to you. Invite children to draw pictures of people who have been prophets to them, and suggest that older worshipers write about such people. As worshipers leave, collect their work for display in a hall near the sanctuary.

2. To explore the world of magic, perform a simple slight-of-hand magic trick. (Check the children's section of the public library for books on such tricks.) Then talk about the dangers of misinterpreting the power of Ouija boards. Most older children have played with one and can sense the way the pointer could be moved in order to use it for someone's own ends. Be clear that God speaks through more dependable means—such as other people.

Cross out one square when you see, hear, sing, say, or do it.
How many ways can you get five in a row today?

Praise the Lord!	Jesus	Sing a Hymn	I Corinthians 8 : 1 - 13	A PROPHET IS . . .
I believe . . .			"Christ have mercy upon us."	
Sing a Hymn	"He spoke with AUTHORITY."	FREE		The Gloria Patri
Mark 1: 21-28		Baptism	ALLELUIA !	Sing a Hymn
PAUL	Benediction		MOSES	

Fourth Sunday After the Epiphany | © 1993 by Abingdon Press.

FIFTH SUNDAY AFTER THE EPIPHANY

To most children, power and love seem to belong to different arenas. People are either powerful or loving. Today's passages describe God as both powerful and loving. God creates the vast world, but knows each star by name and cares for each small creature. God never overlooks even the most hopeless people, but gives them the power they need. Jesus uses his powers to heal unknown people. Paul disciplines his powers to do his loving task. The texts call us both to celebrate God's power and love, and to follow Jesus' and Paul's examples of powerful loving.

From a Child's Point of View

Gospel: Mark 1:29-39. The contrast between these healings and the previous one at the synagogue makes it clear that Jesus did not heal to impress big groups of important people. He simply reached out to do what he could for people he met. When he went home with his friend for supper, he healed the man's sick mother-in-law. When people came to the door asking for help, he healed them.

Fifth- and sixth-graders are ready to take responsibility for their own devotional life. They are able to read the Bible on their own and are independent enough set their own disciplines. Many are learning to take responsibility for individual athletic, dance, or music practice. Just as these disciplines help children develop their athletic and artistic power, daily prayer helps them develop their power to live as God's people. The story of Jesus' withdrawal for prayer is attractive to them.

Old Testament: Isaiah 40:21-31. Children cannot understand this passage as it is read, in any translation. They do, however, empathize with the hopeless exiles. Like the exiles, children often feel overlooked and forgotten. They feel like baggage that is shifted around to suit the adults. Children who are mistreated by the central adults in their lives feel shut out by the whole world. But even those who are loved and well cared for occasionally feel overlooked and overpowered. Isaiah reminds children that God, who created the vast world, pays attention to each creature in it—even to them. God notices them and will give them the power they need in even the most hopeless situations.

Psalm: 147:1-11, 20c. This psalm celebrates both the power and the loving care of God. Children can recognize it as a psalm that might have been sung by Peter's family, or by any of the many people Jesus healed.

Epistle: I Corinthians 9:16-23. It is more effective to summarize Paul's point and illustrate it with current examples of people who are doing as he did, than to attempt to explain the significance of living by the Law and becoming "weak." Paul's point is that he is willing to accept rules he does not really need to accept, if living by those rules will help him do his job of telling people about God.

WARNING: It is important to point out the difference between what Paul did and merely going along with the crowd to make them like you.

Watch Words

Do not let speaking of God's power lead you to

use *omnipotence* or other long "power" words without explaining their meaning.

Let the Children Sing

Both "How Great Thou Art," when sung with feeling by a congregation that loves it, and "For the Beauty of the Earth" describe God's power and love. "All Things Bright and Beautiful," which praises God's attention to both the great and the small, is familiar to most church children.

Though "We Would See Jesus" includes some abstract and obsolete words, older children can sing along. It helps to point out the topic of each verse before the singing begins.

Older children can read and sing the words of "Take Time to Be Holy," in response to Jesus' prayer practices.

The Liturgical Child

1. To emphasize the psalmist's points about God's power and include worshipers in the poet's praising, ask the congregation to say "Praise the Lord!" (1*a*) to begin Psalm 147, and also after a worship leader reads the following sections of the psalm: 1*b*, 2-3, 4, 5, 6, 7, 8-9, and 10-11. This might be printed in its entirety in the bulletin.

2. Invite three older children to read the three stories (verses 29-31; 32-34; and 35-39) in the Gospel text. The New Revised Standard Version can be read without difficulty by most fourth-through sixth-graders. Plan one practice session in the sanctuary to be sure they can pronounce all the words easily, know where to stand, and can use the microphone comfortably.

3. *Prayer of Confession:* Loving God, you have commanded us to love one another, and you have shown us how to do it. When crowds came to the door at the end of a long day, Jesus talked to them and healed them. But when people·come to us when we are tired, we say, "Come back tomorrow. Can't you see I'm busy?" or just "Go away!" Forgive us.

When Paul became a missionary, he was willing to try almost anything to persuade people to listen to God's good news. He obeyed the laws the Jews obeyed, so that they would listen when he told them about Jesus. He ate the strange food the Gentiles ate, so that he could tell them about God's love.

But we are not so eager to help others. We are helpful when we feel like it. We serve others when it is convenient and when serving is interesting or fun. We invite to church only the people we like. We are kind to those who are kind to us. Forgive us. Help us to love one another as you commanded. Amen.

Assurance of Pardon: God loves us even when we are not loving. God loves us even when we are not lovable. God loves and forgives us even when we are at our worst. More than that, God gives us the power to love others when we do not feel like it, to say kind words to people we do not like, even to take care of others when we are tired and want someone to take care of us. When God's power works through us, we are surprised by what can happen. Thanks be to God!

4. As the Benediction, recite Isaiah 40:28-29 and 31. Conclude with, "So go in peace. God is with you."

Sermon Resources

1. To set Paul's point in modern circumstances, tell stories. Tell about teenage American girls who wear skirts instead of shorts while painting a children's home in Jamaica. Because they do not offend the community's customs regarding women's dress, they are able to share God's love with those people.

Tell about an older child who plays little kids' games, maybe "Chutes and Ladders," to care for a younger child. Tell about the eight-year-old who ate barbecued goat when invited to dinner by the Central American refugee boy he befriended at school.

2. Offer specific helps for daily prayer. Name daily devotional guides that have proved useful. If your children's church-school curriculum offers a daily prayer guide, point it out, encourage children to use it, and urge parents to support its use. Another excellent resource is *Pockets*, a monthly magazine for seven- to twelve-year-olds that includes devotional activities for each day of the coming month. (Order *Pockets* from The Upper Room, 1908 Grand ave, P.O. Box 189, Nashville, TN 37202-9929.) Display these resources near the sanctuary.

In old Bibles, artists drew pictures around the first letter of a psalm or story. Listen when **Psalm 147** is read. Then draw a picture on and around the P, showing God's powerful, loving care.

raise the Lord!
How good it is
to sing praises
to our God.

(Psalm 147:1)

Jesus and Paul loved and took care of people.

Jesus healed sick people.
Paul told people the good news about Jesus.

Turn the letters of the word LOVE into pictures of you taking care of people today.

Fifth Sunday After the Epiphany | *© 1993 by Abingdon Press.*

SIXTH SUNDAY AFTER THE EPIPHANY
PROPER ONE

From a Child's Point of View

Two of today's lections describe the healing of lepers. Children are curious about leprosy. They want to know: (1) what leprosy is and what it does to a person; (2) why lepers have to leave their homes and towns (children who depend on their parents for survival are frightened by such separation); and (3) why there are not as many lepers today as there were in the Bible. An encyclopedia can provide concrete answers to such questions.

Gospel: Mark 1:40-45. For children, this is the less interesting of today's healing stories. It simply says that Jesus was able to cure lepers, and he did. Because children have many taboos about touching, Jesus' touching a leper can be explored as a sign of Jesus' love, and as a challenge for us to take risks for others.

Old Testament: II Kings 5:1-14. The story of Namaan's cure appeals to children because the heroine is a little girl. The fact that a little slave girl provided the key information about the cure and that General Namaan and his wife took her suggestion delights children, who often feel that adults do not take their ideas seriously.

The story makes two related points. First, God is at work in everyday events, as well as in extraordinary ones. Children who grow up hearing the spectacular biblical stories often overlook God at work in the love of their families, the activities of their church, and the events of their own lives. This story encourages children to look for God at work in the everyday.

Second, as Namaan's servant pointed out, we should be as willing to do nonspectacular deeds as we are to do the dramatic ones. Children often undervalue their deeds of lovingkindness and playground peacemaking. They want to do heroic deeds and solve big problems in single strokes. They need to be reminded that God is working out the big plan through all our little efforts. Just as God used information from the slave girl and cured Namaan with a bath in a muddy river, God uses our efforts to care for others.

Psalm: 30. Poetic images of death and references to God being angry and hiding from people keep children from following this psalm as a whole. But if they are told before the reading that this is a prayer that a leper might have prayed after being healed, they can hear and understand occasional phrases.

Epistle: I Corinthians 9:24-27. The Corinthians were sports crazy. Their Isthmian games were second only to the Olympics. All of Paul's sports references indicate that he was also an avid fan. Sports-minded children appreciate Paul's interest but are confused by his jumble of sports images and depend upon the preacher to explain them.

In the context of the chapter, Paul makes two points. First, just as discipline is necessary for athletes to win at sports, it is necessary for Christians in order to achieve their goal of proclaiming the good news to all the world. Christians must be just as willing to do what Paul described in the beginning of the chapter as a boxer is willing to take a beating from his sparring partner in order to win in the championship ring.

Second, our goal is longer lasting than that of the athlete. Even if today's trophies are more durable than laurel wreaths, children realize that winning is short-term. This year's champions are replaced by next year's. Every new record is eventually broken. Still, children think winning is worth the discipline. Paul agrees, but insists that because the proclamation of the gospel wins permanent results, it is even more worthy of our discipline.

Finally, Paul throws out a warning worthy of a coach. Wouldn't it be embarrassing if you invited your friends to join you in a big race, and then you were disqualified, while they won all the ribbons? Similarly, wouldn't it be embarrassing if the people you invited to church became great Christian disciples, while you refused to discipline yourself enough to be effective?

Watch Words

When using sports terms metaphorically, remember that children think literally. They often infer from references to "winning the victory" that Christians are playing some sort of game with God and that only those who excel will win God's favor and a place in heaven. To help them understand the metaphors, cite specific ways we can discipline ourselves and specific goals that we, as Christians, aim for.

Let the Children Sing

Good discipline hymns include "Take My Life and Let It Be Consecrated," with it's reference to using our bodies, and "I'm Gonna Live So God Can Use Me." In "God of Grace and God of Glory," young readers can sing the repeated line, "grant us wisdom, grant us courage"; as their reading abilities grow, they will catch more and more of the verses.

Songs about Jesus touching people, such as "He Touched Me," often reduce children to giggles and poking each other.

The Liturgical Child

1. Have the story of Namaan's cure pantomimed as it is read. To emphasize the presence of the little girl and to involve actors able to communicate the feelings of the different characters, type-cast people of all ages. During a practice session, work on expressing feelings with the whole body as well as with the face. (Provide simple costumes, or perhaps one character-defining prop for each player. For example, Namaan's wife could carry a hand mirror; the little slave girl, a hair brush.)

2. *Prayer of Confession:* God our Creator, we all want to be winners, we want to succeed, we want to do great things for you. But we are not as eager to do the work. We are slow to read the Bible and build our understanding of your will. We hardly pay attention in worship and are lazy about making time to pray. We dream of doing big things in your name, but we ignore the needs of people we work and play with every day. We talk about feeding the hungry, building homes for the homeless, and making the world fair, but we always have excuses for not working on church mission projects. We give only our leftover money. Forgive us and discipline us. Help us to shape up into the strong, active Christians you call us to be. In Jesus' name we pray. Amen.

Assurance of Pardon: God knows that we cannot do it on our own. God forgives us when we fail, and even when we do not try. God also promises to work with us and through us, giving us power and discipline we never imagined possible. Thanks be to God!

Sermon Resources

1. Younger children are very sensitive about touching. Teachers insist that they keep their hands to themselves. During this cold and flu season, adults urge them not to touch people with colds. Boys and girls refuse to sit by, stand in line with, or risk any other physical contact with the opposite sex. On the playground, boys and girls chase members of the opposite sex, trying to defile them with a touch. Unpopular children are often teased about having transmittable cooties. Lucy (in the "Peanuts" comics) expresses this fear in her squeamishness about anything that has been touched by dog lips.

2. Take on the role of a coach addressing the team. Point out the goals. Describe specific disciplines necessary to achieve them. Review some current strategies—that is, describe current ministry efforts as parts of the game plan. Urge the team on. Remind them of those who are worthy of Hall of Fame status and encourage others to follow their example. Consider wearing a baseball cap while delivering this charge to your congregational team.

Running is good discipline for athletes.
Practicing is good discipline for musicians.
What is good discipline for Christians?

Draw or write your answer here.

Listen carefully when **II Kings 5:1-14 is read.** Then fill in the blanks in the story below.

_____ (who) **Is Healed!**

Namaan had _____ (a disease).
A little slave girl said there was a
P_____ in Samaria who could
heal him. Namaan decided to
_____
heal him. Namaan decided to

Elisha told him to take _____ (how many?) baths in the muddy J_____.

R_____.

Namaan thought that was a dumb idea.
When his _____ (who?) told him
he should try it anyway, he did.
After his _____, Namaan was
h_____y again.

SEVENTH SUNDAY AFTER THE EPIPHANY
PROPER TWO

From a Child's Point of View

Before hearing today's lections, children need to be introduced to another "used-to-think." People used to think that sickness was caused by sin. They thought that God punished people by making them sick. Today we think that sickness and deformity are caused by germs and genes. But to understand today's readings, we need to realize what they meant to people who thought that sickness was a punishment.

The texts also deal with an issue that is key to children. The lessons insist that God does not give us what we deserve, but loves and forgives us. For elementary children, constantly pushed by adults to earn their privileges and take full responsibility for their sins and failures, this is good news indeed. It is particularly welcome to children who deserve punishment more often than they earn praise. God is not another powerful figure, ready to demand and punish.

Gospel: Mark 2:1-12. The attention of children is first drawn to the friends who opened the roof to lower the sick man into Jesus' presence. They want to know how it was done. A lesson on the roof structure of Palestinian homes helps. Most children will not delve beyond this level of the story. For them, the story focuses on the determination and cleverness of the friends. In the context of today's theme, the friends' grace is a human example of God's grace.

Though they cannot yet understand the abstract debate between Jesus and the scribes, older children can understand what Jesus said: "You know I can heal. But I can do something even better. God and I can, and do, forgive sin."

Old Testament: Isaiah 43:18-25. Again, children will depend upon the preacher to present the message of this passage. Paraphrased, Isaiah says, "You people deserved to be defeated and forced to move to Babylon. And you still have not learned your lesson. Though God has not asked much of you, you have not even done that. You have not worshiped God, and you sin continually. If God gave you what you deserved, you would stay in Babylon forever. But God loves you and is going to take you back home."

To children, this says that God is not a punishing judge. God may discipline us, but God always loves and forgives us.

Psalm: 41. This is a difficult psalm for children to understand. If it is presented as the prayer of a person with a serious illness, they will catch some of the psalmist's requests. The Good News Bible offers the simplest translation for children.

Epistle: II Corinthians 1:18-22. To understand this passage, readers must know the story about Paul's changes of travel plans and that his detractors used those changes to tell the people that if they could not trust the man's travel plans, they should not trust his message. This insidious adult in-fighting is beyond the comprehension of children.

About the only point in these verses that can be explored meaningfully with children is Paul's insistence that Jesus is God's "Yes!" The triumphant "Yes!" moves of today's successful athletes may be the best reference point for children. (See Sermon Resource 3.)

Watch Words

To children, *grace* is a girl's name, the prayer some families say before meals, and the ability to move smoothly. So either avoid using the word or make it the word of the day, defining it and using it repeatedly. Today, *grace* is love that never gives up, love that forgives, and love that takes care of us.

Watch your *forgiveness* vocabulary. *Mercy, compassion, pardon,* and so forth are confusing and unfamiliar. To be *forgiven* means that the person you have hurt refuses to hold what you did against you.

Let the Children Sing

Forgiveness hymns tend to be based on atonement images that children take literally and therefore find confusing, so choose carefully. Children do enjoy singing "Amazing Grace" with adults who sing it often and with great feeling. They do not, however, understand its abstract words or its cognitive meaning until they are older.

Celebrate Paul's Yes! by singing "O Sing a Song of Bethlehem" to review Jesus' life in simple words. It might also be a good day to sing "Jesus Loves Me."

Invite the congregation to join a soloist and the choir in singing the spiritual "Amen, Amen." The soloist could sing the verses, with the choir and congregation singing the Amens. *The Presbyterian Hymnal* includes an easy arrangement of this hymn.

The Liturgical Child

1. Affirm your faith responsively. Have a worship leader make a series of "I believe . . . " statements (perhaps the lines of a familiar creed). The congregation responds to each statement with a resounding, "Amen!" or "Yes!" Before making this affirmation, briefly explain the meaning of *Amen*: "I believe that!"; "Me too!"; "Count me in on that!"; or "Let it be just as you said." Or connect the "Yes!" to Paul's message to the Corinthians.

2. If you focus on forgiveness today, and if you include a prayer of confession, assurance of pardon, kyrie, and congregational response in weekly worship, take time just before that part of the service to talk about its significance. Instruct people to find it in their bulletins. Explain why it is located where it is in worship. Pay attention to the big words, but paraphrase what is going on in simple terms. For example: "We tell God we are sorry and ask God to forgive us. When we are reminded that God promises to forgive us, we naturally want to say thank you and hurray!" Then invite worshipers to confess their sins and accept God's forgiveness.

3. Before reading the Gospel lesson, invite children to listen carefully and then draw a picture of what happened. As they leave worship, speak briefly with them about their pictures and save those of willing artists to post on a bulletin board.

Sermon Resources

1. A prophet is rather like a coach. Isaiah was coaching the Jewish people in Babylon. So begin your sermon with several versions of a coach's speech to an errant team. In one version, have the coach resign because the team is not worth the coach's time and work. In another, have the coach kick offending players off the team. In the last, have the coach forgive and give the team more chances, as God did through Isaiah. Children, who have heard similar speeches from their teachers, coaches, and parents, are relieved to hear the final coach's forgiveness and to know that God is like that coach.

2. *The Giving Tree,* by Shel Silverstein, describes a tree that gives everything it has to a boy as that boy grows up. Though the word is not used, the tree also forgives the boy for his continual selfish use of the tree. In some congregations, this story is so familiar that you need only refer to it. In others, worshipers of all ages may enjoy hearing it read.

3. Demonstrate some of the ways athletes express their "Yes!" after sinking a hard basket, completing a difficult gymnastic trick, making a perfect dive, and so on. Point out that the athletes are saying with their triumphant fists and smiles, "There. That is how it's supposed to be done!" or "That is exactly what I have been trying to do!" or "That is my very best!" Imagine God making such gestures, as Jesus heals and forgives, then dies and rises.

Listen
carefully
as
Mark 2:1-12
is read
today.

Draw a
picture
of what
happened.

You may have heard of contests for counting
the beans in a jar. Today, count the AMENS
in our worship. Write AMEN on a bean each
time you hear, sing, or say AMEN.

There are ____ AMENs in
our worship today.

EIGHTH SUNDAY AFTER THE EPIPHANY
PROPER THREE

From a Child's Point of View

Old Testament: Hosea 2:14-20. This is a difficult but fascinating text for children. Their interest in weddings makes the passage attractive, but the comparison of God's relationship with people to that of a man wooing an estranged girlfriend/wife is beyond them. They rely on the preacher to say literally what Hosea said poetically.

Verses 18-20 can be introduced as friendship promises (marriage partners are one kind of best friends) describing the relationship God wants with us. God wants us to be at peace with the animals (the environment) and with one another. God's friendship, unlike the fickle friendships of some people, lasts forever. God insists that friends be treated fairly and that no one be hurt. God is a friend who understands and forgives. Such a friendship with such a God attracts children, who value friends and friendship highly.

Psalm: 103:1-13, 22. Children hear the psalmist's opening call to bless God, but quickly get lost in his words and images as he cites his reasons for praising God. Paraphrase, rather than explain those reasons to children: God forgives me, God healed me when I was sick, God saves me when I'm headed for trouble, and so on.

The psalmist's thoughts about God's response to our sins (verses 8-12) are important to children. The psalmist says that God does not become angry too easily—that is, God is patient with us. When we do something that does make God angry, God does not punish us as severely as we deserve and does not stay angry with us forever (God does not keep grudges). Based on their concrete understanding of such images, children enjoy and find security in the promise that in forgiving us, God pushes our sin as far away as the sky is from the earth, as far as the east is from the west.

Epistle: II Corinthians 3:1-6. Paul's situation, his use of the letter of recommendation, and the questions about pastoral authority that sparked the passage baffle children. It is, however, possible to highlight Paul's idea that faith is like a friendship with God. Through God's Spirit, we feel God with us and at work through us.

Gospel: Mark 2:13-22. Jesus' conversation with the scribes about the people he ate with hits home with elementary-school children. They tend to be picky about who they eat with in the lunch room and who they sit with on the bus or in the car pool. They jockey for seats with friends or people they want for friends. They are delighted when the right people choose to sit with them and horrified when an undesirable plops down beside them. They can stubbornly refuse to sit in the only place left, if it is beside such an undesirable; loudly tell an intruder that "these seats are saved," even if there are more "saved" seats than people to take them; and pout if forced to accept an unwanted seatmate. Jesus speaks directly to such children.

On the other hand, Mark's point in verses 18-22, that people should not use old standards to judge the new thing God was doing in Jesus, says little to children. Mark was addressing adults who were clinging to the old ways, not to children who are learning the "ways" for the first time. Mark's examples of fasting (a religious practice few children recognize), shrinking patches, and wineskins make these stories even harder for today's children.

Watch Words

If you focus on the Old Testament texts, consider introducing and using the word *shalom* to describe a right relationship with God.

Watch the wedding words. Speak of *engagement* or *wedding promises* rather than *betrothal*. (Older children are interested in the difference between biblical betrothals and today's more breakable engagements.)

Let the Children Sing

General praise hymns tend to be filled with difficult vocabulary. Choose carefully. Praise God for loving relationships with "For the Beauty of the Earth." If you sing "O Worship the King," invite children to illustrate one line or verse they especially like. Talk with children about their drawings as they leave the sanctuary.

Celebrate God's offer of friendship with "What a Friend We Have in Jesus" only if your children sing it often. The difficult vocabulary requires that children learn the words by ear rather than reading them.

The Liturgical Child

1. Feature Psalm 103:11-12 as the Assurance of Pardon, especially if you use the verses regularly. Tailor the following to your sanctuary:

Look up. Imagine that you can see through the roof to the sky. If it were night, we could see thousands of stars. Scientists tell us that the closest of those stars is millions of light years away. The psalmist says, "As high as the sky is above the earth, so great is [God's] love to those who have reverence for him" (GNB).

Look to the right. Imagine that you can see east through the wall, down the street, across the interstate highway, past Richmond to the Atlantic Ocean and beyond. Now turn to the left. Imagine that you can see west up the bypass, across the mountains, all the way to the Pacific Ocean. The psalmist says, "As far as the east is from the west, so far does [God] remove our sins from us."

Look straight ahead, and remember that God does forgive us. We can forget about our sins. They have been removed farther than the farthest star, farther than from east to west. Thanks be to God!

2. To create a litany prayer of praise, a worship leader describes a series of reasons for which your congregation can praise God. After each, the congregation responds, "Bless the Lord, O my soul, and all that is within me, bless his holy name." Include children's reasons for praising God. Ask a children's class to prepare some of the prayers.

3. If you celebrate Holy Communion, connect Jesus' meal at Levi's home with the invitation to the table. Point out that Jesus invites us, even when we feel most unworthy of coming to his table; that Jesus even invites some people we think do not deserve to be included. Jesus wants all of us to sit down together as friends.

Sermon Resources

1. Pick up on Valentine's Day interests. Describe the valentine wishes and gifts that God sends to the people through Hosea: peace between people and animals (ecological peace), peace among people (no more fighting), justice, forgiveness, and loyalty. You might even display, or give to someone in the congregation, a big paper heart inscribed with key words or pictures for each of God's valentines.

2. Help children who wear preshrunk clothing and see wine only in bottles get Jesus' point in Mark 2:21-22, by providing more familiar parables. For example, it is a waste to put fancy new shoelaces in tennis shoes that have holes and are so small they hurt your feet. It is also useless to wear your very best clothes for a piano recital for which you have not been practicing. Looking good will not make you sound any better.

3. Write each Hebrew letter in the word *shalom*, שָׁלוֹם or each letter in the English word *peace* on separate posters.

Invite one child forward to hold each poster. After spelling and defining the word, turn one child away from the congregation. Suggest that we don't need "ol' _____ (name)." Pause. Realize aloud that the word is no longer right. We no longer have shalom/peace. Maybe we do need "ol' _____" after all. Make the point about needing everyone to have the shalom/peace God offers. As the children return to their seats, give "ol' _____" a hug and some reassuring words.

51

Listen carefully as Psalm 103 is read. The poet lists reasons for praising God. To make your own psalm, write your reasons for praising God on the lines below.

A Psalm of _____

(your name)

Bless the Lord, O my soul,
and all that is within me,
bless his holy name.
Bless the Lord because

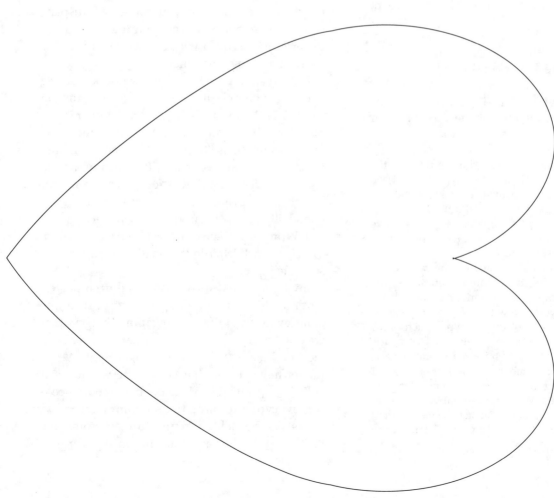

Valentine's Day is over, but no one would mind getting a valentine on any day. Draw a valentine, or write a valentine wish for God.

LAST SUNDAY AFTER THE EPIPHANY
TRANSFIGURATION

From a Child's Point of View

The focus of Transfiguration Sunday is that Jesus is the divine Son of God. Halfway between the celebration of "God with us" in the baby born in a barn, and the celebration of the resurrected Christ with us forever, we are reminded that Jesus was not just a good person, or even a new prophet. Jesus is God's Son who lived among us. With this in mind, we prepare for Lent. For children who are less likely to attend Ash Wednesday services, this preparation is important.

Gospel: Mark 9:2-9. In the Transfiguration, Mark tells us who Jesus is by how he looked and who stood with him. Unfortunately, Mark assumes that his readers know the significance of Jesus' appearance and of Moses' and Elijah's presence. Children do not, and they get lost in extensive explanations. All they need to know is that no human being ever looked like Jesus did on that mountain; that being seen with Moses and Elijah meant that Jesus was God's Messiah; and that God's voice confirmed what the disciples saw.

The disciples did understand and were impressed. Jesus then told them to tell no one what they had seen. In children's words, "You now know for sure that I am the Son of God, but you do not yet know what that means. It is not just looking superhuman and knowing long-dead leaders like Moses and Elijah. The important part of being the Son of God is suffering, even dying, to save people."

Old Testament: II Kings 2:1-12. The story of Elijah's fiery chariot is read today because of Elijah's appearance at the Transfiguration and because of the spectacular way he departed this life. Chil-

dren, however, are mainly attracted to Elisha's bravery in sticking with Elijah, and his boldness in asking for twice as much power as Elijah had. So the lesson may distract them. Furthermore, the fiery chariot, when connected to the divine dramatics of Transfiguration, leads children to ask why God did such things for people in the Bible, but not for us today. They wonder, "Were those people that much better than we are?" or "What would I have to do or be to rate such treatment?" or "Did God love the disciples more than us, and so gave them special proof about Jesus that we/I do not share?" Though there are few answers that satisfy literal thinkers, children appreciate hearing their questions recognized as valid.

Epistle: II Corinthians 4:3-6. The only idea in the passage that is meaningful to children is the suggestion that some people "veil their eyes"— that is, they do not see God standing before them because they are paying so much attention to other things (toys, TV, what others think of them, etc.). Or they insist that God can appear only in certain ways, and they refuse to see God in other ways. We are to watch for and recognize "God with us."

WARNING: Mixing Paul's poetic-light images in this text with the physical light in the Transfiguration story confuses literal thinkers.

Psalm: 50:1-6. This is another word picture of God appearing with great power. The New Jerusalem Bible paints a particularly clear picture for children. When the text is read in majestic tones, children sense God's greatness. But literal thinkers also respond that they have never seen God come with storming fire, so they need descriptions of other ways that God appears: God speaking through a Bible story; God's power displayed in the beauty and power of nature; God's presence felt during campfire vespers.

Watch Words

Some dictionaries define *Transfiguration* only with reference to this event in Jesus' life. So you might want to omit the long, strange word entirely. If you do use it, introduce it as the name of this day of the church year or as the title of this story about Jesus.

If you speak of *incarnation* or *Emmanuel* in talking about who Jesus is, do not expect children to recall these words from Christmas without coaching. Do reintroduce the terms to reenforce a growing worship vocabulary.

Let the Children Sing

Not one of the Transfiguration hymns is easy for children to sing with understanding. Before singing "Swiftly Pass the Clouds of Glory," paraphrase the last verse.

To praise Christ in more general terms, sing "Come, Christians, Join to Sing," with all its Alleluias; "When Morning Gilds the Skies," with its repeated "May Jesus Christ be praised!"; or "Fairest Lord Jesus," if spring seems near.

To review Jesus' life, sing "We Would See Jesus," "I Love to Tell the Story," or "O Sing a Song of Bethlehem."

The Liturgical Child

1. For the Call to Worship, read Mark 9:2,3, and 7, then say simply, "Let us worship God and Jesus, God's Son." For the Charge and Benediction, say:

As they came down from the mountain, Jesus told Peter, James, and John not to talk about what they had seen there. Though they knew Jesus was God's Son, they did not yet know what being God's Son meant. But you do. You know that God's Son was arrested, beaten, and killed. And you know that he rose on Easter. So do not be silent. Tell everyone! Tell people at school, people at work, and people in your neighborhood. Invite them to worship with you. Take care of them in Jesus' name. And remember that Jesus the Christ, God's Son, is with you always. Amen. ("Go, Tell It on the Mountain" is an appropriate choral response.)

2. Celebrate Jesus' divinity with a litany reviewing ways we know "God with us" in Jesus' life. The worship leader describes a series of things Jesus said and did. To each, the congregation responds, "God is with us!" Mention Jesus' birth as a helpless baby, his powerful healings, the way he made friends with people others looked down on, his teachings, and the confrontations of Holy Week and Easter. For example:

Jesus taught us that God loves us and wants us to love one another. He told a story about a father who waited for a son who had run away from home, and he said that God loves us as much as that father loved his son. He told us about a man who rescued a foreigner who had been beaten by bandits, and he said that we are to be like that man. When we hear Jesus' teachings, we know that . . . (CONGREGATIONAL RESPONSE)

3. See more suggestions for Transfiguration Sunday in Years A and C of this series.

Sermon Resources

1. The Transfiguration invites careful comparisons between Jesus and Superman. Superman was a being from the planet Krypton who lived on earth as "mild-mannered Clark Kent." Few people (except comic-book readers and movie-goers) ever saw him transformed into the powerful Superman. Similarly, Jesus of Nazareth was the divine Son of God. Only Peter, James, and John saw his divine appearance. Invite worshipers to recognize Jesus' true identity.

2. Speak about the church year. Recall how you celebrated Jesus' birth during Advent, Christmas, and Epiphany. Look ahead to Lent and Easter. Point out that Transfiguration Sunday is about halfway between Christmas and Easter. Talk about the importance of remembering who the Christmas baby was and of beginning Lent by remembering what that baby did when he grew up. Introduce any Lenten disciplines your congregation is urging this year, and point out Lenten opportunities to celebrate the life of Jesus, the Son of God.

Today we are about half way from Christmas to Easter.

Draw one picture of Jesus as a baby or boy.

Draw one picture of something Jesus did when he was a man.

Today we are thinking about who Jesus is. Listen for the names we give Jesus in worship. Fit one on each letter of JESUS.

1. J _ _ _ _

2. _ E _ _ _ _ _ _

3. S _ _

4. _ _ _ U _

5. _ _ _ _ S _ _

1. The name his friends called him

2. His job title

3. What God called him

4. What we call him at Christmas

5. A title used so often that some people think it is his last name

Answer: Jesus, Messiah, Son, Emmanuel, Christ

Last Sunday After the Epiphany | © 1993 by Abingdon Press.

FIRST SUNDAY IN LENT

From a Child's Point of View

Gospel: Mark 1:9-15. For children, this text might be titled, "How Jesus Got His Start." Children, because they are at such beginning points, are interested in what great people did as they began their careers. From these three brief stories, they learn that Jesus began with a personal decision. His baptism was like signing up to be on a team or going to a first club meeting. He decided to give himself to God. Apparently he was not sure what that would involve, but he went to be baptized as a way of saying that he was ready to try. God approved Jesus' decision by speaking to him. (Some perceptive children wonder how Mark knew about a voice that only Jesus heard.) After this decision came a time of disciplined preparation in the wilderness. Then Jesus began to preach. He called people to change their ways because the kingdom of God was coming. And he told them to trust God's love.

Epistle: I Peter 3:18-22. This passage, which puzzles scholars, overwhelms children with its profusion of unfamiliar concepts. The comment on Christ's preaching to the already dead raises for literal thinkers unanswerable questions about a peripheral Christian doctrine. Older children can begin to see a similarity between Noah's family, which floated through the flood waters to new lives, and Christians, who come through baptism to a new life in God's family. With adult help, children can connect the overview of Jesus' mission in verse 18*a* with his baptismal commitment and wilderness preparation. But a case can also made for simply reading this text for the adults.

Old Testament: Genesis 9:8-17. Children are fascinated by rainbows and love to draw them. Most church children are familiar with Noah's story. The story and the rainbow tell them that God loves and cares for us. Perhaps because of the way the story is generally presented to children, their attention focuses on the people and animals who were saved, rather than the people whose drownings were God's punishment or the innocent animals who died with them.

Psalm: 25:1-10. Children enjoy the alphabet format of this psalm when it is pointed out. The New Jerusalem Bible makes this format especially clear by starting each phrase with a word that begins with the sequence of letters in the English alphabet: "Adoration," "But," "Calling," and so on. Unfortunately, the psalmist's meaning is not as clear in that translation as in the New Revised Standard Version or the Good News Bible. With some help, children can sense the psalmist's dependence upon God's care and forgiveness.

Watch Words

Do not expect children to recognize the word *Lent*. Remember that it may sound like fuzzy *lint*. The derivation of the word interests worshipers of all ages.

Commitment is a big word that means to decide to do something. Discussions about such *decisions* are easier for young children to understand. If you do speak of *commitment*, begin by describing commitments to meet a friend for a movie, to play on a team, or to be a good club member.

If you focus on Jesus' preparation for his *min-*

56

istry, define *ministry* as a task to which God calls a person. Point out that every Christian, not just the professional *minister,* has an important ministry.

Let the Children Sing

Recall Jesus' time in the wilderness and begin the season of Lenten disciplines with "Jesus Walked This Lonesome Valley."

To sing your commitments, "Here I Am, Lord" (even nonreaders can sing the chorus) calls worshipers to make commitments similar to those Jesus made. The new hymn "Whom Shall I Send" can be sung by fifth-and sixth-graders, especially if it has been explored during the sermon (perhaps with hymnals open). But hymns such as "I Am Thine, O Lord," filled with difficult words and abstract ideas, do not reflect the experience of children and should be avoided. "Lord, I Want to Be a Christian" is probably the best commitment song for children.

Praise Noah's God with "All Creatures of Our God and King" or "All Things Bright and Beautiful."

The Liturgical Child

1. Begin worship by removing the white paraments of Epiphany or the green paraments of the pre-Lenten weeks and replacing them with the purple paraments of Lent. Some students from an older children's class could process in to receive the old paraments as worship leaders remove them, while other students process in with purple paraments to give to the leaders. During the change, a worship leader can describe the change of season in simple language. When the change is completed, the Call to Worship is given:

> At Christmas we celebrate the birth of the baby Jesus. But Jesus did not stay a baby. He grew up. He became a teacher, a preacher, a healer, a loving friend, and our Savior. During Lent, we celebrate his ministry, and we try to do a better job with the ministries to which we are called. Jesus is our Lord! Let us worship God.

2. If you focus on Noah's story, ask a younger children's class to prepare paper rainbows to arch over the sanctuary doors. Draw rainbow stripes with pencil on nonglossy shelf paper, which can be cut into sections to fit the doors. Children then paint the rainbows with tempera paints and large brushes.

3. The format of Psalm 25 suggests two presentations: (1) To emphasize and enjoy the acrostic, ask an older children's class to present the New Jerusalem Bible translation. Each child, in succession, says one letter or holds up a poster with one letter, then reads or recites that phrase of the psalm; (2) Use the psalm as the Prayer of Confession. Invite the congregation to read and pray verses 1-7 in unison. The worship leader then reads verses 8-10 as the Assurance of Pardon. Use the Good News Bible or the New Revised Standard Version.

4. After preaching about Lenten disciplines that prepare us for ministry, challenge worshipers of all ages to write or draw on a slip of paper one discipline they will try during Lent. Invite them to place the paper in the offering plate as a sign of their commitment. Promise confidentiality and instruct the ushers to respect it.

Sermon Resources

1. Compare Jesus' time of prayer in the wilderness to: (1) the discipline of a sports camps, with early morning exercises, practice sessions, and classes; or (2) the orientation during which new missionaries learn about the country where they will go, learn a new language, worship together, and prepare for the work they will do. Finally, describe some of the activities of your congregation that prepare people for ministry at home, work, and school.

2. Lent is traditionally the time for baptism and confirmation preparation. Especially if such preparation is beginning in your congregation, speak to the congregation of its meaning and significance. Link it to Jesus' preparation for ministry. Speak specifically about what is involved, so that younger children have something to grow up toward. Spend time on big unfamiliar terms—confirmation, commissioning, and profession of faith.

3. A three-point sermon on "How to Keep Lent," based on today's texts about Jesus' preparation for ministry, could urge worshipers of all ages to commit themselves to one or more disciplines or changes they want to make during Lent, remember God's love every day, and share the good news with others.

Jesus spent 40 days alone in the wilderness to prepare for his work.

Make a picture poem. On the mountains, rocks, and trees, write:

2 things Jesus did in the wilderness
2 things you think he thought about
2 feelings he felt

JESUS
into the wilderness

out of the wilderness
CHRIST

SECOND SUNDAY IN LENT

From a Child's Point of View

Today's texts are loosely gathered around the meaning of life in covenant with God.

Old Testament: Genesis 17:1-7, 15-16. The story of God's announcing the covenant to Abram is simple, especially as presented in The Good News Bible. Abram and Sarai are promised that from them will come great nations, and they are given new names as a sign of that promise. Children are fascinated with names, especially those with special meaning. They like Native American names and often adopt secret names among themselves. So they tend to focus on the new names and, unless they are pointed out, are likely to overlook God's introductory instructions: "Obey me and always do what is right." In so doing, they miss a key part of what it means to live in covenant with God.

Gospel: Mark 8:31-38 or Mark 9:2-9. While the Genesis account focuses on God's covenant promises, the Gospel lesson focuses on what living in covenant with God requires. Unfortunately, Jesus' symbolic talk about finding life and taking up crosses is hard for children to understand. They depend on the preacher to describe the temptation to take the easy, selfish way, rather than do God's hard work of loving and caring for others. They need to hear that sometimes, to love and care for others, God asks us to take stands that make us unpopular or to give up what we want and need.

Jesus also points to a strange surprise. When we are hurt because we obey God or when we give up what is ours in order to take care of others, we find a special kind of happiness that makes the pain more bearable. Adults who try to use the thoughts of this happiness to bribe children, or who force them to admit to experiencing it when they have been coerced into a self-sacrificing deed they did not want to do, steal the joy. It is more effective to present the happiness as a mystery which Jesus told us about, and then alert children to watch for it when they choose to do self-sacrificing deeds.

Commentary and suggestions for using Mark 9:2-9 (the Transfiguration Story) are offered on the last Sunday of Epiphany, for which it is also the suggested Gospel.

Epistle: Romans 4:13-25. Paul's point, that we take up crosses not in order to gain God's salvation (or earn the covenant promises) but in response to God's salvation, is too subtle for children. For them, faith such as Abraham and Sarah had means deciding to follow God—even when it causes discomfort. Abraham and Sarah decided that following God was worth the risks of the travel and all the comforts they gave up. They decided that there were things more important than a comfortable home, good food, and even being safe. Jesus and Paul agreed. All of them took many risks and suffered for their decisions. But all said they were happy with their decisions, and they call us to obey God, no matter what it costs.

Paul assumes that his readers know the story of Abraham and Sarah in detail. While children may have heard most of it, they will need to hear it again, with attention focused on the specific risks and hardships involved.

Psalm: 22:23-31. Children will catch occasional phrases of this hymn of praise, but neither the phrases nor the whole will grab their attention.

Watch Words

Covenant, a key Christian term that is not familiar to children, is an agreement. People make covenants when they marry, or when nations sign agreements about what they will and will not do. The Bible describes several covenants that God offers to people.

In today's texts, *faith* means trusting God so completely that we will risk our comfort and safety to obey God. *Faith* is acting as if the self-giving ways of God are better than self-serving ones.

For children, a *cross* is a wooden means of execution. Jesus was killed on a *cross.* Calls to *take up your cross* need to be illustrated with specific examples of ways we can give up our own wants, comfort, and even safety, in order to take care of others.

Let the Children Sing

Be careful with hymns about taking up crosses. Their symbolic, often obsolete language confuses children. To introduce the new hymn "Take Up Your Cross, the Savior Said," read and put into your own words the first verse or two. (The verses become progressively more difficult for children to understand.)

"Jesus Walked This Lonesome Valley" is the easiest song about suffering obedience for children. If the story sequence of the verses of "Go to Dark Gethsemane" is pointed out, older children can begin to learn it.

The Liturgical Child

1. Middle-elementary readers can join in reading this Prayer of Confession:

God of Abraham and Sarah, Abraham and Sarah obeyed you. They left their comfortable home to live in an unknown country. But we love our homes. We want to keep all our clothes, toys, and comforts. We are quick with excuses about giving any of them up. Forgive us.

God of Paul, Paul spoke about you everywhere he went. For what he said, he was whipped, put in jail, and even stoned. But we are slow to speak up about you. We are afraid we will be embarrassed, or teased, or laughed at. Forgive us.

Lord Jesus, you prayed not to have to die on the cross, but you obeyed. When we are called to do hard, frightening disciple's work, we make excuses or hide. Forgive us.

Lord God, you call us to be disciples. Be with us. Give us the courage we need; for we pray in your name. Amen.

2. Give worshipers small plastic or metal crosses to carry in a pocket or purse during Lent, as a reminder that they are to be ready to do self-giving disciple's work.

Sermon Resources

1. If you focus on bearing crosses, display a variety of crosses in the chancel. Include crosses of various sizes, materials, and styles. Use their meanings to explore what it means to "bear a cross."

2. Cite as examples of suffering discipleship the children and teenagers who integrated public schools in the South. Robert Coles describes their experiences in *Children of Crisis, Vol. 1: A Study of Courage and Fear.* Chapters 2 ("When I Draw the Lord, He'll Be a Real Big Man") and 3 ("The Students") offer children's accounts of what they experienced.

3. These two stories about self-sacrificing animals are appreciated by people of all ages: "Barrington Bunny," found in *The Way of the Wolf* by Martin Bell; and *The Story of Jumping Mouse* by John Steptoe.

4. Speak about the practice of "giving something up for Lent." Encourage worshipers of all ages to give up some pleasure in order to raise their contribution to the congregation's Lenten offering. Children can give up movie money or snack money or part of their pocket money so that others may have basic necessities.

Artists in Central America paint pictures of Jesus and of people being disciples on crosses. One cross may have a different picture on each arm.

Create a cross of your own by drawing pictures of Jesus and of people being disciples.

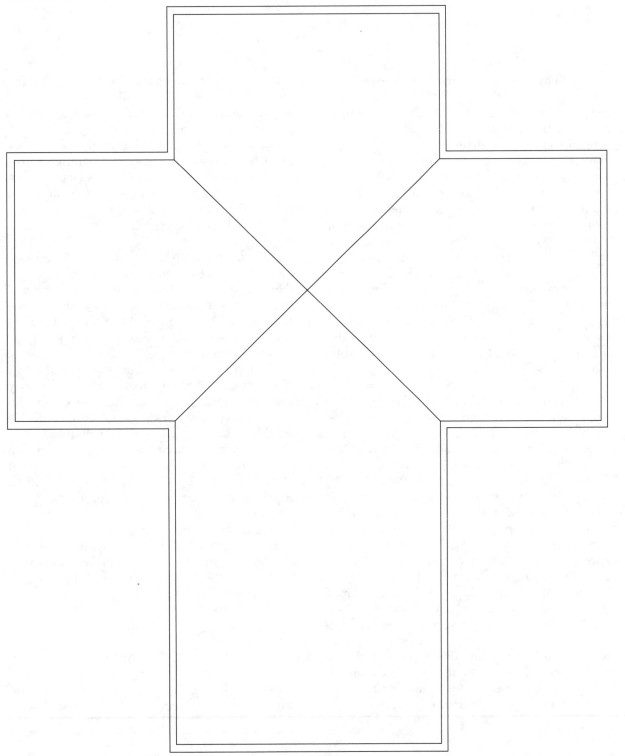

Second Sunday in Lent | © 1993 by Abingdon Press.

THIRD SUNDAY IN LENT

From a Child's Point of View

Epistle: I Corinthians 1:18-25. A case can be made for using this text as the summary text for worship, celebrating the wisdom of God, which, though it looks foolish by the standards of this world, is wiser than any human wisdom. Children will, however, have trouble with Paul's examples. For them, Paul's comments about the Jewish wish for miracles and the Greek interest in philosophy are foreign. They find more meaning in a comparison between the "foolish" Ten Commandments and the "wise" look-out-for-yourself mentality of today's world. Use specific examples, such as comparing the short-term wisdom of stealing what you want with the long-term wisdom of living among people who can trust one another not to steal. Children appreciate the summary in verse 25.

Old Testament: Exodus 20:1-17. Children place high value on, and have great interest in rules. They learn Scout, club, class, and team rules. Though they are not aware of it, they often evaluate groups by the quality of their rules. The Ten Commandments, viewed as the rules of God's people, tell much about God and God's people. They can be used in the context of today's other texts as a standard for measuring the wisdom or foolishness of God and God's people. Unfortunately, in a world in which most school children feel that cheating is all right if you don't get caught; more than half the children have divorced or single parents; and ads urge children to want more and more of everything, the Ten Commandments make God's people and God look pretty foolish. It is best to admit this honestly, and then explore examples of real strength and wisdom. (See Year A, Proper 22, for Commandment-by-Commandment commentary for children.)

Psalm: 19. In the context of today's themes, verses 7-14 are key. Once children have explored and evaluated the Ten Commandments, they are generally ready to praise God for these "wise" rules. Before they can do so using this psalm, they need help in identifying the six strange words that are synonyms for God's rules (*laws, decrees,* etc.). Then they will catch the meaning of one or two of the phrases and will enjoy celebrating God's good rules in general.

Gospel: John 2:13-22. Children are impressed by Jesus' strong action in the Temple. The Jesus they see here knows what is right and wrong, and protests strongly when he sees things that are terribly wrong. He is not afraid to turn over tables and make a scene to make an important point.

Read in the context of the other texts, Jesus' action in the Temple is a fine example of God's "foolishness." When he turned over the money changers' tables, Jesus made some very powerful people angry. It was not a "wise" thing to do. He would not have gotten into so much trouble if he had written a letter or talked quietly to people in private. But Jesus was thinking from God's point of view and making God's point as clearly as he could. Making that point was worth getting into trouble.

Also in the context of the other readings, Jesus' conversation with the leaders about rebuilding the Temple is a joke on the foolish leaders who thought they were smart. They called Jesus foolish, but since the resurrection, we know who the real fools were.

Watch Words

Do not speak of the *foolishness of the cross* without describing it specifically—that is, Jesus, God's

Son, who could have forced everyone to obey, did not. Instead, he loved them. He did not stop loving them, even when they killed him.

Law, decrees, precepts, Commandments, fear, ordinances—all these words are synonyms (words that mean the same as) for God's rules, or *Torah* (Psalm 19).

Explain the function of the *money changers* before telling the Gospel story.

Let the Children Sing

The repeated chorus of "God of Grace and God of Glory" is a prayer ("grant us wisdom, grant us courage . . .") which even nonreaders can sing. But the vocabulary of "Immortal, Invisible, God Only Wise" makes it strictly an adult hymn about God's wisdom. If you featured "Guide Me, O Thou Great Jehovah" during the reading of Exodus last fall, this is a good Sunday to sing it again.

Once they know that in "O God, What You Ordain Is Right," *ordain* means what God decides or declares (rather than to ordain a minister or church officer), children can follow the simple language. If they sing it frequently in other settings in which its meaning is explored, children can sing of God's wisdom and power with "How Great Thou Art."

The Liturgical Child

1. Have a children's class "read" the Old Testament lesson. Each of ten children recites one of the Ten Commandments. Have the children stand in the correct order so that they need to remember only their Commandment and its number.

2. See the third Sunday after the Epiphany, Year C of this series, which provides a script for six children to read Psalm 19:7-14.

3. As an Affirmation of Faith in God's wisdom, the congregation reads I Corinthians 1:25 in response to each of the Ten Commandments read by the worship leader. The New Revised Standard Version offers a translation that is clear to worshipers of all ages. For example:

Leader: I am the Lord your God, who brought you out of the land of Egypt, out of the house of slavery; you shall have no other gods before me.

People: We believe that "God's foolishness is wiser than human wisdom, and God's weakness is stronger than human strength."

4. Be daring! Invite an adult clown in full makeup and costume (featuring a large cross or other Christian symbol) to be present and move about being helpful before and at the beginning of the service by escorting people to their places, dusting their seats, handing them hymnbooks, holding the hand of the first person in the processional, straightening the minister's notes or the organist's music, and so forth. Then at the appropriate time, the clown comes to the lectern to read the Epistle lesson—for emphasis, reading verse 25 both first and last. During the sermon, compare the clown's "foolishness" with God's "foolishness." Try this only if you can find a clown who will do the job with both creativity and sensitivity.

Sermon Resources

1. Create some opposites for each of the Ten Commandments. Let each reflect the "wisdom" of our world and the "foolishness" of God's rules. For example, opposites for "Do not steal" could be "Finders keepers," "If I can take it, it's mine!" and "If you want it, figure out how to get it."

2. Hans Christian Anderson speaks about wisdom and foolishness in "The Emperor's New Clothes," in which scoundrels promise the emperor a set of magic clothes that those who are "stupid" and "unfit for their jobs" (i.e., foolish) cannot see. When the scoundrels provide the clothes, no one, including the emperor, can see them, but everyone who wants to be wise pretends to see them and comments on their beauty. It is a "foolish" child who finally blurts out the truth, as the emperor parades through the streets in his "magic" clothes.

More Worship Worksheet Ideas: Proper 22 in Year A includes a Ten Commandments puzzle. The Third Sunday After the Epiphany in Year C offers a coded version of Psalm 19:14.

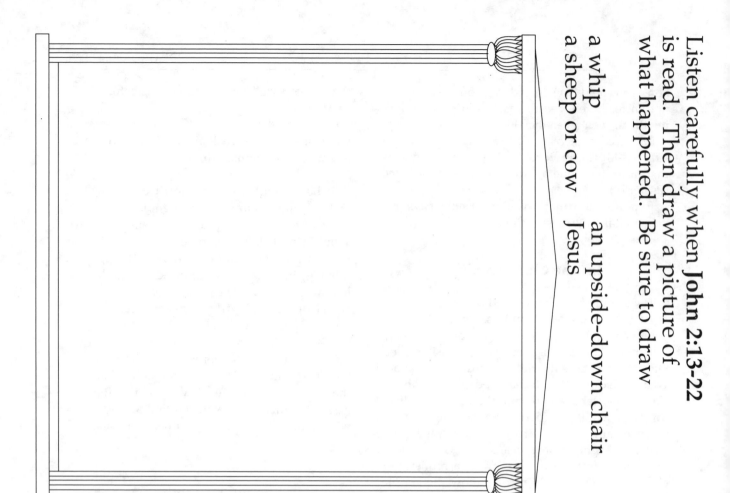

Listen carefully when **John 2:13-22** is read. Then draw a picture of what happened. Be sure to draw

a whip   an upside-down chair
a sheep or cow   Jesus

Each of the words below is upside down and backwards. Fix them to find a truth about God's wisdom.

THAN WISER IS FOOLISHNESS GOD'S

_ _ _ _ ' _

WEAKNESS GOD'S AND, WISDOM HUMAN

_ _ _ _ _ _ _ _ _ _ _ ; _ _ _ ' _ _ _ _ _ _ _

STRENGTH HUMAN THAN STRONGER IS

_ .

Third Sunday in Lent / © *1993 by Abingdon Press.*

FOURTH SUNDAY
IN LENT

From a Child's Point of View

Old Testament: Numbers 21:4-9. This is the story of the bronze snake which Moses erected to heal those bitten by poisonous snakes. Because both the psalm and the Gospel refer to this not-very-familiar story, it should be read early in the service. Before reading it, remind worshipers both of the difficulties the Hebrews faced during their desert travels and of the special way God had cared for them in the desert, giving them manna and quail. With such background, even young children can follow and understand the story.

Psalm: 107:1-3, 17-22. This psalm was sung by pilgrims as they walked together to religious festivals in Jerusalem. It is not unlike the songs and games families enjoy to pass the time on long car trips. Verses 1-3 introduce the song by pointing out that God saves us from our own messes. The stanzas that follow describe how God saves travelers, prisoners, the sick, and sailors. Today's reading includes the introduction and the stanza about the sick. Do not expect children to understand the belief that sin caused sickness. Instead, suggest that this stanza be sung for the people who were bitten by the snakes in the desert.

Gospel: John 3:14-21. John's message is like a two-sided coin. On one side is the truth that God sends Jesus to save people. On the other is the paradoxical truth that those who do not want to be saved find themselves judged instead. The combined message is too subtle for children. They will need to examine each side separately.

The first side tells us that God loves us and sent Jesus to save us. God gave us Jesus as a perfect example of how to live. God then forgave the human race for not following Jesus' example, and even for killing him. Then and now, God's forgiveness saves us from punishment we deserve. It also saves us from trying to be good enough for God.

The second half of the message is most clearly put to children in verses 20 and 21. While they may miss the symbolic meaning of dark and light (v. 20), they do have experience with trying to hide in a dark closet or under the covers to do something they know is wrong. And any children who have fidgeted through the presentation of a project that did not get their best efforts knows what the judgment of "coming to the light" (v.21) feels like. Just as they judge their projects before the teacher grades them, they can understand that we may judge our own actions before God does.

Epistle: Ephesians 2:1-10. Children will not follow this abstract theological discussion as it is read. With help, they can, however, explore two of its points.

Children have experienced being stuck in a variety of hopeless situations, ranging from long late-winter weekends trapped indoors with squabbling siblings, to parental abuse and fighting. After such experiences, they can empathize with the hopeless cry, "I wish I were dead." Concrete examples of sinful activity that lead people to feeling dead, or wishing they were dead, bring the phrase "dead in sin" more vividly to life than does expounding on the details of this argument.

The other point that speaks to children is that we do not need to earn God's respect. God loves and forgives us just as we are. God knows all the awful things we have done and thought, but God also knows the things we have been created able to do. God is more interested in the good we can do than in the bad we have done.

Watch Words

Today's texts are a mine field of abstract theological terms. Focus on one and avoid the others.

All children are *judged* by their teachers, coaches, peers, and even parents. The Good News is that they do not need to impress God. God does not want to *judge* them.

Literal-thinking children have a hard time grasping *how God saves us.* That we are "saved" as a result of Jesus' death and resurrection makes little sense. For them today, it means that we are saved from having to be good enough for God.

Grace is a girl's name and the ability to **move** beautifully. For Christian children, it may be a prayer before meals. *Grace* is also receiving good things you do not deserve—specifically, it is receiving God's forgiveness and love, even though you do not deserve them.

Let the Children Sing

"Help Us Accept Each Other" uses the language of acceptance, rather than salvation, to sing about the message of John 3:16-21. Acceptance is more meaningful to ten- to twelve-year-olds intent on relationships.

Using simple language, "O Sing a Song of Bethlehem" tells about Jesus saving us. Children will sing along if the story format is pointed out before the hymn is sung.

The spiritual "I Want Jesus to Walk with Me" is a simple prayer for the saving God to be with us. The repeated words make it easy for young readers.

The Liturgical Child

1. Introduce the context of Psalm 107, then have it read by a group, a different person reading each stanza. Verses 1-3 may be read in unison by the readers or by the worship leader who introduces the psalm. The other verses:

  verses 4-9—desert travelers
  verses 10-16—prisoners
  verses 17-22—the sick
  verses 23-32—sailors

Help readers express with their voices the change that occurred when God's saving actions solved their problems. A group of fifth- or sixth-graders would enjoy preparing such a reading.

2. In confession, a leader describes a series of situations in which we are "dead in sin." Worshipers respond to each, "It makes us wish we were dead." For example:

Leader: God of Truth, our world is tied up in lies. Countries lie to each other. Leaders lie to their people. Bosses and employees lie on the job. Even friends and families lie. Often, lies become so entangled that they seem hopeless.
People: It makes us wish we were dead.

Assurance of Pardon: God says to all of us, "Do not give up. I will save you. I forgive you. I will change you. I love you." Thanks be to God. Amen.

3. To pray for those in need of God's saving action today, a leader offers a series of prayers for people in specific desperate situations. After each, the congregation responds by singing the chorus of "Kum Ba Yah."

Sermon Resources

1. The focal word today is *save.* The dictionary offers a variety of definitions for *save* which can be related both to everyday activities and to God's saving of us. For example:

• "to save from danger": A person can be saved from a river that is tumbling toward a waterfall. A girl or boy can be saved from getting in trouble with a street gang if he or she is offered the opportunity to work and play with friends in sports or youth clubs. People in Moses' camp who had been bitten by poisonous snakes were saved when they looked at the bronze snake. God saves us from lives that make us wish we were dead by forgiving us and giving us the power to change.
• "to set aside for special use": A family saves pennies in a jar for vacation treats. Many children put money into savings accounts for special purchases. God saves us, or sets us aside, for special work. God does not want our lives to be wasted, but to be saved for important activities.

Listen carefully when **Numbers 21 : 4 – 9** is read. Then draw a picture of what happened. Where will you put the most important snake?

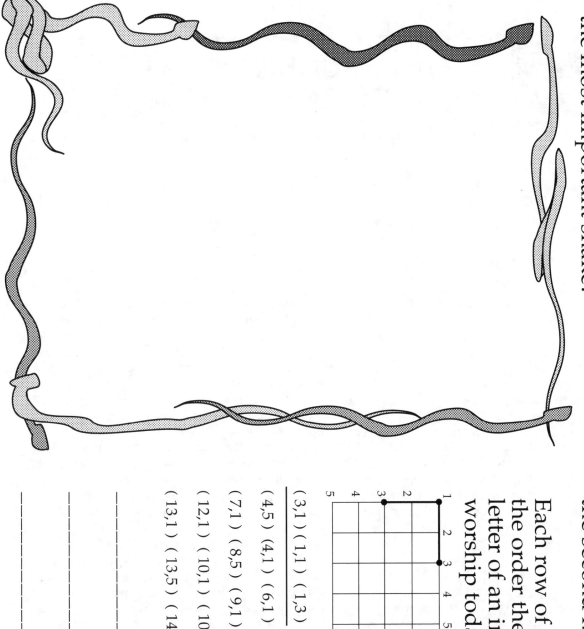

The 2 numbers in each ( ) show the point where 2 lines meet. To find the first number, count across the lines. To find the second number, count down.

Each row of points, when connected in the order they are listed, form 1 letter of an important word in our worship today.

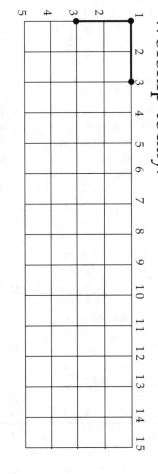

(3,1) (1,1) (1,3) (3,3) (3,5) (1,5) = ___

(4,5) (4,1) (6,1) (6,5) and (4,3) (6,3) = ___

(7,1) (8,5) (9,1) = ___

(12,1) (10,1) (10,5) (12,5) and (10,3) (11,3) = ___

(13,1) (13,5) (14,5) (15,4) (15,2) (14,1) (13,1) = ___

___ ___ ___ ___ ___ to me means ___ ___

FIFTH SUNDAY
IN LENT

From a Child's Point of View

In planning today's worship, consider the following:

Children are quickly overwhelmed when confronted with all these texts. It is better to explore either the New Testament crucifixion texts or the Old Testament "heart" lessons.

During Lent, all worshipers need to encounter the crucifixion story. If you celebrate Palm Sunday next week, and few children participate in Good Friday worship, this Sunday would be a good time to focus on the crucifixion. If, on the other hand, you celebrate Passion Sunday next week, you may prefer to work with the Old Testament texts this week.

Old Testament: Jeremiah 31:31-34. For literal thinkers, the possibility of having their heart cleaned creates a strange, rather humorous picture. But at an early age, children send valentines and begin to understand such phrases as "I give my heart to you." Therefore when it is approached deliberately, the clean heart, or a covenant written on the heart, begins to make sense to children.

Children know the difference between keeping rules someone else forces on you and keeping rules you have chosen. You keep the first because you have to; you keep the second because you want to. Sometimes, as the Hebrews carried the Ten Commandment stones with them, they were happy to have the rules. But sometimes they felt as if God had forced the rules on them, and because of this, they often broke the rules. Jeremiah said that one day God would make a covenant with us that we would keep because we want to, not because we have to.

Psalm: 51:1-12 or 119:9-16. Psalm 51 is one of those familiar prayers that is loved in part for its beautiful language. Unfortunately, that language is often foreign to children. The challenge is to introduce such prayers effectively to children while preserving their beauty for adults. In this case, it is more meaningful to tell the story behind the psalm than to explain the difficult words and phrases. When children have heard that David had murdered a man in order to steal his wife, even the youngest ones recognize the repentant mood of the psalm and understand a few of the phrases. As their vocabularies grow, they catch the meaning of more and more of the confessional phrases.

The compelling story behind Psalm 51 makes it a better choice for children than Psalm 119's eight loosely connected verses expressing love for God's Law. If you do read this psalm portion, point out all the synonyms for God's covenant, or Law, that are written in our hearts. (The New Jerusalem Bible provides an especially clear translation.)

Gospel: John 12:20-33. To explain why Jesus accepted the cross, John tells this complicated story instead of the Gethsemane story. While the Gethsemane story is easier for children to understand, this one can make sense with some adult help. Like the Jews of that time, and many adults today, children wish for a hero who will conquer all their enemies and solve all their problems.

They can understand Jesus' insistence that God did not send him to be that kind of hero. Jesus taught us to love our enemies into friends and to solve our problems by taking care of one another. Jesus accepted the cross because he knew that self-giving love was what we needed.

Epistle: Hebrews 5:5-10. For children, the crux of this lesson is found in verses 7-9. They will not grasp its message as it is read, but with help, they can appreciate how hard it was for Jesus to accept being crucified. He, like anyone, wanted to run from the horror of being crucified. If these horrors are described in detail, children are impressed by Jesus' willingness to carry out his terrifying mission.

Watch Words

If you focus on the Old Testament texts, avoid *penitence* and *repentance.* Speak of *feeling sorry about* and *confessing* what we did wrong, and promising to do better.

A *covenant* is an agreement. Avoid using the word repeatedly unless it is featured in your children's church school curriculum.

Remember that in everyday use, *passion* refers to sexual feelings. If you use the term to describe Jesus' self-sacrifice, redefine it accordingly.

Crucifixion, fortunately, is no longer used as a method of execution. Children need to hear how a person was crucified, how crucifixion killed, and why it was so terrible.

Let the Children Sing

Choose Passion hymns carefully. Children are baffled by those that speak symbolically about the cross. "Were You There" is probably the best because it tells the story simply and with great feeling. While children cannot understand the meaning of "O Sacred Head Now Wounded," they do pick up on its strong emotions. Older children can follow the Passion story as it is presented in "Go to Dark Gethsemane," especially if they are alerted to the story line before singing it.

"O for a Heart to Praise My God" is filled with references to hearts that belong to God. Instruct worshipers to listen for those references as they sing.

The Liturgical Child

1. For a powerful beginning for worship focused on the Passion, have a soloist sing the first two verses of "What Wondrous Love Is This?" a cappella as he or she walks down the aisle, lights any candles in the chancel, and takes a seat. If the choir normally processes, it may silently follow the singer. Though children understand little more than the first phrase of each verse, they respond strongly to the mood created.

2. Pray a responsive Prayer of Confession, with the congregation responding, "Create in me a clean heart, O God, and put a new and right spirit within me," to confessions voiced by a worship leader. If the prayer follows the reading of Psalm 51, relate it to David's confession. For example:

Leader: God, like David, we see things we want. We want cars and homes and clothes and toys. We want to have good jobs and be on the winning team. We want to have popular, interesting friends. All our wants get us in trouble.

People: Create in me a clean heart, O God, and put a new and right spirit within me.

Leader: God, like David, we know what is right and wrong but we forget . . .

Sermon Resources

1. To explore the meaning of the clean heart, have fun imagining the literal possibility of removing a person's heart, scrubbing it down, then stuffing it back into place. Next tell about an old car engine or bicycle clogged up with dirt and rust. Describe how poorly it works, how it can be cleaned up, and how it works afterwards. Finally, point out ways we can get too clogged up with bad feelings to work properly. We feel so terrible about mean things we have done, we forget we can do kind deeds. We have been so mean to someone that we hide from them. Describe how we can let God clean us up so that we work again, like a clean heart or bike or engine. Be concrete and specific.

2. Compare the Son of Man (as the Jews expected him to be) with cartoon heroes who win the day with force. Popeye, for example, after eating spinach, beats up Brutus the bully. But in the next episode, Brutus is back, still the enemy. So the problem really has not been solved. Jesus, in the crucifixion, chooses another way to deal with enemies and bullies.

Use the cross-code key to decode this message.

✝ ✝✝✝✝ PU✝ ✝Y ✝✝✝ ✝✝✝✝✝✝ ✝ ✝✝✝

__ ____ ___ __ ___ ___ _____ _ ____

✝ ✝✝✝✝ ✝✝✝✝✝ ✝✝ ✝✝ ✝✝✝✝✝ ✝✝✝✝✝S.

__ ____ ___ __ __ _____ _____ ____.

⊕ =A	=E	⚓ =H	✝ =I	=L
=M	=N	=R	=T	=W

Listen when Jeremiah 31:33 is read. Who is the "I"?

Find the 9 crucifixion words hidden in the letters below.

```
P R Q D J C R O S S
A Z K I X R R A Q P
S M J E S U S L W H
S G L Q C R O W N M
I F O R G I V E J S
O W T S F W H I P S
N H E J D Y M L H J
```

PASSION DIE CROWN
FORGIVE (JESUS) WHIP
CRUCIFY LOVE CROSS

Circle each word every time
you hear it, sing it, or
say it in worship today.

Fifth Sunday in Lent | © 1993 by Abingdon Press.

PALM/PASSION SUNDAY

Consider the children when deciding whether to celebrate Palm or Passion Sunday. If they will not worship around the Passion stories on Holy (Maundy) Thursday or Good Friday, and worship last Sunday did not focus on the crucifixion, celebrate Passion Sunday rather than Palm Sunday. No worshiper of any age can fully understand or share in Easter joy without first exploring the betrayals and crucifixion.

Only the Gospel texts for Palm/Passion Sunday differ from year to year. Check other cycles of this series for additional commentary and suggestions.

From a Child's Point of View

Gospel: (Palm) Mark 11:1-11 or John 12:12-16. Mark's account of the triumphal entry is filled with details that make it the more interesting of these two for children. But both focus on what might be called the Palm Sunday Misunderstanding. That misunderstanding began with what Jesus "said" to the crowd as he came to Jerusalem. By riding on a donkey he "said" that he came in peace, as a humble rather than a warrior king. But the people "heard" only that Jesus was coming as a king. So they expected him to save them as a warrior king would. John points out that it was not until after Easter that the disciples understood what Jesus was "saying" and realized that he had indeed saved them—but not the way they expected.

Gospel: (Passion) Mark 14:1–15:47 or Mark 15:1-39 (40-47). Two themes stand out in Mark's text: The King is crucified; the loving friend is betrayed and killed by those he loved. The second

speaks more clearly to children, who value the loyalty of friends highly and know first-hand the pain of betrayals by those they have trusted. This theme is announced in verse 14:27, in language children understand: "You will all become deserters" (NRSV) or "All of you will run away and leave me" (GNB).

It is then detailed in the disciples failing to stay awake with Jesus as he prayed, Judas helping Jesus' enemies arrest him, Peter disowning his best friend, Pilate refusing to protect Jesus, the once welcoming crowd calling for his death, and finally Jesus' cry from the cross, wondering if even God had abandoned him. Children feel this kind of pain keenly and are impressed that God and Jesus could forgive these people. Though they cannot yet feel solidarity with the deserters and accept God's forgiveness with them, they can conclude that if God would forgive those who betrayed and deserted Jesus, then God will forgive them (the children) for their betrayals and desertions.

Epistle: Philippians 2:5-11. Children will grasp neither the language nor the theology of this hymn as it is read. They depend on the preacher to explain it's message. If the focus of worship is on Jesus' mission of forgiveness, verses 6-8 become a description of Jesus' commitment to forgive all those who betrayed and abandoned him during Holy Week. Jesus, who could have fought back, chose to love and forgive. Children appreciate such tenacious forgiveness. They also can be challenged to follow Jesus' example in forgiving their friends.

Psalm: (Palm) 118:1-2, 19-29; (Passion) Psalm 31:9-16 and Isaiah 50:4-9a. If either of these poems is well read, children will hear in them phrases related to the New Testament stories and Holy Week themes.

Watch Words

Hosanna may be used simply as a greeting meant only for Jesus, or it's meaning, *save us*, may be explored.

For most children, *passion* is related to sexual feelings. Go back to the dictionary definitions that speak of caring very strongly about and being ready to make sacrifices on behalf of, some object. In his crucifixion, Jesus showed *passion* for loving forgiveness.

Let the Children Sing

On the last Sunday in Lent, chuckle about the possibility of having a thousand tongues, imagine a choir of a thousand people singing God's praises, then sing "O for a Thousand Tongues to Sing." "To God Be the Glory," if the difficult verse that begins "O perfect redemption" is omitted, is another good choice.

Palm Sunday: "All Glory Laud and Honor" and "Hosanna, Loud Hosanna" are the most familiar Palm Sunday hymns for children. "Tell Me the Stories of Jesus," which many children know, also includes a verse about Palm Sunday.

Passion Sunday: "Were You There?" is the most understandable and emotionally powerful crucifixion song for children. Remember that children have difficulty understanding hymns that speak symbolically of the cross and use abstract atonement language.

The Liturgical Child

1. Turn the crowd's shouts into an intergenerational Call to Worship. An adult choir might respond to a children's class or choir. Or the adults in the congregation, led by an adult, could respond to the children, led by a child or a children's class. A processional hymn led by palm-waving children follows naturally. For example:

Children: Hosanna!

Adults: Blessed is he who comes in the name of the Lord!

Children: Hosanna!

Children and Adults: Let us worship God together.

2. Use the part of the Apostles' Creed about Jesus as an Affirmation of Faith. After a worship leader recites each phrase, the congregation responds, "Hosanna, Blessed is he who comes in the name of the Lord!":

Leader: I believe in Jesus Christ, his only Son, our Lord.

People: Hosanna! Blessed is he who comes in the name of the Lord!

Leader: Who was conceived of the Holy Ghost and born of the virgin Mary.

People: Hosanna! Blessed is he who comes in the name of the Lord!

3. As the Passion is read, present a series of tableaus of events. Position the actors for each scene to emphasize the rejections by facing them away from Jesus, folding arms over chests and/or putting hands palms out to separate themselves from Jesus. Help actors show appropriate facial expressions. To keep the focus on rejection, dress actors in dark turtlenecks and pants rather than biblical costumes. Children pay close attention to such tableaus, but are not mature enough to do the acting. Well-prepared youths and adults are needed for these strong scenes.

Sermon Resources

1. Peter, the rough and ready fishing disciple, is a character to whom children relate. He was always first to rush in and frequently got into things he could not complete. He was one of Jesus' very best friends. So devote the sermon to telling and interpreting the stories of Holy Week from his point of view. Speak from the pre-Easter point of view to communicate the strength of Peter's feelings about his failures and about what happened.

2. If you explore the Palm Sunday Misunder-

standing, begin by citing ways people want to be saved and things from which they want to be saved. Include some children's wishes, such as being saved from homework by simply not having to do it (rather than by getting needed help with it), or being saved from a pesty or bullying sibling by someone who would make the sibling "be nice" (rather than by someone who would help the child learn to get along better).

Add a Palm Sunday prayer or greeting for Jesus to each letter of HOSANNA!

H _____
O _____
S *ave us!*
A _____
N _____
*Jesus is our Ki*N *g!*
A _____

Hint: Most of the letters in HOSANNA are also in THANK.

Listen to the Holy Week stories. Draw lines between the people and the words that tell how they deserted Jesus. Some people deserted in more than one way.

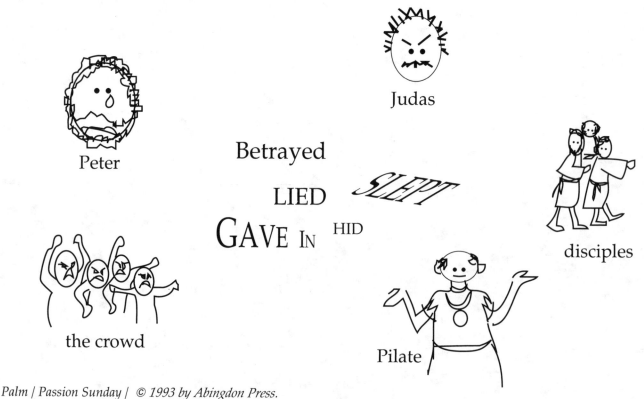

Peter

Judas

Betrayed

LIED   SLEPT

GAVE IN   HID

disciples

the crowd

Pilate

HOLY THURSDAY

From a Child's Point of View

Three of these texts present three different aspects of the Holy Thursday celebration. The Exodus text points to the Passover theme (God acts to save us); John's account of the last supper includes footwashing and a new Commandment, but no bread or wine; Paul's words of institution in I Corinthians tell the story and meaning of the communion sacrament. To avoid overwhelming children, focus on one of these aspects, rather than trying to cover all of them.

Old Testament: Exodus 12:1-14. This text invites us to remember the Passover context of the last supper. Unfortunately, it assumes that worshipers know the whole Exodus saga. Few children do. For them, a worship leader will need to sketch, in his or her own words, the broad sweep of events. The key theme in those events is that God saved the people when they could not save themselves. The two clearest examples of this are the death of the first-born Egyptians and the crossing of the Red Sea.

The killing of the first-born often frightens children, especially first-born children. It seems unfair to them that God would kill children in order to make a stubborn, evil king do what God wanted. They wonder if God would kill them for such purposes. The blood on the doorposts to save the first-born slaves is some comfort, but many children are concerned for the dead Egyptian children. For that reason, it may be best to focus on God saving the people when they were hopelessly trapped between Pharoah's army and the Red Sea.

Psalm: 116:1-2, 12-19. This piece of a psalm is for the adults. It is so filled with the language of

Temple sacrifices and poetic images that it is impossible for children to make sense of it.

Gospel: John 13:1-17, 31b-35. Children can follow the events in this story as they are read. But to understand their significance, they need to know that foot washing was one of the dirtiest jobs in the house in Jesus' day. Everyone tried to avoid the job. As the disciples gathered to celebrate Passover, they all needed to have their feet washed, but everyone was sitting around, hoping someone else would do the dirty work. By what he did and said, Jesus taught a lesson. Though he, of all people, should have been the one having his feet washed, he was willing to do it for them. In verse 14, Jesus used his example to redefine what it means to love, reminding his disciples that they were to love others with this same kind of love.

Adults, hearing the story from the other side of Easter, see the connection between this dirty work and the dirty work of being crucified. Children cannot, because making that connection requires critical thinking of which they are not yet capable. So for children, this is primarily a story about what it means to love one another.

Epistle: I Corinthians 11:23-26. Paul's words point to the breaking of bread and drinking of wine as a way of remembering Jesus and his love. Although young children cannot understand why broken bread and poured-out wine are good reminders of Jesus, they can share in the remembering.

Watch Words

Watch your Passover vocabulary. *Passover, unleavened bread,* and *Passover Lamb* are probably new.

The cup is a verbal symbol loaded with abstract connections to Jesus' crucifixion. Speak instead of *drinking wine*.

Let the Children Sing

The simplest communion hymn, "Let Us Break Bread Together on Our Knees," is especially effective when communion is received kneeling. "For the Bread Which You Have Broken" (esp. verses 1-2) reflects both communion and the great Commandment. The Ghanian hymn, "Jesu, Jesu, Fill Us with Your Love," may be new to many congregations but lifts up Jesus' new Commandment and foot washing.

Children, as well as youths, respond to "In Remembrance of Me" from the cantata *Celebrate*, by Buryl Red (Broadman Press).

The Liturgical Child

1. To emphasize the parallel truths of Passover and communion, and to get the feel of the last supper, set Holy Thursday services around tables at a church supper featuring traditional Jewish Passover foods. (A group of church cooks may enjoy the challenge of preparing this meal.) Set each table with standard dinner ware and a piece of matzo placed beside a goblet of wine or grape juice in the center. After all are seated at tables, remind people that when Jesus and his friends gathered to celebrate Passover that night, Jesus gave it new meaning. Tell briefly the story of Exodus, stressing God's action to save the Hebrew slaves. Then point out the significance of some of the foods. Offer a blessing and invite all to enjoy their meal. After all have finished, rise and, using Paul's words about communion, tell the story of the last supper and celebrate communion around the tables. Worshipers may break off a piece of matzo and dip it in the goblet as it is passed around the table. Conclude with prayers and a hymn.

If a full church supper is not feasible, gather worshipers around table(s) in the fellowship hall, set with communion elements and a single prepared Seder plate.

2. To explore how God has loved us, create a litany that cites examples of that love. A worship leader describes such things as the created world, the Exodus, the community of the church, and Jesus' self-giving love, as well as specific local signs of God's love. After each description, the congregation responds, "God loves us that much!"

3. If your congregation has experienced clowns in worship, invite several clowns to pantomime the Gospel story. You may want to read the passage and then watch the clowns silently reenact the event. Clowns, by overstating the response of Peter and the other disciples, can drive home Jesus' point with great power.

4. If your congregation will not offer a Good Friday service at which you expect children, follow the celebration of communion with a Tenebrae service. See Tenebrae directions in the Good Friday materials in Year C of this series.

Sermon Resources

1. Introduce foot washing by asking worshipers to identify the housework they most dislike (cleaning the cat's litter? weeding? taking out the garbage?). Describe common feelings about changing diapers, emptying bedpans, and other onerous but necessary tasks. Then explore what it felt like to wash someone's dirty feet.

2. Explain the meaning of the term *Maundy* Thursday. *Maundy* comes from the Latin word *mandatae*, which means "commandment." So Maundy Thursday is Commandment Thursday.

There is no Worship Worksheet for Holy Thursday; the service should be so active and appealing to the senses that paper and pencils would be in the way.

EASTER

From a Child's Point of View

Gospel: John 20:1-18 or Mark 16:1-8. According to Mark, when the women found the tomb empty and heard what the angels said, they were not happy but frightened. According to John, Peter scratched his head and slowly walked away, Mary Magdalene sat down and cried (thinking that Jesus' body had been stolen), and only John "believed." All this skepticism makes sense to elementary-aged children who want to know "what really happened." They need to be told that nobody knows what really happened or how it happened. All we know is that Jesus was dead and buried on Friday evening, but was alive in a new way on Sunday morning. Exactly *what* happened and *how* it happened is God's secret. But we do know *why* it happened. Easter is God's proof that love is more powerful than selfishness, hate, and all other evils. (God would not let the evil that killed Jesus win in the end.) Easter is also God's way of showing us that we are forgiven—no matter what we do.

First Reading: Acts 10:34-43 or Isaiah 25:6-9. In its context in Acts, Peter's sermon focuses on God's salvation of the whole world, not just Jews. In its Easter liturgy context, it is a summary of the good news about Jesus. Unfortunately, its generally stated list of categories of stories about Jesus—for example, "He went about doing good and healing," is difficult for children to understand. To help them, cite specific, familiar examples in each category.

Isaiah's prophecy, with its references to obsolete mourning garb and a symbolic feast on a mountain, is beyond the understanding of children. Read it for the adults.

Psalm: 118:1-2, 14-24. Children will hear this psalm as a jumbled collection of praises, several of which make special sense on Easter. Verse 24 is probably the best known.

Second Reading: I Corinthians 15:1-11 or Acts 10:34-43. Children can follow, but do not appreciate Paul's "Easter Creed" in I Corinthians until the setting and the meaning of each phrase is explored.

They must be reminded of Paul's story as an outsider, who, though he had met the risen Jesus, was not an eyewitness to Jesus' life on earth. He learned about what happened from others. (It helps to compare the way Paul learned the stories of Jesus' life with the way we learned the same stories, and to emphasize that we and Paul are in the same situation.)

One helpful way to translate "Christ died for our sins" for children is to say, "Christ died because of our sins." When all the sins of the disciples and Jesus' enemies are recalled, children agree that those sins caused Jesus' death. In other words, the bad that other people did hurt and killed Jesus. Similarly, the sinful things we do hurt other people and God.

In the resurrection appearances that Paul highlights, Jesus forgives. After Peter had denied that he knew Jesus, the resurrected Jesus gave him a chance to admit that he really loved Jesus, and then put him to work. After Paul persecuted the church, the resurrected Jesus appeared to him, forgave him, and sent him out as a missionary. The creed suggests to children that the resurrected Jesus is willing to forgive them also and put them to work.

Watch Words

Resurrection is a word used only at church and usually during Easter. So use it frequently today to build familiarity. Use it to refer to what happened to Jesus, rather than to describe what will happen to us at death. (See Easter in Year C of this series for a discussion about children's understanding of our death and resurrection.)

Alleluia is another word to use frequently and to invite worshipers to use in response to the Easter story. *Alleluia* means "Hurray for God!"; "Look what God has done now!"; "Thank you, God"; and more.

Let the Children Sing

Both "Christ the Lord Is Risen Today!" and "Jesus Christ Is Risen Today!" follow every phrase with "Alleluia." Non-readers can join on the Alleluias. Readers will understand more of the phrases each time they sing them. The phrases of "Jesus Christ Is Risen Today!" are, however, easier.

The simple words and ideas of "Good Christians All, Rejoice and Sing!" make it child-accessible. If you are reluctant to try a possibly unfamiliar hymn on Easter Sunday, save it for another Sunday of this Easter season.

The Liturgical Child

1. Young children respond more to the mood of Easter than to its meaning. So fill the sanctuary with sparkling white and gold paraments, fresh flowers, and joyful music. Then be sure that all children participate at least briefly. There is no way to reproduce the feel of the Easter sanctuary in a classroom or children's chapel. Kindergartners may come only long enough to hear an anthem (especially if it is the "Hallelujah Chorus"). If children's choirs sing, they should spend a little time there before they sing or remain afterward, to take in the Easter sanctuary.

2. Children participate more readily in services that are held at unusual times and in unusual places. Easter suggests early morning and outside worship.

• For an early service, dramatize the change from Good Friday to Easter Sunday. Begin the service with the sanctuary stripped of paraments (except possibly the Good Friday black drapes). Briefly recall the events of Good Friday and sing "Were You There?" Then read the Easter Gospel for the day. Follow the reading immediately with a trumpet fanfare and an Easter hymn. During the hymn, have the Easter paraments and flowers carried in and arranged appropriately. (Adults may receive and arrange paraments brought in procession by older children.)

• Sunrise services that are outside, story-oriented, and brief can be the best Easter worship for children. If an Easter breakfast follows, instruct worshipers to greet one another with the traditional Easter greetings:

> Greeting: Christ is risen!
> Response: Christ is risen, indeed!

3. Ask a young trumpeter to play a simple fanfare for a responsive Call to Worship with the congregation:

FANFARE Christ is risen!
FANFARE This is the day the Lord has made!
FANFARE Let us rejoice and be glad in it!

Sermon Resource

Show the congregation a large beautifully decorated egg-shaped container. (This could be a stocking-container "egg" that has been decorated for Easter by an artistic adult.) Describe different ways we present Easter candy and gifts in egg-shaped packages. Range from the plastic eggs that contain jelly beans to the delicate jeweled eggs of the Russian czars.

Then open your egg to produce a small New Testament. Point out that the first Easter gift is the Easter story. Whether it is a great gift or a disappointment depends on what we do with it. Then proceed to tell how different people responded to the Easter story. Include some, like Temple priests, who ignored it or decided it was a lie, and others like Peter and Paul, who let it change their whole lives. Finally, ask worshipers of all ages what they are going to do with their gift.

Peter told what he knew.
Paul said what he believed.
Write what you think about Easter.

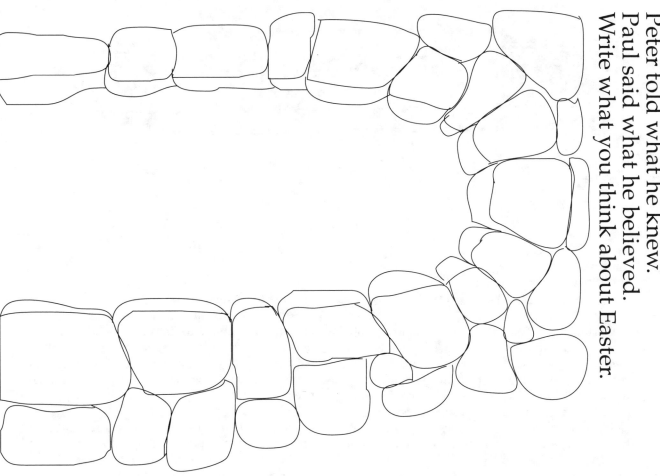

Fit the 12 Easter words below on the
letters of the most important Easter
word of all.

R _ _ _
E _ _ _ _
S _ _
U _ _
R _ _ _
R _ _ _ _ _
E _ _ _ _
C _ _ _ _
T _ _ _
I _ _ _ _ _ _ _ _ _ _
O _ _
N _ _ _ _ _ _ _ _ _ _ _

Jesus   forgiveness   sunrise
Mary   sin   death
Peter   Alleluia   crucify
cross   tomb   risen

SECOND SUNDAY OF EASTER

From a Child's Point of View

During their elementary years, children join clubs, teams, and other groups. They know that members of each of these groups share a common interest or experience that holds the group together. Today's texts describe the Christian church as a group that shares the experience of God's love and forgiveness in Jesus' resurrection. Each passage describes how the church lives in response to God's Easter work.

Gospel: John 20:19-31. (The Gospel text for the Second Sunday of Easter is the same in all three years of the lectionary cycle. Review other years of this series for further ideas.) This is one of the most appealing of the resurrection stories for children because it deals with questions about what Jesus' body was like after the resurrection. It was different. He could walk through locked doors. But it also was the same. He was recognized by his friends and still carried the wounds from his crucifixion. Children can understand that for the disciples (including Thomas) seeing was necessary for believing. It is reassuring to them that Jesus understood this need to see, and he knew that in many ways it would be harder for us to believe than it was for the disciples, who did see.

Unless they are pointed out, children will overlook the two Easter gifts (peace and the Holy Spirit) and the Easter task (forgiving) described in verses 21-23. Both the gifts and the task are given to the disciples as a group (the church).

First Reading: Acts 4:32-35. To children, this passage says simply that God's people took care of one another. Because children do not become entangled in adult concerns about finances, they are free to identify ways the church responds to all kinds of needs. Just as Barnabas sold land and brought the money to help those with financial needs, children can spend time and effort befriending those without friends, taking care of younger children, and helping others with special needs.

Epistle: I John 1:1–2:2. The "children of darkness" and the "children of light" are best presented as two very different groups. Light and darkness are symbols for the way each group lives. Children of darkness do sneaky things and hide them so they will not be seen. Children of light try to do loving things. Sometimes they fail, but when they do, children of light do not try to hide their sinful deeds. Instead, they confess them, because they know that they can be forgiven. The church is meant to be the "children of light."

Psalm: 133. The Good News Bible's "How wonderful it is, how pleasant, for God's people to live together in harmony" makes it the best translation for the day. Children hear clearly the value placed on the joys of living together as God's people. They enjoy hearing about times when their church enjoyed that kind of unity (maybe on a retreat, on clean-up days, or during baptisms, weddings, or funerals).

Both of the psalmist's descriptions of "how good it is" are strange to children. So briefly describe the old treat of being anointed with sweet smelling oil, admit that it sounds pretty awful to us today, and point out that several hundred years from now, some of the things we consider treats (e.g., swimming pools and ice cream sundaes) probably will seem just as undesirable.

Next, ask worshipers to remember some of the beautiful places they have visited. Explain that the psalmist thought the dew on Mount Hermon was just as beautiful.

Watch Words

There are no central words in today's texts or themes that require special explanations for children.

Let the Children Sing

"O Sons and Daughters, Let Us Sing" includes verses which tell today's Gospel stories, interspersed with lots of Alleluias. The Presbyterian hymnal offers an especially good arrangement of the verses. Older children will try harder to keep up if they are told in advance that this is a storytelling hymn. Younger children catch some of the story and join in on the Alleluias.

The words of "Blest Be the Tie That Binds" are not easy for children. To help them learn the meaning of the song, illustrate it by instructing worshipers to hold the hand of, or put a hand on the shoulder of, their neighbor while singing this hymn.

If the focus is on Jesus' gift of peace, sing "I've Got Peace Like a River" or "Dona Nobis Pacem." For the anthem, a children's choir or class might sing the latter as a round.

The Liturgical Child

1. Base a prayer of confession on the differences between the children of light and the children of darkness:

> Lord, you have called us to be children of light, and we want to be, but sometimes we act more like children of darkness. Children of light love and care for others, but too often we love ourselves most and take care only of ourselves. Children of light are honest in all things, but we sometimes twist the truth to get our own way. Children of light admit it when they are wrong, but we try to cover up our sins or pretend that they are only mistakes. Forgive us.

Assurance of Pardon: Because we are children of light, we know that we are not perfect. We also know that God loves us. Indeed, Jesus lived, died, and has risen so that we might know that God forgives us. When we admit our sins, God promises to forgive us. Thanks be to God. Amen.

2. Highlight the offering. Just before it is collected, speak specifically about how the money is used to care for those in need. Name institutions and projects with which children as well as adults are familiar. If you gathered a special Easter offering, tell how much was given and describe how it will be used. In the prayer of dedication, mention some of the ways the church cares for those in need, and pray for their effectiveness.

Sermon Resources

1. To explain Jesus' Easter peace, compare rolling down a hill or spinning in circles until you are dizzy to the spins and tricks done by dancers, skaters, gymnasts, or divers. Athletes learn to focus on a single point, around which their movements revolve. Dancers focus their eyes on one spot, to which they keep returning as they spin. Divers and gymnasts find a balanced position, to which their bodies return after each trick. These focus points make their movements possible. Without them, the athletes would become dizzy and fall. On Easter, God gave us a focus point— the knowledge that we are loved and forgiven by God. No matter where we go or what we do, if we keep reminding ourselves of that fact, we will keep our balance. That balance is the peace that Jesus promised.

2. Try writing, and challenging worshipers to write, new versions of Psalm 133 which describe "how wonderful it is, how pleasant when God's people live together in harmony." Suggest that they write about images that make sense today, or descriptions of the times they have sensed that harmony in your congregation. Display worshipers' psalms on a bulletin board.

Note: If you focus on the giving of the Spirit, consult Pentecost for additional liturgical and sermon resources.

Make an X across each box below after you do it or answer the question in it. Go for 3 in a row in any direction. Or be a Worship Whiz and go for the whole card.

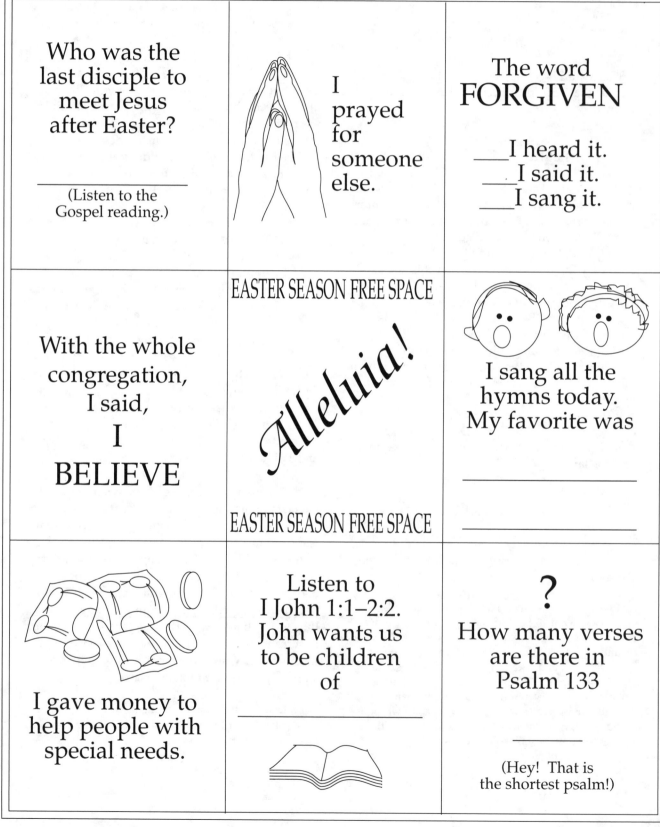

Who was the last disciple to meet Jesus after Easter?

_____
(Listen to the Gospel reading.)

I prayed for someone else.

The word FORGIVEN

____ I heard it.
____ I said it.
____ I sang it.

With the whole congregation, I said,
I
BELIEVE

EASTER SEASON FREE SPACE

Alleluia!

EASTER SEASON FREE SPACE

I sang all the hymns today. My favorite was

_____
_____

I gave money to help people with special needs.

Listen to I John 1:1–2:2. John wants us to be children of

_____

?

How many verses are there in Psalm 133

_____

(Hey! That is the shortest psalm!)

Second Sunday of Easter / © 1993 by Abingdon Press.

THIRD SUNDAY OF EASTER

From a Child's Point of View

First Reading: Acts 3:12-19. Children need to hear the preceding story of the healing of the lame man (vss. 1-11) to make sense of Peter's sermon. Once they know what had happened, they are impressed by Peter's refusal to take any credit for the healing. They need some adult help to follow Peter's subtle series of accusations and promises.

Psalm: 4. The complex progression of speakers and general language of this psalm make it an interesting puzzle for adult Bible scholars, but a confusing jumble for children. It is, however, possible to explore the last three verses as a prayer we can pray during Easter. In that prayer, we praise God for the invaluable gift of Jesus' resurrection, and we put our trust in God's care whether we are awake or asleep, alive or beyond death.

Epistle: I John 3:1-7. John is dealing with an obsolete Greek heresy that is beyond the understanding and interest of children. What they *can* glean from this passage is that to be Christian is to be like Jesus. We are like Jesus in two ways—we will be resurrected, and we can fight sin. John's point about obedience in the fight against sin is particularly clear to elementary children, who tend to understand sin as "breaking the rules."

If you worked with "the children of light" last week, children will be ready to hear "children of God" as another name for God's people and think about the privileges (resurrection) and responsibilities (fight against sin) of being one of "the children of God."

Gospel: Luke 24:36b-48. Few children recognize their own mortality or respond with the relieved joy of adults to the promise of resurrection. But most children are curious about what happens to people when they die and what happened to Jesus' body on Easter. Luke speaks concretely to their curiosity. He insists that after the resurrection, Jesus' body was totally new and different. He could appear inside a locked room, but was not a ghost. He had skin the disciples could touch, and his body functioned in some of the old ways—for example, he could eat, and it still bore the crucifixion wounds. His friends recognized him (most of the time) by the way his body looked. In short, Jesus' resurrected body was unique, something totally new and different. Because we know about Jesus' resurrected body, we know the answers to some of our questions, but not to all of them.

As another tack to take with children, explore Jesus' explanation of the meaning of his Easter resurrection. Adults, aware of the brevity and vulnerability of life, appreciate the Easter promise of life beyond death. Children, struggling to learn how to live in this world, appreciate more deeply Jesus' explanation in verse 47—that his resurrection means we are forgiven (even when we desert Jesus) and can try again (repent). For them, resurrection is a fresh start, another try.

Watch Words

Today, speak either of *resurrection* of the body, or of *resurrection* to forgiveness and new life. If you explore both on the same day, children are overwhelmed and confused.

Introduce *repent* and *forgiven* as an Easter word

pair. Describe how and why the words go together.

Let the Children Sing

"The Day of Resurrection!" ties in closely with John's demands for obedience. Before singing it, walk through the verses, putting them into your own words and connecting them to the day's message. Downplay the Passover references in the first verse to emphasize the prayer request in verse 2 and the praise in verse 3. Children follow such walk-throughs better with their hymnals open.

If you focus on resurrection of the body, sing "Thine Is the Glory" or "Up from the Grave He Arose." "Thine Is the Glory" is a song the disciples could have sung after the events and discussion in today's Gospel story. You might suggest that worshipers imagine themselves singing it with the disciples. Children enjoy the dramatic change from the somber verses of "Up from the Grave He Arose" to the upbeat chorus that celebrates Jesus' victory over death.

The Liturgical Child

1. To clarify the events in Acts 3, ask a group of costumed clowns to pantomime the whole story (vss. 1-19) as it is read. Peter should be an adult who can dramatize what is said with both body and face. The lame man, John, and two or three crowd clowns may played by older children or teenagers. Peter and John pull their empty pockets inside out when the lame man begs. Peter points up, with assurance, to speak of God; points accusingly at the crowd, which cowers; turns a thumb to himself, as a witness, and nods his head. As verses 17-19 are read, Peter uses inclusive arm gestures, then raises the crowd clowns from their cowering positions, dusts them off a little, and turns them to face the worship center. The reading ends with Peter standing with his arms around them, facing the worship center. (If you have never involved clowns in presenting Scripture, this is a good text with which to begin. Clowns can make clear what a story suggests, but which many hearers fail to catch.)

2. In this Affirmation of Faith, the congregation's response is, "We Believe in the Resurrection of the Body." (If your congregation recites the Apostles' Creed frequently, point out this line.)

When people die, we bury or cremate their bodies. Some of us have decided to donate parts of our bodies when we die, to save others. And some of us will give our bodies to be used in medical studies or research, but . . . (RESPONSE)

No one knows exactly what happens after we die, but . . . (RESPONSE)

On Easter, three days after he had been killed on a cross, Jesus was alive again. His friends saw him, ate with him, and talked with him. So . . . (RESPONSE)

His body was different. He could appear and disappear. But he was the same Jesus. He still loved and cared for people. He explained to his friends what had happened. And though they never really understood it all, the disciples began to say . . . (RESPONSE)

Jesus promised that we too will experience resurrection of our bodies, so . . . (RESPONSE)

None of us knows exactly what will happen after we die, but we do not need to be afraid. We know that God will be with us and take care of us . . . (RESPONSE)

Sermon Resources

1. Today's Gospel suggests a sermon focused on bodies. Some children get the idea from Christian adults that God is not interested in our bodies, or even that our bodies are dangerous and can get us into trouble. The biblical message is that God created us with bodies, and part of God's plan is the resurrection of our bodies. This means that we are to respect and care for our bodies. The beginning of spring sports opens the way for talking about the joy of using our bodies and the importance of disciplining them. The end of the school year often involves sixth-graders in their first "teenage" parties, at which they may face pressure to try alcohol or drugs.

2. *Mary Poppins* tells about a father who has a "resurrection," or fresh start. When he loses his bank job because his children Jane and Michael accidentally start a run on the bank during a visit, he repents and plans to pay more attention to his family. Try creating a next chapter which describes the changes he made. What would he look for in a new nanny? What problems might he encounter back at work?

Decode John's message to us.

☐ ☐ ☐ ☐ ☐ ☐

⌐ _ _ ⌐ _ _ ⌐ _ _ _ .

A	B	C		J	K	L		S	T	U
D	E	F		M	N	O		V	W	X
E/H	F	I		P	Q	R		Y	Z	

(1 John 3 : 2)

Draw a picture of one way you can be like Jesus now. Or write a prayer about being like Jesus.

Listen when Luke 24:36b-48 is read. Pretend you are one of Jesus' disciples. What would you write in your diary that day?

My day
What happened: _____

How I feel: _____

What I will do tomorrow: _____

FOURTH SUNDAY OF EASTER

From a Child's Point of View

First Reading: Acts 4:5-12. Children do not understand this story unless it is read in the context of the healing of the lame man (vss. 1-11). They also need to be told that the Temple leaders were not happy about the healing because they felt that God should work only through them. They were, after all, the Temple officers! With this background, children are quite impressed by the bravery of Peter and John.

Before they can understand the Old Testament reference, children need a description of the function and importance of a cornerstone. (If your building has a cornerstone that really is a cornerstone, rather than a decorative inset, it makes a good example.) Even then, children will count on the preacher to explain Peter's point.

Psalm: 23. The Good News Bible's translation of this familiar psalm is most child-accessible and also offers adults—even those who prefer more aesthetic versions—some fresh insights. The poet's trust in the shepherd's care (vss.1-4) can be understood by all worshipers, even those with minimal knowledge of shepherding. But the banquet images of verses 5-6 speak uniquely to children. Children, often sent to eat in the kitchen or at a special table for youngsters, appreciate being welcomed to the banquet table as honored guests. Those whose cups are often half-filled (to avoid spills) long for the day when they will be given cups filled "to the brim." (Translations are critical in verse 6. While The Good News Bible promises something a child desires—a cup full "to the brim"—the New Revised Standard Version promises something that gets most children into trouble—a cup that "overflows.")

Epistle: I John 3:16-24. Children quickly become lost in this string of abstract pronouncements. They depend on the preacher to select one or two for illustration with everyday examples. Probably the most influential with children is the teaching that we are to put our love into action. Love is not just what we say, but what we do. To say we love a person, pet, or possession, but then fail to treat it lovingly, proves that we do not really mean what we have said.

Gospel: John 10:11-18. John's point, that we can trust Jesus because Jesus is a shepherd/owner rather than a hired shepherd, makes great sense to adults but is puzzling to children, who are interested in the various jobs people do and are learning to do all their assigned jobs well. They assume that any good worker will do the very best on any job. So children are more impressed by Jesus' statement that he loves us enough to risk his life to save us (like a shepherd, protecting the sheep from a wolf).

Watch Words

Children who attend church school usually collect shepherd vocabulary fairly early. But do not count on all children understanding it. *Rod* is most often a boy's name. The *staff* is the group of adult leaders at the church or day-care center. And the only *shepherd* most urban kids have met is a large, sometimes fierce, dog. Remember too that a *sheepfold* is a *pen* or *yard* for sheep.

To *lay down my life for you* means *to be killed* while protecting you.

Let the Children Sing

Sing the version of Psalm 23 that is most familiar to your congregation. Choose other shepherd hymns carefully. Children have trouble with the complex theological language of "He Leadeth Me" and "The King of Love My Shepherd Is." The more concrete language of "Savior, Like a Shepherd Lead Us" makes it a better choice.

"Go Forth for God" is a good hymn with which to send worshipers out to imitate the brave witness of Peter and John. The simple language and the repeated opening and closing lines in each verse are easy for middle-elementary readers.

The Liturgical Child

1. Before reading the Gospel, call a small group of people to sit or stand with you. If there are steps leading to the chancel, ask them to sit around you. Carry a Bible from the lectern to open in your lap. Point out that these people, by their presence, remind everyone that though Jesus was speaking about sheep, he was really talking about how he cares for each of us. While reading the appropriate phrases in verses 14-15, reach out to pat an adult or older child on the back, or give a younger child a hug. If possible, include people of all ages.

2. Before reading Acts 4:5-16, read or tell about the healing of the lame man and briefly point out that the Temple leaders were not pleased. Then read today's text dramatically. Assuming an authoritarian posture, read about the gathering of the important leaders. State the question in verse 7 with appropriate condescension. Then turn slightly to take the role of Peter. Read his words with persuasive enthusiasm. Use your hands to emphasize both the leaders' contempt for Peter and Peter's strong feelings about what he was saying.

3. Create an Easter Affirmation of Faith based on the rejected stone. The worship leader cites a series of the ways Jesus, though he was rejected, turned out to be right. Some statements can focus on what Jesus said, while others focus on what happened. To each statement the congregation responds, "The stone the builders rejected turned out to be the most important of all." For example:

Jesus said, "Love one another." But everyone replied, "No, it is smarter to love your friends and hate your enemies." (RESPONSE)

The Temple leaders turned Jesus over to the Romans to be crucified. But on the third day, God raised Jesus from the dead. Jesus is Lord! (RESPONSE)

4. See The Liturgical Child, Fourth Sunday of Easter, Year C, for a way to use Psalm 23 as a prayer outline.

Sermon Resources

1. Our care of pets is today's parallel to the shepherd's care of the sheep. Pet owners provide food, water, and shelter for their animals. In cities they take them for walks in all kinds of weather, and many carry scoops to clean up after them. When they are injured or sick, people pay to take pets to veterinarians and may even take time off from work or school to care for them. Newspaper pictures of firemen rescuing kittens from tall trees illustrate the lengths we go to for our pets. (If you have pets, speak specifically of your loving "shepherding" of those animals.)

2. *And Now Miguel . . .*, by Joseph Krumgold, offers interesting information about the care of sheep (esp. chaps. 4 and 5). Miguel and his family are shepherds in New Mexico. One task at lambing time is to paint matching numbers on the lambs and ewes so that they do not become separated in the crowded sheep pens.

3. Set the banquet images of Psalm 23 in a school lunchroom. Often the problems and joys of children's interpersonal relationships are emphasized there. Who one eats with is critical. All children know the humiliation of being crowded out of the group with which they wanted to sit and the joy of having a seat saved for them by a desirable friend. They truly do eat "in the presence of their enemies" every day. The poet says that God is like a friend who welcomes you and treats you as the guest of honor every day, no matter who is watching or what they think.

Psalm 23 says that God takes care of us like shepherds take care of their sheep. Write your own psalm, telling at least one way God takes care of you.

The Lord is
my shepherd

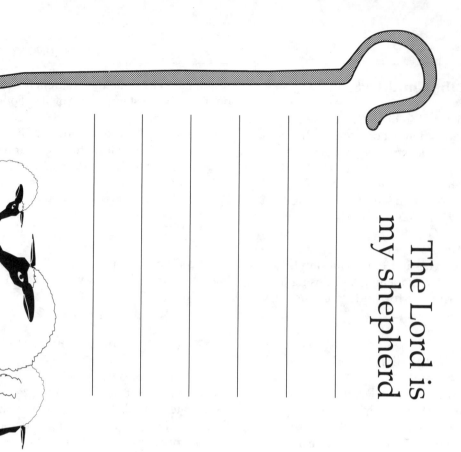

The letters in the words below are all mixed up. Unscramble them to find a message about the words we say.

"URO EVOL DOLUSH

TON EB TJUS

ROWDS NAD KLAT."

(See I John 3:18.)

IF you really listen, you know our love should also be seen in our
C A T O N I S !

_____ !

Fourth Sunday of Easter / © *1993 by Abingdon Press.*

FIFTH SUNDAY OF EASTER

From a Child's Point of View

First Reading: Acts 8:26-40. Some older children will recognize Ethiopia as a modern country. Others will need to have this pointed out. (Identifying Ethiopia on a globe or map enhances everyone's sense of its reality.) In any case, Ethiopia seems as far away and foreign to children today as it did to Luke. So they can appreciate Luke's point that God sent Jesus not just for people "like us," but for people as far away and as different as the Ethiopians. By sending Philip to tell the Ethiopian about Jesus and to baptize him, God further insisted that people of all nations and races be included in the church.

Psalm: 22:25-31. This is a complex passage filled with difficult poetic images. Children are more likely to catch occasional phrases that describe people who should praise God than they are to hear the whole text. The New Jerusalem Bible offers the most, though not completely, satisfactory translation for children.

Epistle: I John 4:7-21. Worshipers of all ages have the same problem with this passage. It overwhelms us with good one-liners about God and love, all of which are true and important, but we need to pick each one up and examine it alone. Some speak more powerfully than others to children.

"Let us love one another because love comes from God" speaks more clearly to literal thinkers than does "God is love." The latter associates a "person" with an activity or feeling. The former suggests an activity that God inspires and endorses.

"Those who say they love God but hate their brothers and sisters are liars" and "Those who love God must love their brothers and sisters" are related to one of children's daily concerns. They need to hear that this applies both to our brothers and sisters at home and to all our brothers and sisters in God's worldwide family. They also need to be reminded that love describes a way we treat people, not just how we feel about them. We can treat with respect even people we do not like or admire.

Gospel: John 15:1-8. Urban children, except those with gardening parents, have little experience with the process and purpose of pruning. It will need to be explained, and then its relation to the way God works in and through us must also be explained. (That's a lot of explaining!)

Provide specific examples of what it means for a person to be pruned. Bad habits can be cut out. The way we spend our time can be changed—for example, we can watch less TV so that there is time for more stimulating and giving activities. We can learn something new that will change the way we do things (a good reason to go to church school).

Watch Words

Speak of *the Ethiopian official*, to avoid dealing with the definition of a eunuch. Or define a *eunuch* as a man who had an operation so that he would never have children. Point out that often eunuchs were the only men allowed to serve queens. Still, few men chose to become eunuches, even in order to obtain the high office of the Ethiopian Philip met. So the Ethiopian probably had had an unhappy life and knew what Isaiah was talking about when he wrote of being humiliated and denied justice.

Abide is not a commonly used word today, especially among children. The New Jerusalem Bible's translation of today's Gospel does not use the word at all. If you use it, define it as *staying close to*, and provide lots of specific examples—babies must abide with their parents to survive; dedicated students may abide with or "shadow" their teachers in order to learn everything they can from them; Christians abide in their church in order to grow as a disciples. Some children will have heard the exclamation, "I can't abide him!"

Children often define *love* in terms of sexual passion or drippy sentimentality. Be sure they know that John is talking about *caring about people* and being ready to *give up what you want so that others can have what they need.*

Let the Children Sing

For children, "Come Christians Join to Sing," with all its Alleluias, is the best hymn for the latter part of the Easter season.

Invite a children's choir or class to present, as an anthem, one of the many songs about love from its Bible school and church camp repertoire. "We Love Because God First Loved Us" and "Love, Love, Love" are two that are generally well known. "For the Beauty of the Earth" is one of the easier hymnbook hymns that list the ways God loves us.

Many new hymnals intentionally include hymns from other cultures, and even other languages, to celebrate the worldwide Christian family. Sing one of them to celebrate Philip's encounter with the Ethiopian. The simple words and melody of "Jesu, Jesu, Fill Us with Your Love," a Ghanian hymn, make it a particularly good choice.

Children have trouble with some of the traditional hymns about God's presence. "Abide with Me" is filled with impossible poetic images. Though the language of "I Need Thee Every Hour" is certainly child-accessible, the melody and passion with which some adults sing it can lead many children to sing it overdramatically, through giggles.

The Liturgical Child

1. Feature Ethiopia in your worship center. Display a map or globe with Ethiopia highlighted. Hang a banner or other art by Ethiopian artists. Display flowers similar to those that bloom in Ethiopia.

2. Be ready to tell worshipers about your denomination's connection to the church in Ethiopia. Pray specifically for the church in Ethiopia and for the people of Ethiopia in general. As I write, Ethiopians face both famine and war.

Another prayerful response to the story of the Ethiopian is to pray not only for Ethiopians, but for people all over the world. Pray your way around the globe, noting specifically the joys and needs of national and ethnic groups. To participate more fully, the congregation can respond to each prayer, "Lord, hear our prayers for our brothers and sisters."

3. To keep the Easter Alleluias going, turn the psalm into a praise litany. During the reading, the congregation says, "Alleluia!" after each of the following verses: 25, 26, 28, 29*a*, 29*b*, and 31 (based on the versification of The New Jerusalem Bible).

Sermon Resources

1. Display prominently a large potted plant that has been allowed to grow profusely. During the sermon, demonstrate, or ask a gardener in your congregation to demonstrate, while you describe the pruning of this plant. Work in the order of the verses of the Gospel text. The result should be an attractive plant that will grace rather than disgrace the chancel.

2. When churches welcome refugee families, it is often the children on both sides who form the quickest, strongest bridges. Because children can play and work together with few words, refugee children often learn American ways by mimicking American children, and then they teach their parents. Children also learn new languages more readily than most adults. If the story of Philip and the Ethiopian leads you to speak of refugee resettlement, be sure to include stories about the ways children have helped. Point out to children that because they can do what adults cannot, they have special responsibilities in reaching out to "foreigners."

Before you can understand John 15: 1-8, you must know that Jesus was speaking in a kind of code. He spoke about vines, and their fruit, to tell us about being disciples.

The writer of I John was not speaking in code. But what he said is hidden in the telephone code below.

"43* 22 72 73 71 43 53 81 22
"L __ __ __ __ __ __ __ __

53 52 22 11 52 53 72 32 22 63
__ __ __ __ __ __ __ __ __ __

12 22 13 11 73 71 22 43 53 81 22
__ __ __ __ __ __ __ __ __ __ __

33 71 23 63 53 51 31 53 21 ."
__ __ __ __ __ __ __ __ __ ""

Jesus said, "I am the vine, you are the branches. Those who abide in me and I in them, bear much fruit."

What do you think Jesus was trying to tell us?

_____
_____
_____
_____
_____

Hint: Listen for ideas in the SERMON

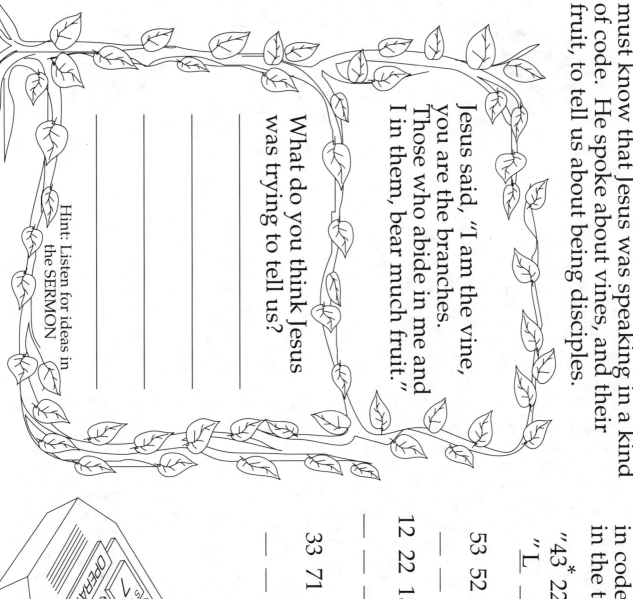

* 43 is button #4 and the 3rd letter on that button.

SIXTH SUNDAY OF EASTER

From a Child's Point of View

First Reading: Acts 10:44-48. This is a story about a time the church changed its ways to keep up with what God was doing—that is, including the Gentiles, upon whom the Holy Spirit had been poured. For adults, who tend to be threatened by calls to change their ways, this is challenging reading. But for children, who are continually changing their ways as they age into new groups and come under the influence of new adults, the story has less power. For them, it is simply another story which restates God's insistence that all people be welcomed into the church. Last week's story about Philip and the Ethiopian is a more intriguing one with which to explore this theme. If you do explore this text in depth, be sure to present it in the context of the whole story of Peter's encounter with Cornelius.

Psalm: 98. This psalm is a series of happy shouts, praising God, who brings all the people of the world together into one united group. It is meant to be felt and experienced rather than intellectually understood. So, presentation is key. If they hear it read in a stately monotone, children will fail to grasp its message. But if they are invited to join in an upbeat reading, they will catch on immediately.

Though the content and feelings of the psalm are child-accessible, the language used in most translations is not. The Good News Bible, however, uses words that children understand and that older children can read fairly readily.

Gospel and Epistle: John 15:9-17 and I John 5:1-6. Children understand John's linking of love (or friendship) and obedience, because children obey people rather than rules. An adult or bigger child whom they neither like nor respect may force them to obey a set of rules to avoid punishment—at least while that person is there to make good on threats. But the rules they truly accept and follow by choice are those that come from people they like and want to imitate. A Scout is more likely to adopt the Scout laws if the leaders who present them live them out in ways that are attractive to the younger Scouts. Young athletes follow the disciplines that are followed by their sports heroes. Similarly, Christians show their love of God by obeying God. Our "heroic example" is Jesus, who followed God's law of love, even when it led to his death.

Children have trouble with traditional explanations of how Jesus' death affects them (he "laid down his life for you"). Because they have not grown up with the sacrificial systems of first-century religious life, they do not understand why someone else's death would appease God for their sins. Especially if they have grown up hearing about God's forgiving love, atonement and expiation theology do not make much sense. So for children, Jesus sets the example—not by going to the cross on their behalf, but by obeying God even at the cost of his life. God said we should love, even when people hurt us rather than love us back. Jesus did. And we are to follow his example.

Watch Words

The *circumcised* believers in Acts are simply *Jewish* believers.

92

Most children hear *lyre* (e.g., praise God with the lyre) as *liar*.

Abide means *stay close to*. To *lay down my life* means to *be killed*.

Let the Children Sing

Singing Christmas songs at Easter is fun. So point out that "Joy to the World!" is based on Psalm 98 and celebrates God at work in the world—not just at Christmas, but every day. Then enjoy singing it for the Risen Christ.

"Earth and All Stars" also is based on Psalm 98, but adds calls for praise to modern groups of people and situations. (If this is used as an opening hymn, precede it with a Call to Worship based on Psalm 98:1, 4-9.)

"Lord, I Want to Be a Christian," with its verses about being "like Jesus" and "more loving" is the best children's hymn about loving obedience. The chorus of "Trust and Obey" is easy for children, but the vocabulary of the verses is difficult. If you sing it, take time to explain one or two key phrases.

The Ghanaian hymn, "Jesu, Jesu Fill Us with Your Love," which was suggested for last Sunday, is also fitting for today. Singing it two Sundays in a row is a good way to learn a new hymn.

The Liturgical Child

1. Psalm 98 might have been shouted responsively by the Jewish and Gentile Christians after the latter were baptized. The Good News Bible offers a translation that lends itself to responsive reading between choir and congregation or two halves of the congregation. Be sure each group has strong leadership to set the exuberant tone of the psalm:

> All: Verse 1a (Sing a new song to the Lord!)
> Group 1: Verse 1b (He has done wonderful things!)
> Group 2: Verse 1c (By his own power and holy strength,
> he has won the victory.)
> Group 1: the "a" part of verses 2 through 8, with
> Group 2: responding with the "b" part of verses 2 through 8
> All: Verse 9

2. Prayer of Confession:

Loving God, we say we love you, but then most of the time, we ignore you. We say you are Lord of our lives, but then we allow our jobs, school work, and family responsibilities to take up so much time that we have none left for church, or even for prayer. We say we want to be like Jesus, but we also want to be the most popular, the best dressed, the most outstanding. Somehow, we let you get crowded out.

Forgive us for our weak love. Do not treat us the way we have treated you. Instead, help us to make time for your work and worship. Remind us of your rules when we are making everyday decisions, and be with us. For we pray in the name of Jesus, who loves us. Amen

Sermon Resources

1. Cite as examples of obedience young athletes or musicians who move across the country or around the world in order to be near the very best coach or teacher. Frequently, young gymnasts or skaters preparing for the Olympics will literally move in with a coach. During that period, they eat with those coaches, practice under their direction, study with them, and play with them. In short, they obey them in all things. Just as it takes this kind of obedience to win Olympic medals, it takes total obedience to God to be able to love as God calls us to love.

2. One Christmas Eve, Andrew M. Barr bought and personally delivered 100 sleeping bags to homeless people in his city. At another time, he read that while a group of teenagers were visiting his city on a church trip, their van, with all their clothes and money, had been stolen. He found out where they were staying and wrote them a check to replace their loss.

When he was interviewed, Mr. Barr said, "When I see someone in trouble, my brain goes on red alert, looking for something I might do to help. There's usually something you can do if you really look and see what's going on around you, if you make up your mind to do what you can, if you just listen." Mr. Barr is an example of a person who obediently loves others. (This story comes from a July 24, 1991, column by William Rasberry.)

Psalm 98 calls on the people of Israel to praise God. It names musical instruments with which they might praise God. It also calls on the seas and hills to praise God.

Rewrite Psalm 98. Who and what will you ask to praise God? How could they do their praising?

Psalm of Praise

Sing the Lord a new song!

by _____

_____
(Who?)

_____
(How?)

Sing the Lord a new song!

_____
(What?)

_____
(How?)

Shade in every space that has a dot (•) in it to find 2 very important words today. Listen for these words in our songs, prayers, and sermon.

SEVENTH SUNDAY OF EASTER

Note: The Revised Common Lectionary suggests that the texts for Ascension of the Lord may be used on the seventh Sunday of Easter. That may be especially wise for children, because it offers an opportunity to explore the Ascension story, and also because the texts for the seventh Sunday of Easter are rather difficult for them. See Year C of this series for Ascension of the Lord resources.

From a Child's Point of View

First Reading: Acts 1:15-17, 21-26. Children ask some of the same questions adults ask of this story, but they look for different kinds of answers. They ask, "Why did the disciples feel the need to replace Judas?" The scholar's answer about preserving the number 12 is only partially satisfying, because such concern seems out of character for God. God, it seems to children, would be more interested in love than in getting the details, like the number 12, just right.

They also ask, "What was 'casting lots,' and why did they use that way to make such an important decision?" Few adults want to present making important decisions by rolling dice or flipping a coin as an example for children to follow. But children, like adults, are tempted to fall back on this way of deciding what God wants us to do.

Finally, children often ask one question that adults do not: "How do you suppose Justus felt about not being chosen?" Explore this one by comparing it to being nominated for an award. Like those who are nominated for but do not win the Heisman Trophy or an Academy Award, Justus was probably disappointed not to be elected but proud and happy to have been nominated.

Psalm: 1. Children appreciate this stark comparison of good and evil people. While older worshipers realize that the psalmist oversimplifies things (few people wear perfectly white hats or totally black hats), children do not. They are still learning the major differences between good and evil, rather than sorting out the finer distinctions. So, while we sometimes read passages for the adults because it is more appropriate for them, this is one to read mainly for the children. Adults, however, benefit from the psalmist's emphasis on the simplicity of the differences between good and evil, rather than the complexities.

Although their mental development keeps younger children from appreciating the plant images fully, they can understand the leafy tree as the group plant (like a state flower or bird) of the good, and the dry weeds as the group plant of the wicked. Given the choice, they will choose the "good" plant.

Epistle: I John 5:9-13. For adults, this abstract argument makes a fine summary of the Easter faith with which to conclude the season. But it makes little sense to children. Attempts to explain the passage in terms of courtroom testimony can get hopelessly bogged down. This is one to read for the adults.

Gospel: John 17:6-19. Like many adults, most children quickly become lost in the repetitive short phrases of this prayer. Before they can follow it, they need to hear that just before Jesus was arrested and killed, he was praying for his disciples, who were also his best friends. Given the situation, children are impressed that Jesus loved his disciples so much that he was worrying about and praying for them, rather than for himself.

They can find great security in the possibility that Jesus cares that much for them, too.

Watch Words

Older children often wonder about the difference between *apostles* and *disciples*. The terms may be used interchangeably in children's Bible storybooks. Point out that all people who follow Jesus are *disciples*. But only the twelve men who actually lived and traveled with Jesus during his life, and Paul, who was the first missionary, are called *apostles*. This provides an opportunity to explain how The Apostles' Creed got it's name.

Psalm 1, in all translations, is filled with unfamiliar words about good and evil: *scornful, scoffers, mockers, cynics,* and even *righteous.* Put the message of the psalm into simple, everyday terms.

Let the Children Sing

Conclude the Easter season with "Come, Christians, Join to Sing." In response to Jesus' loving care, sing "Jesus Loves Me!"

If the focus is on discipleship, sing "Go Forth for God," with its repeated simple phrases, or "I Sing a Song of the Saints of God."

The Liturgical Child

1. In the worship center, feature two arrangements: the first, of a flowering, or even a fruit-bearing plant; the other, of dry weeds, or a dead branch stuck in a bucket of sand. Refer to them in exploring Psalm 1.

2. To emphasize the comparison made in Psalm 1, ask two readers to present it as follows. Before they read, point out the character each is describing.

"Good" Reader: verses 1-3
"Wicked" Reader: verses 4-5
"Good" Reader: verse 6a
"Wicked" Reader: verse 6b

3. If you celebrate the witness of the apostles, point out how the Apostles' Creed got its name, and invite worshipers to stand with Matthias and all the other apostles, to repeat it.

4. Continue Jesus' prayer for disciples. A worship leader offers prayers for various groups of disciples, including church-school classes, groups of Christians who face hardships around the world, and so forth. To each, the congregation responds, "Holy Father, keep them safe in your name." Be sure to include groups of children among the mentioned disciples.

5. Know when school lets out for most of your children. On the appropriate Sundays, include prayers for their concerns at this intense time. There is the excitement of end-of-year field trips, parties, and awards assemblies. For those who do not excel, there is an extra worry about final tests and the possibility of flunking, or the stress of watching others get all the awards. There are also hopes and fears about summer—hopes for a change of pace, relief from homework, and maybe a trip; fears about new day-care arrangements or going away to camp alone.

Sermon Resources

1. Psalm 1 tells us that good people recognize bad advice and do not follow it and that they refuse to follow people who are bad examples. Christians of all ages must continually evaluate and respond to both advice and examples. Cite the bad advice offered in current commercials aimed at people of different ages. Recall all the bad advice Alice received in Wonderland. When she ate and drank what was suggested, she grew or shrank much more than she wished. Describe the bad examples who tempt us to follow their ways.

The popular Ninja Turtles, for example, are admirable in working for justice, but their methods are not acceptable for Christians. Jesus calls us to get rid of our enemies by turning them into friends, rather than beating them into submission. (If you tackle the Turtles, realize that to many children they are personal heroes. Watch at least one Turtle video, so that you can call them by name and describe their methods specifically.)

The same 4 words are missing in each line of Jesus' prayer for his disciples. Write them in the correct places on each line.

WORLD INTO THE SENT

"I _____ them _____ ___ _____

just as

You _____ me _____ ___ _____."

Jesus prayed: I sent them into the world just as you sent me into the world.

BEING GOOD

Psalm 1 is about **being good**. Write your own prayer about being good. Tell God what is hardest for you about being good. Ask God's help. Make God one promise about being good this week.

PENTECOST

Note: Consult other books in this series for additional ideas for the celebration of Pentecost. Year C offers most suggestions about the overall celebration of Pentecost.

From a Child's Point of View

Acts 2:1-21 Children are more interested in the story of Pentecost than in Peter's sermon. Before reading the story, help them recognize the difference that God's Spirit made in the lives of the disciples by reminding them that the disciples had been hiding out together, excited and frightened about what happened at Easter, but even more frightened about what might happen to them next. There are really two Pentecost miracles: (1) the uneducated disciples spoke foreign languages; and (2) the frightened disciples spoke bravely and publicly about Jesus. The second miracle is the one that children are most likely to experience.

The first and last lines of Peter's sermon are key for children. God's Spirit was poured out on everyone, and everyone who welcomed God's Spirit was saved (belonged to God). To complete the story, add verse 41 and perhaps 42.

Romans 8:22-27. The apocalyptic background and big words (adoption, redemption, etc.) make this text nearly impossible for children to understand as it is read. Its message for children is that the activity of the Holy Spirit gives us hope. Hope, however, needs to be carefully defined so that it refers not to our hope for such things as a Nintendo for a birthday, but to our hope for things such as a time when everyone will get along happily, a time when all the hungry are fed,

and so forth. We have God's promise that each of these things will one day happen, and we can tell stories that prove that God is working to make them happen, although sometimes it seems impossible that they will ever happen. The Holy Spirit reminds us of God's promises and gives us the courage to keep on working and hoping, even when it looks as if the problems are too big to be solved. And the Spirit works through us to do more than we could do on our own.

The intercession of the Holy Spirit (vss. 26-27) is hard to explain to children without making God seem like a fearsome judge, from whom we need the protection of the more understanding Spirit. It is clearer simply to say that the Holy Spirit lets us know that God is close to us, loving and caring for us.

John 15:26-27; 16:4b-15. John's abstract language and sophisticated theology also lose children. But he has two related things to say to them about the Holy Spirit. First, the Holy Spirit is God's way of being with us after Jesus was no longer with us. So on Pentecost, we remember that God is with us always, in every situation. Second, the Holy Spirit also helps us to know what is true. Even young children are confronted by a dizzying array of claims about what is right and good. Ads tell them they need certain cereal, clothes, and toys to be happy. Teachers tell them what they must do to be successful. Other children urge them into all sorts of activities—from cheating to hunger-relief walkathons—saying that they are fun and acceptable. God's Holy Spirit works deep within each of us, helping us to know which claims are really true.

Ezekiel 37:1-14. Children delight in the mental

picture of dry bones coming together into skeletons, to which muscles and skin are added before God breathes life into them. Once they have had a chance to enjoy this picture and have identified the power that can achieve such a feat, older children are ready to hear the Pentecost point: that the Holy Spirit not only can bring dry bones back to life, the Holy Spirit can resolve situations that look hopeless. For example, the Spirit can lead people who are prisoners of war in a foreign country back home. We can count on the Holy Spirit to be with us in the worst of our problems and to work through us to solve them. Celebrating the power of the Holy Spirit gives us the hope of which Paul spoke.

Psalm: 104:24-34, 35b. The psalmist praises the Spirit's work in creation. On a day devoted to the Spirit's role in the church, this is peripheral, so save this psalm for a day when God's creation can be the focus of worship.

Watch Words

Use *Pentecost* frequently today to build familiarity with this holy day that is not celebrated at all in the larger society. *Tongues of fire* are small flames.

Speak of the *Holy Spirit,* rather than the *Holy Ghost,* which sounds like a somewhat friendly Halloween spook.

Let the Children Sing

"Breathe on Me, Breath of God" and "Spirit of the Living God" are good Pentecost hymns for children. And though they miss most of the verses, children do catch the repeated opening line and changing titles for the Holy Spirit in "Holy Spirit, Truth Divine."

"Open My Eyes That I May See" is a natural choice when the focus is on the Romans text. Children pick up the repeated chorus quickly and follow the verses about different parts of the body. They do need a paraphrase of *illumine me*—perhaps "Fill me with understanding."

For an intergenerational Pentecost celebration:

• Ask a children's choir or class to sing the first two verses (the storytelling verses) of "On Pen-

tecost They Gathered," with the adult choir or congregation singing verses 3 and 4 (the commentary verses). Or

• Invite a kindergarten choir or class to sing the choruses of "We Are the Church" (maybe with hand motions), with the congregation singing the verses. Sing the verses in reverse order starting with the verse about Pentecost.

Singing "Happy Birthday" to the church remains the most meaningful Pentecost song for young children.

The Liturgical Child

1. Ask each household to bring one candle (red if possible) in a sturdy holder to place on the central table. As worshipers arrive, have ushers instruct them to place their candles on the table before taking seats. (Provide candles for those who arrive without.) Begin worship by reading Acts 2:1-4*a*, and continue with: "Come, let us worship God. Let us be alert for God's Holy Spirit moving among us, filling us with the power to be God's people."

Then during an opening Pentecost hymn of praise, have acolytes or a class of younger teenagers light all the candles. At the close of the service, have them extinguish the candles. Invite worshipers to take their candle home and light it at mealtime each day this week, as a reminder that God's Spirit rests on each one of us, every day.

2. A prayer leader could describe a series of seemingly hopeless situations which children worry about, to each of which the congregation would respond: "Holy Spirit, come stay in us. Give us courage and hope. Work through us until your will is done." For example:

God, you gave us families as gifts. But often we treat our brothers and sisters worse than we treat bullies on the street, and we treat our husbands and wives with less respect than we give strangers. Simple chores cause major battles. Instead of friendly conversation, gripes about "Who gets what" and "Who gets to do what," instead of friendly conversation dominate the dinner table. Too often, our families seem like a terrible burden instead of a wonderful gift. (RESPONSE)

God, it's hard to imagine being really hungry

and not knowing when or if you're going to eat again. But we see pictures of people in faraway places, and in our own town, who know exactly how it feels. We want to help, but we do not know how. The problem seems hopelessly big for us. (RESPONSE)

Sermon Resources

1. Describe before and after experiences with the Holy Spirit: the disciples before and after Pentecost; the Hebrews in exile and returned (Ezekiel); feelings when we are trapped in a hopeless situation and when that situation is resolved through God's Spirit working in us (e.g., we accidentally make friends with someone who had been making our life miserable).

2. Cite claims made in specific current commercials and describe how God's Spirit (the Spirit of truth) helps us to know which claims are "true." Cite several commercials, each aimed at viewers of a different age. Watching children's programs for an hour on Saturday morning will provide several good examples of what will promote happiness, friends, and strength.

HAPPY PENTECOST !

Pentecost is the birthday of the church. Write each Pentecost word below on one candle. When you hear, say, or sing each word, draw a flame on its candle.

Disciple   Preach   Spirit   Courage   Wind

Flame   Peter   Power   Hope

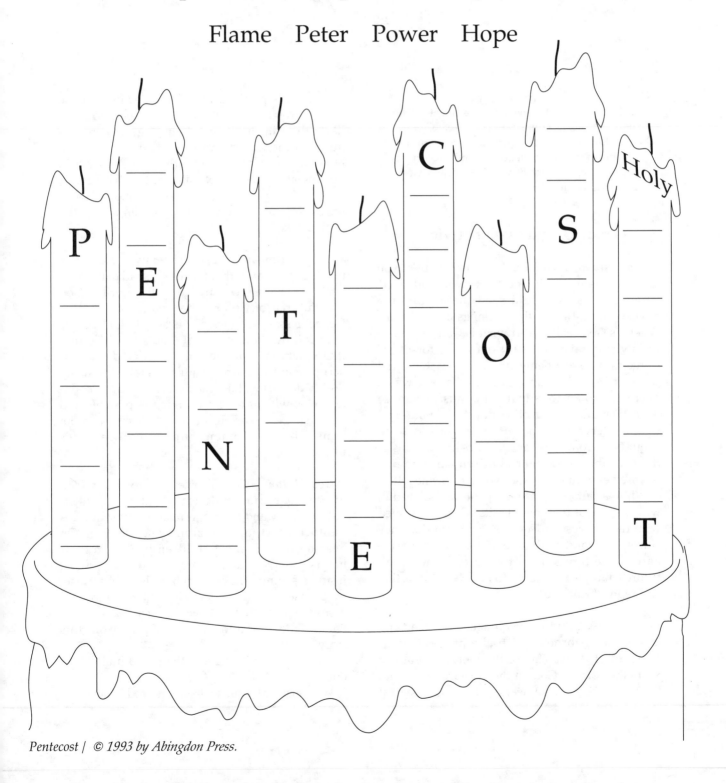

TRINITY SUNDAY

Note: *Trinity* is not a particularly easy concept for most adults, and it is even more challenging for children. Consult Trinity Sunday in Year C of this series for information about children's understanding of the Trinity in general and suggestions for building an order of worship around God's Trinitarian nature.

From a Child's Point of View

Old Testament: Isaiah 6:1-8. "But I thought you said God is invisible and everywhere at once. How come Isaiah could see God sitting on a throne with all those flying things around him? Where is God really? And what is God like?" Isaiah's vision raises difficult questions for literal thinkers who are being urged by teachers and parents to understand God in abstract ways. There are no answers that truly satisfy them, so focus their attention in other directions. Fifth- and sixth-graders can begin to decipher what we learn about God from the characteristics and actions of the seraphim. Younger children can imagine themselves with Isaiah and wonder how he felt.

While adults naturally respond as Isaiah did, with a sense of their own limits when confronted with the holiness of God, few children do. They simply respond with awe and wonder. Fortunately, the limits do not need to be accepted before children are willing to hear God's question and reply, "Send me."

Psalm: 29. Children of all ages both fear and love thunderstorms. This psalm praises God as the Lord of storms. In the thunder, the psalmist hears the voice of God. In the powerful wind and lightning, the psalmist hears and sees God's great power. This particular storm comes in over the sea, crosses the mountains (which seem to jump like calves in the strobic lightning), and moves out into the desert. Adults and older children benefit from tracing the path of the storm and hearing about the use of this psalm in the Temple as the rainy season began. But everyone can share in the feelings of awe and wonder which the psalmist expresses.

Epistle: Romans 8:12-17. The only verse in this theological treatise that makes sense to children is verse 14: "For all who are led by the Spirit of God are children of God." When explored with the Gospel lesson, the message is simply that people who follow the urgings of God's Spirit within them (who are pushed along in God's wind) become God's children. Paul's call to put to death fleshly desires will not make sense until later adolescence, when abstract thinking is possible and personal experience has made it clear that problems do arise when human nature rules unchecked.

Gospel: John 3:1-17. This text is chosen for Trinity Sunday because it deals with all three persons of the Trinity and their interrelationships, but it is a difficult text for both adults and children. On hearing it read, most children throw up their hands with Nicodemus, unable to follow what Jesus is saying. They are helped less by phrase-by-phrase explanations of the text and more by comments about what we can learn about the Father, the Son, and the Holy Spirit from this story.

We learn that God loves the world and everyone in it.

We learn that Jesus was sent by God to save us.

We learn that the Holy Spirit brings us new life.

And as they learn to think of God abstractly, children appreciate comparing God's Holy Spirit to the wind. Both are invisible. We can't tell where either comes from or goes, but we can feel and see the effects of its presence.

Watch Words

Children first understand *Trinity* and *Triune* simply as words we use at church to talk about God. The connection to a *triangle* helps them recall and define the words.

Holy, the seraph's greeting and description of God, means *completely perfect* or *set apart* (nothing and no one is even close to being equal to God). *Hallowed*, in the Lord's Prayer, is another old word that means *holy*. Point out any places the word *holy* is painted, stitched, or carved in your sanctuary and explain why it is there.

God is neither male nor female. If you prefer not to use feminine images for God, avoid overusing masculine images and pronouns.

Let the Children Sing

Help children learn their way into "Holy, Holy, Holy" by calling on all worshipers to sing the Holy, Holy, Holy greeting to God at the beginning of each verse—even if they cannot keep up with all the words of the verses.

The Presbyterian hymnal includes a simpler, but less familiar, Trinitarian praise hymn, "Holy, Holy."

Although "Let All Mortal Flesh Keep Silence" is generally sung during Advent, it captures the mood of Isaiah's worship of God and therefore makes a good call to worship for Trinity Sunday. Children pay special attention to any song sung "out of season."

Older children easily read the simple vocabulary of "Here I Am, Lord," based on Isaiah's response to God.

The Liturgical Child

1. Children respond more to the feelings expressed in Isaiah's vision than to its content, so plan a reading that emphasizes Isaiah's awe. Take the role of the prophet, recalling and telling this event. Let your feelings about what happened show in your voice. Practice reading the seraph's song in a booming voice that would shake the Temple. Plan how you will read, "Here am I. Send me."

2. The Liturgical Child, in the first Sunday after Epiphany, Year C of this series, gives directions for a congregational reading of Psalm 29 that includes a hand choir, creating storm sounds. Relaxed summer congregations with fresh experience with thunderstorms especially enjoy participating in such praise of God's power.

3. Create a prayer or praise litany in which the worship leader lists God's attributes or work. The congregation responds to each with the seraphim song in Isaiah 6:3 NRSV, or by singing that song as it is presented in the chorus of the hymn "Day Is Dying in the West." For example, if a prayer:

> We praise you, Creator God. When we see a canyon carved out by a stream over millions of years, or watch a tiny spider spinning its web between two leaves, we are amazed by the beauty of your plan for the earth and for all on it. (RESPONSE)

Sermon Resources

1. Build a sermon around the ways God is like the wind: comforting us when we are in difficult situations, as a cool breeze comforts us on a hot day; pushing us to let go of bad habits and wrong ideas, as a strong wind prunes the dead wood from trees; supporting and pushing us along faster than we dreamed possible, as the wind supports a kite or sends a sailboat speeding across the water; surprising us by being present when we least expect it, like a wind springing up when we least expect it. Children will need to hear specific examples of God's activity in each comparison. For example, repeat the comment sometimes heard after worship, "Today's Bible reading was aimed at me," to illustrate God's Spirit at work, demanding that people change their ways.

2. Explain the Worship Worksheet task to the whole congregation, and tell the children you are looking forward to reading their poems as they leave the sanctuary. You might give the worksheet to all worshipers today and display all shared poems on a hallway bulletin board.

Today we are thinking, singing, and praying about God. Make up a poem that tells what YOU think about God. Listen to our songs, prayers, and Bible readings for ideas or words.

What goes in this poem?

A title

2 words that describe God

3 things God does
(Make them end in "ing.")

What you want to say to God

Another name for God

GOD

_____

_____

_____

by _____
(your name)

PROPER FOUR

(Sunday between May 29 and June 4 inclusive, if after Trinity Sunday)

Note: If the Sunday between May 24 and 28 inclusive happens to follow Trinity Sunday, the lections for the Eighth Sunday After the Epiphany should be used on that day.

From a Child's Point of View

Old Testament: I Samuel 3:1-10 (11-20). In this story a much older man and a young boy are presented as partners who possess the same important ability. Both listened for and obeyed God. Eli taught Samuel how to listen for and respond to God. But God spoke to the student, not the teacher. Children first focus with delight on God speaking to Samuel, rather than to Eli. It raises the possibility that God might use them *now*—not after they grow up. Walter Brueggemann, in *First and Second Samuel* (Westminster John Knox, 1990), insists that this is indeed the main point of this story. The priests had always been the leaders of Israel, and Eli's sons were next in line to be priests. But God was changing the leadership. Samuel, a "nobody" who listened to God, was chosen to be the prophet and eventually would anoint the kings of Israel. Though children cannot yet comprehend the political significance of this change, they do appreciate the fact that God passed over other candidates to choose a child as spokesperson.

Once they have savored this, they, like Samuel, are impressed by Eli's acceptance of God's terrible message. Eli sets a memorable example by following God's will—even when it is hard to do. That example must have helped Samuel face his disappointments—for example, the failure of Saul—and can help children face theirs.

This passage is also read on the Second Sunday

After Epiphany this year. Look there for additional commentary and worship suggestions.

Psalm: 139:1-6, 13-18. This is a good prayer for building the self-esteem of Christian children. It recounts all the ways God knows us, plans for our lives, and cares for us. The children who pray this prayer sense themselves as some of God's treasures (perhaps treasures stored in clay pots). Vocabulary, especially in verses 13-18, can present problems. The Good News Bible's translation is easiest for children.

Epistle: II Corinthians 4:5-12. Children will not catch Paul's point as they hear this passage read. But when the point is presented in simpler terms, it is one children need to explore. Paul's image of the clay pot is probably the best starting point. Average children who compare themselves to children who are TV stars, athletic champions, or the kids who win all the prizes, do indeed feel like common clay pots. Paul insists that God works through average "clay-pot" people, in our ordinary lives, to do important work.

Gospel: Mark 2:23–3:6. This generation of American children is the first to grow up in a culture entirely free of "sabbath restrictions." Stores are open, sports events are held, and, in many households, the laundry is done. While adults appreciate exploring Jesus' indictment of the way the religious leaders of his day were abusing the sabbath, children have more need of a positive presentation of Jesus' belief that we all need to set aside times for reflection, worship, and "doing good." While adults understand the need for a rhythm of work and re-creative leisure, children more readily recognize that what we do affects who we are and who we become—for instance, athletes and musicians spend all their time practicing. So if we want to be strong Christians, we need to set aside time for worship and "doing good." For children, keeping the sabbath means setting aside time every week to worship and participate in church activities.

Watch Words

Sabbath will be a new term for most children, even church children. If it is recognized at all, it will be as an old-fashioned word for Sunday. The purpose of *sabbath*, as Jesus understood it, will need to be explained in concrete terms, with examples of ways to keep such a *sabbath* today.

Let the Children Sing

"Lord, Speak to Me, That I May Speak" is an easy hymn to sing with Paul and Samuel, to commit ourselves to hear and do God's will.

"Now Thank We All Our God" celebrates God's care and presence, in words children understand.

Though it does not use the word *sabbath*, "Take Time to Be Holy" illustrates, with everyday examples, what it means to keep the sabbath as Jesus understood it.

The Liturgical Child

1. Ask that chancel flowers be displayed in plain pottery pots or bowls. Refer to the floral treasure in clay pots during the service.

2. Instruct worshipers to put themselves in the "I" of Psalm 139:1-6, 13-18. Begin the reading with, "Let us pray," as you pray it in unison or line it out.

3. Remember to include the children's end-of-school concerns in the church's prayers on the appropriate Sunday.

4. *Charge and Benediction:* Today could be a sabbath. Remember that, and keep the day holy. As you leave worship, continue to live this day in God's presence. Do good deeds to share God's love. And as you do, may you know the sabbath peace of God which lasts through the whole week.

Sermon Resources

1. Display at least one fancy vase or bowl and one clay flowerpot on the pulpit. Describe celebrities who are more like the fancy piece. Then describe Paul, with his handicapping "thorn" and rather abrasive personality, and young, unknown Samuel as clay pots. Describe the ways God can use all of us who are clay pots to do important work in our ordinary, everyday lives.

2. The following true story took place in a small town in central North Carolina in 1985:

For months, the members of Cross Roads Presbyterian Church had been preparing to welcome a refugee family. One Saturday afternoon, a sudden call announced that the family would arrive on Monday morning. On Sunday at church, everyone made last-minute plans, and that afternoon, Elder Howard Young loaded his lawnmower on a truck and went to mow the grass at the newly rented house. He was surprised when a policeman stopped and told him that if he continued to mow, he would get a ticket. It seems there was a law against mowing grass on the sabbath. Everyone laughed about that and had fun imagining how the newspaper would have reported the event, if Mr. Young had kept mowing. But everyone also thought that in court, God would have sided with Mr. Young and the good deed he did on the sabbath.

3. Summer has a sabbath quality. Most children are out of school and have more time for the activities they choose. Many organizations stop or curtail activities during the summer, giving adults more time, too. Summer is also vacation time. As the summer begins, challenge worshipers to make this summer a true sabbath. Encourage them to plan time for worship and "doing good." Describe the "sabbath" experiences and feelings of individuals and families who have spent their free time on mission projects.

Note: Remember that the lectionary texts during Ordinary Time are less related to one another. On some weeks, you may want to enlarge the half of the Worship Worksheet that fits your plans, rather than reproduce the entire sheet.

Draw a picture or fill in a letter to take the place of each word missing from Psalm 139.

"Lord, ___(letter) have ___(letter) + amined me and kn + ___(letter) me."

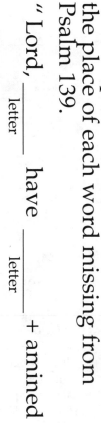

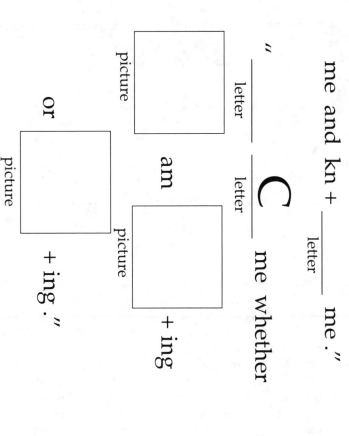

"___(letter) ___(letter) C me whether ___(picture) am + ing or ___(picture) + ing."

"kn + ___(letter) all ___(letter) + ing."

m +  + ions."

Listen as **Mark 2: 23 ʌ 3: 6** is read. Jesus talks about good things to do on the sabbath. Draw or write about at least 2 things YOU can do to keep the sabbath today.

PROPER FIVE

(Sunday between June 5 and 11 inclusive, if after Trinity Sunday)

From a Child's Point of View

Old Testament: I Samuel 8:4-11 (12-15), 16-20 (11:14-15). The questions about political power raised by this text are important and fascinating to adults, but beyond the understanding of children. To children, God's indictment of all kings seems unfair. They prefer to judge each king or queen on performance. Their judgments are colored by the fact that most of their knowledge of kings and queens comes from children's stories, rather than from historical studies. This lack of experience with and understanding of real political systems makes it impossible for them to consider the problem raised in the text. Perhaps the clearest point they can decipher from listening in on this adult conversation is that all political powers, be they monarchs or presidents, are secondary to God. Our first allegiance is always to God.

Psalm: 138. Though this psalm offers no particular problems, neither does it speak with any power to children about things that concern them. It is a psalm for them to read, but not explore in any great depth.

Epistle: II Corinthians 4:13–5:1. Basically, Paul claims that he can put up with all kinds of suffering now, because he knows that the unseen things (like God's plan being carried out and resurrection in the future) are what is really important. That is a tough message for children to accept. Because they live so much in the present and have so little sense of their own mortality, promises about life beyond death do not have much power for them.

The claim of verse 18 that what is unseen is more important than what is seen may make most sense to children. In their world, it means that "seen" things do not last—great toys get broken, wonderful clothes wear out or are outgrown, this year's trophies mean very little next year, and so forth. Because they do not last, we should not be so upset about obtaining or losing them. Instead, we should pay attention to the unseen things— loving friendships, peace in our families and in the world, and so on. Paul insists that those unseen things are the ones that last forever. The Good News Bible offers children the most understandable translation of this verse.

Gospel: Mark 3:20-35. Because children are not sure about either the function or the reality of demons, the part of this reading that deals with Jesus' ability to cast out demons is not very meaningful for them. Fifth- and sixth-graders begin to understand Jesus' response to the scribes and appreciate its cleverness. But the whole incident raises questions about first-century and twentieth-century understanding of demons that cannot be answered to their satisfaction. So either skip the story entirely or read it and pass on.

The confrontation between Jesus and his family has more to offer children. Though some children, who are after all totally dependent on their families, worry about Jesus' refusal to respond to his family, most focus on the fact that Jesus calls us to join an extended family. That family includes all the people at church and all the people all around the world who do God's will.

Watch Words

Children hear about *demons* as mischievous little critters (*Gremlins*), serious malevolent forces that disrupt life (*The Exorcist*), sports teams named Demons, and overenergetic children with a penchant for trouble.

Let the Children Sing

Praise God as ruler of all with "Rejoice, the Lord Is King!" or "Come, Christians, Join to Sing," with its "Alleluia! Amen!" nine times for nonreaders. Even if it is not evening, sing "The Day Thou Gavest, Lord, Is Ended" to celebrate God's rule over all nations on this slowly revolving planet.

Avoid singing patriotic hymns in worship. Children interpret the inclusion of such hymns, no matter what the words of the hymn might say to the contrary, as proof that God is on the side of their country. One alternative, with language simple enough for fifth- and sixth-graders, is "O God of Every Nation."

"Bless Be the Tie That Binds" and "I Come with Joy" (if communion is celebrated) are good choices when the focus is on Jesus' extended family.

The Liturgical Child

1. Ask the congregation to read the part of the people in I Samuel 8. Have one worship leader prepared to read the narrator's part and another to read Samuel's part. Print the whole passage in the bulletin, with the people's lines in **bold type** if possible (to shorten Samuel's part, omit verses 12-15).

Narrator: 8:4-5*a*
People: 5*b*
Narrator: 6-10
Samuel: 11-18
Narrator: 19*a*
People: 19-20
Samuel: 11:14
Narrator: 15

2. Pray for a series of nations with different kinds of leadership—Saudi Arabia with its royal family, Canada with its prime minister, even Cuba with its dictator. Conclude by praying for your own nation and government leaders by name.

3. Create a responsive prayer for God's family. The worship leader offers prayers for a series of groups, to which the congregation responds, "God, hear our prayers for our brothers and sisters." For example:

God of the cities, we pray for our brothers and sisters who run soup kitchens and shelters and help centers. Give them hope when it feels as if all their work makes no difference. Inspire them with new ideas to solve old problems. Protect them from angry people who carry knives and guns. (RESPONSE)

God, who created us with bodies that jump, run, and swim, we pray for those who try to do your will in the locker room, on the playing field, and in the pool. Help the players to recognize those on the other team as brothers and sisters. Help the coaches to treat the players as sons and daughters, from whom they try to draw the very best. Give the referees a spirit of fairness and quick eyes. (RESPONSE)

4. If there is to be a baptism today, before it takes place, invite children to stand or sit near the font. Talk briefly with them about the meaning of baptism, with emphasis on identifying the baptized as one of God's family. The parents and any older siblings of an infant being baptized may be willing to join the group so that the children can see and even touch the baby. Family members, the worship leader, and children can name some of the things they will do to welcome this child into God's family. If possible, allow all the children to stay where they can see well during the baptism.

5. Remember to include the children's end-of-school concerns in the church's prayers on the appropriate Sunday.

Sermon Resource

Recall the parts of your baptismal rite which focus on the baptized being identified as one of the family of God. Paraphrase sentences that are not immediately clear to children. Describe how people of all ages can keep the vows they make during the baptism of another. Use examples from everyday life.

Psalm 138 is like a thank-you note to God. It begins, "I give you thanks, O Lord, with my whole heart." Use that as the first sentence in a thank-you note YOU write for God today.

_____ (date)

Dear God,

I give you thanks for

_____
_____
_____
_____
_____
_____

love,
_____

Follow the chain of people to find Jesus' family. Write the letter in each face in the correct space.

" _ _ _ _ _ _ _ _ _ _ _ _ _ _ _

_ _ _ _ _ _ _ _ _ _ _ _ _ _ _ ."

PROPER SIX

(Sunday between June 12 and 18 inclusive, if after Trinity Sunday)

From a Child's Point of View

Old Testament: I Samuel 15:34–16:13. Children, who have been left at home while older family members go to interesting-sounding events, or have eaten in the kitchen while the grown-ups eat in the dining room, delight in God's choice of the youngest kid, who was left behind to tend the sheep while the rest of the family went to the sacrifice with the important visitor. It gives them hope that God is aware of them and values their abilities, too. Teachers, coaches, older siblings, friends, and even parents may overlook them, but God, who "looks on the heart," knows who they really are and appreciates their dreams and intentions.

It is, however, important for children to be reminded that being chosen by God did not immediately change David's life. A few years later when all his older brothers went off to fight, David was still left at home to take care of the sheep and was sent to the battle camp only to take extra food to his brothers. God's plan for David began with years of doing the chores of the youngest brother in a large, busy household.

Psalm: 20. If they are told before the reading that this is a prayer for a king, children catch at least some of its petitions. Though the psalm is peppered with references to Temple sacrifices with which children are unfamiliar, the verb phrases of the petitions—"protect," "send you help," "give you support"—state the requests clearly.

Gospel: Mark 4:26-34. These two parables about growing seeds can either stand alone or comple-

ment the story about David. God uses small things like seeds, a shepherd boy, and us, to do important things, such as produce flowers, rule a nation, and build God's kingdom. For children, that means that they can do important work for God in seemingly little ways. Just as God works on seeds, God works on their kind words, small offerings, and attempts to do God's will every day. This is especially important for middle- and older-elementary children who long to do big things in big ways and tend to devalue the small things they can do now.

Epistle: II Corinthians 5:6-10 (11-13), 14-17. This is the hardest of today's passages for children to understand. To older children attentive enough to sift through all the abstract vocabulary, Paul seems to say that he would rather be dead ("with God") than alive, but he is willing to live in order to do God's work. To children, and to many adults, this is not compelling logic.

The New Jerusalem Bible, however, offers a translation of verse 10 which fits well with the David story: "At the judgment seat of Christ, *we are all to be seen for what we are*" (italics added). This reminds us that because God sees us as we are and does not overlook us, we are responsible for what we do and say. Because Paul believed that he was responsible for doing the job Christ had given him (to start new churches), he was willing for people to say he was crazy. He knew that Christ's opinion of him mattered more than theirs. We are to be as responsible to Christ as Paul was.

Watch Words

If your congregation does not *anoint* in worship, introduce it simply as a way of identifying a person who will be king. If your congregation does *anoint* at baptism and confirmation, compare the way David was identified to become king with the way baptism and confirmation identify us and set us aside to do God's work.

Kingdom of God is a term children easily understand. However, many adults, interested in promoting less monarchical and patriarchal visions of the world, urge that we limit our use of such terms to describe God's action in the world. So try using more "farming" words than "kingdom" words. Speak of God as tending the world and its inhabitants, identify seeds that God is bringing to life, and so forth.

Let the Children Sing

Praise God, who pays attention to both the great and the small, with "All Things Bright and Beautiful."

Sing "Here I Am, Lord" to commit yourselves, with David and Paul, to doing God's will.

Fifth- and sixth-graders can read the vocabulary of "Eternal God, Whose Power Upholds" and, when it is pointed out in advance, appreciate the description in each verse of one human activity through which God may work.

The Liturgical Child

1. Ask the person who provides flowers for the chancel to also provide one seed of that kind of flower for each worshiper. Seeds may be given out by children at the time the Gospel is read, or taped into the bulletins by an older children's class before worship. Point out the mystery of the growth of seed into flower. Then read the Gospel lesson.

2. Anoint worshipers, to show that as God chose David to be king, God has also chosen them for certain service. (Draw a cross on the forehead of each worshiper with one finger dipped in a dish of olive oil.) People may be anointed either as they leave the communion rail or as they leave the sanctuary. Say to each one, "God set David aside to be king. God has a task for you." If this is

done at the end of the service, the following would be an appropriate Charge and Benediction:

Go forth to live for God. Make a difference in the world. Remember that no need is too small to deserve your attention and no problem is too big for you to tackle with God's power. God has set you apart and called you. God is working through you and will be with you always. So, go in peace. Amen.

3. To get into the feeling of Psalm 20, invite the congregation to imagine itself among those greeting David when he later became king. Then read the psalm, with halves of the congregation reading the crowd shouts responsively.

4. Remember to include the children's end-of-school concerns in the church's prayers on the appropriate Sunday.

Sermon Resources

1. It takes 54 people, holding hands, to stand in a circle around the trunk of a giant sequoia tree. Two people can put their arms around the trunk of a lodgepole pine tree. The surprise is that the seed-bearing cone of the second tree is 8 to 12 inches long, while the cone of the sequoia is less than 3 inches long. Since many children have seen sequoia trees or pictures of them, they are a good modern example with which to make the point of the mustard-seed parable.

2. Compare the growth of a seed to the results when a child puts a dollar in the offering. Describe what one dollar's worth of food can mean for a hungry child, what a Bible could mean to a family in a refugee camp, what communion means when brought to a homebound member, and so forth.

3. *The Quarreling Book,* by Charlotte Zolotow, describes a series of small events that ruin the day, as each in a series of people lash out at someone after being hurt by someone else, until the process is reversed when a dog licks Eddie's hand, regardless of the way Eddie had treated it. It is everyday proof that little deeds, like the seeds referred to in the parable, produce significant results. Bring this very short story to life as you read it, showing the feelings of each person with your facial expressions.

Listen to Jesus' story about planting seeds. Then draw or write about 1 "seed" you want to plant this week. It might be being a friend to someone who needs a friend, or something you can do to solve a problem.

When the offering is collected,
● tell God about your "seed" and
● ask God to make it grow.

When God looks at us, God sees more than people do. Listen to the story about Samuel and David. Decode the message below to learn how God looks at David and at us.

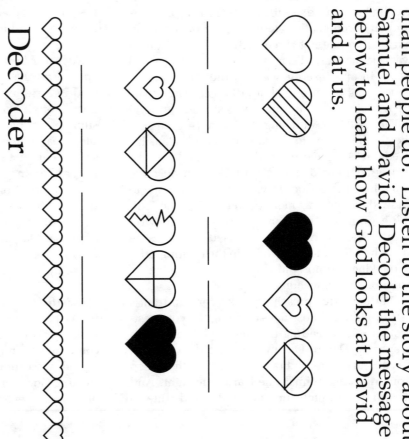

Decoder

=H   =R   =N

=T   =O   =A   =E

PROPER SEVEN

(Sunday between June 19 and 25 inclusive, if after Trinity Sunday)

From a Child's Point of View

Old Testament: I Samuel 17:(1a, 4-11, 19-23), 32-49. Most church children have heard and enjoy this story. They like it because it is action-oriented and because a child acts courageously and successfully, while the adults sit around frightened. They want to be like David.

They are interested in Goliath's size. Translate his height and the weight of his armor into recognizable measurements. Compare the weight of his javelin, 19 pounds, with the weight of javelins thrown in competitions today, 1 1/2 pounds. Point out that we are not sure exactly how tall Goliath was. He may have been as short as 7 feet or as tall as 10. In any case, he was not the taller-than-a-house giant of cartoons, but just a very large man. He was big and mean, but he was still human.

The challenge in telling this story is to be sure the children listen to David's words as well as his deeds. It is his words that tell why and how he did what he did. He fought Goliath because Goliath belittled God. David wanted everyone to know that God was more powerful than any bullying giant or threatening army. David won because he trusted God and used the skills he knew best. He did not give in to the exciting offer of the king's armor, but, knowing what he had to do, chose his slingshot.

One powerful preaching point for children is that through all those days of doing the youngest-brother job of tending the sheep, God had been preparing David. During the long dark nights, David learned to be brave. Protecting the sheep from attacking animals, he learned to fight. And spending so much time alone, he had time to

think about God and God's world. At times, he must have longed to do something more interesting and exciting, but by sticking with his assigned job, he learned skills and attitudes he would need as a warrior and king. By doing boring school work and tedious chores, or practicing exercises instead of playing songs, today's children can achieve the same results.

Psalm: 9:9-20. This psalm is a rather disjointed collection of statements about God's trustworthiness and people and nations who do and do not trust God. Children can catch only a few phrases.

Gospel: Mark 4:35-41. Children may fantasize about bravely fighting a giant bully, but trusting God in a summer storm is closer to reality. Most people of all ages are frightened of the power of summer storms and can easily imagine the disciples' fear when caught out on a big lake, in a small boat, in a storm, in the middle of the night. It's hard to imagine a scarier situation.

Jesus' question to the fearful disciples, and to us, is "Why are you afraid?" Children know that people are injured or killed in storms, and they appreciate hearing such realities identified as the reasons we might rightly be afraid, before listening to the faith reasons for not being afraid.

Epistle: II Corinthians 6:1-13. This passage is too complicated for children to follow as it is read. Read on its own, it offers an example of commitment and discipleship. Read in the context of today's other texts, it offers an example of trusting God from day to day, rather than at times of dramatic events. Paul was brave and faithful enough to stick with one task for years. His task was to tell the Gentiles about Jesus, and he stuck with it even when frightening things happened. He stuck with it when he was hurt and discouraged. He stuck with it when people did not listen to him. And he never let anything else get in the way of his doing the best job he could. Paul was faithful and trusting from day to day.

Watch Words

Before speaking symbolically of *fighting giants*, describe one or two non-literal *giants* with which people battle—for example, a fear of beginning some new activity.

Faith, for David, Paul, and Jesus, was putting what they knew about God into action. Because David had faith in God's power, he fought Goliath. Because Jesus had faith in God's care, he slept through the storm. Because Paul had faith that he was doing work that was important to God, he gave it his best and never gave up.

Let the Children Sing

Invite a young children's class or choir to sing "Only a Boy Named David" as an anthem, perhaps with hand motions.

Remind worshipers of the ways David and/or Paul trusted God with their bodies, before singing "Take My Life and Let It Be Consecrated." Recall the trust David learned as a shepherd by singing the hymn version of Psalm 23 most familiar to your congregation.

Choose storm hymns carefully. The vocabulary of "Eternal Father, Strong to Save" is very difficult for children to read. The storm images of "Lonely the Boat" alternate between the literal and symbolic. "Jesus, Savior, Pilot Me" is so symbolic that children cannot interpret it.

The repeated lines in the chorus of "God of Grace and God of Glory" can be sung as a prayer by even nonreaders.

The Liturgical Child

1. Read I Samuel 17 in good storyteller style.

Use a booming voice for Goliath, a younger, more enthusiastic tone for David, and a sad, resigned voice for Saul. You may want to gather children on the steps to hear this story which has been a favorite for thousands of years.

2. Because Psalm 9 is part of an acrostic poem, have each "letter" read by a different reader. The change in readers helps children catch more phrases. Suggest that older listeners decide to whom, in the story of David and Goliath, each "letter" applies. (The New Jerusalem Bible prints the Hebrew letters in the margins beside the verses.)

3. Prayer of Confession:

God of David, we would like to be brave like David, but we see too quickly the things we think we cannot do and ignore what we might do with your power working through us. Forgive us when we are too hesitant, too unsure, too cautious.

Savior of the disciples, we too are easily frightened. Forgive us when we are afraid—afraid we will be hurt, afraid we will be misunderstood, afraid we will fail. Give us the courage to face our fears and move past them.

Lord of Paul, unlike Paul, we give up too easily. Forgive us when we forget what you have called us to do, when we are ready to "chicken out" on being disciples, when we have lost hope and feel like failures. Give us the kind of commitment Paul had and the courage to keep trying, even when we are not succeeding.

Forgive us, and give us new power and strength to rise up as your people. For we pray in Jesus' name. Amen.

Sermon Resources

1. Summer is filled with opportunities to trust God: going away to camp for the first time; standing up for God's ways at camp and in locker rooms; trying new feats (jumping off the diving board), and so on.

2. David learned how to kill a giant by tending his father's sheep. Similarly, in the movie *The Karate Kid*, a man offers to teach a boy karate, but puts the boy to work polishing cars and painting a fence. The boy protests, until the man proves to him that by doing the work, he has perfected several movements that are critical to karate.

Listen as **I Samuel 17** is read. Then draw pictures of Goliath and David.

What did they wear?

What did they carry?

How did their faces look?

David **trusted** God to defeat Goliath.

Jesus told the disciples to **trust** God during a storm.

Draw or write about one time you need to **trust** God. (Listen to the sermon for ideas.)

PROPER EIGHT

(Sunday between June 26 and July 2 inclusive)

From a Child's Point of View

Old Testament: II Samuel 1:1, 17-27. David's grief for Saul and Jonathan provides adults a counterpoint to the Gospel story about healing and resurrection. But the poem assumes a detailed knowledge of the relationships between Saul, Jonathan, and David, and a mature understanding of death and grieving. Consequently, it is not a compelling reading for children.

The alternative Old Testament readings (I Samuel 18:1-5 and Psalm 133) focus on the friendship of David and Jonathan, featured nowhere else in this cycle of David texts. Telling additional stories about David and Jonathan, preaching about their unlikely friendship, and building liturgy focused on friendship, can produce a worship experience in which both children and adults can participate fully.

Psalm: 130. When it is read with great emotion, children hear this as a prayer which might have been prayed by David after Saul and Jonathan died, by Jarius while his daughter was so ill, or by the woman who had been sick for twelve years. They gather this more from the feeling of phrases such as "Out of the depths I cry to you," than from intellectual understanding of the poem as a whole. Much of the vocabulary and many of the concepts require more explanation than is possible in worship.

Gospel: Mark 5:21-43. This double story offers two more examples of faith in action. Children love the synagogue leader, a father who risked his office and what his friends might think, to ask Jesus to heal his terminally ill daughter. Shy children, especially, admire the woman who quietly reached out to touch Jesus, believing he could heal her. Preaching on these stories, however, generally leads to discussions of adult concerns (wholeness, uncleanness, the meaning of new life) and abstract ideas (the link between faith and healing), which are beyond children. Last week's examples—fighting a giant and facing a storm—are easier to use in meaningfully exploring faith with both adults and children.

Epistle: II Corinthians 8:7-15. This is basically a passage about sharing. Paul wants the Corinthians to share some of what they have with Christians in Jerusalem who have great need at the moment. He promises that when the Corinthians are the needy ones, the Christians in Jerusalem will take up an offering for them. He is not calling for sacrificial giving, but sharing some of our plenty.

It is possible to tie in such sharing with the friendship between David and Jonathan. Generous sharing among friends is not something duty forces us to do, but something we want to do.

Watch Words

Believing and *having faith* mean putting your thoughts into action.

To *heal* is to cure a person of a disease. *To make whole* is interpreted literally and thus produces interesting but not very useful mental pictures of the woman who had been bleeding for years. Today, *save* means either to rescue from identifiable trouble or to set aside for future use. Use it carefully in exploring the Gospel story.

Though II Corinthians suggests a stewardship sermon, do not use the word *stewardship* which relates to doing our *duties* well. Speak instead of *sharing,* which arises from *generous concern* for people we care about. If you use *benevolences* or *benevolent* frequently in your worship, take time to define the terms and paraphrase the sentences in which they are used.

Let the Children Sing

Sing about Christ's power with the hymns you sang during Easter. The repeated phrases make "When Morning Gilds the Skies" a first choice.

Most church-school and vacation-Bible-school songbooks contain songs about generous love. "Love, Love, Love, That's What It's All About," and other such songs may be sung by children's classes or Bible-school groups as anthems.

If you feature the friendship of David and Jonathan on a communion Sunday, sing "I Come with Joy." Alert the children to listen for lines about friendship among God's people.

The Liturgical Child

1. To emphasize the story-within-a-story in Mark, have the passage read by two readers. The first reads from the usual lectern. The second reads either from the pulpit or stands beside or in front of the lectern, to highlight the interruption. The readers should practice reading the verses in order to communicate their urgency.

> male reader:21-24
> female reader: 25-34
> male reader: 35-43

2. Before reading the Epistle, describe the situation in Jerusalem and in Corinth. Ask worshipers to listen for what Paul wanted the people in Corinth to do and why he wanted them to do it. Begin the sermon with comments on that.

3. Before collecting the offering, briefly describe several specific ways your congregation will use the money to share what you have with others. If possible, name sharing efforts with which the children are familiar and in which they have shared time and energy, as well as money.

4. Offer a series of bidding prayers about friends, pausing after each for worshipers to follow the worship leader's directions. Bid worshipers to identify and pray for friends who are older; then younger; then the same age they are. Instruct them to think about and pray for a friend who lives in another town. Ask them to name to themselves, and to God, one friend with whom they are not getting along at the moment. Urge them to think, with God, of ways to work things out with that friend. Suggest that they name to God all their friends in your congregation, and then thank God for something special about each one. Encourage them to identify a person who needs their friendship, and to make a promise to God about offering that friendship this week.

Sermon Resources

1. Explore the spirit of generosity that lay beneath Paul's call to share, by describing two brothers who shared a bedroom. They had their own dressers and desks, but most of their toys and important things were scattered all over the room and under the beds. Stuff was everywhere. At homework time, one brother's "Have you seen my pencil?" generally was answered, "Who knows! Try this one." Though they had their fusses, they usually got along.

Then trace a spiral of selfishness that began when one brother said, "This is mine. Don't even touch it!" and escalated, with each one identifying what was his, until they drew a line down the middle of the room and posted STAY OUT signs. From that time on, there was constant bickering and checking, to make sure that one did not have anything that was the other's.

2. Jess and Leslie, in *Bridge to Terabithia,* by Katherine Paterson, provide a modern example of friendship like that of David and Jonathan. Jess, from a poor rural family, and Leslie, whose family is well-off financially and educationally, forge a creative friendship which ends with Leslie's accidental death. Both their friendship and Jess's grief parallel that of David and Jonathan. This award winner has been read by many fifth- and sixth-graders.

3. If you give the children the puzzle on the Worship Worksheet, use the word *benevolent* repeatedly, to help build their familiarity with it.

Listen as **II Corinthians 8:7-15** is read. Find the words you hear in the letters below. Then find more words that tell what Paul wants us to be and do.

```
K O J G I V E E K G
R F M E J Q X A Y I
O F O N M L J G L F
B E N E V O L E N T
C R E R R V S R Q Z
A I Y O Y E P O O R
R N Y U R I C H Y W
E G Z S H A R I N G
```

GIVE
RICH
CARE
POOR

LOVE
EAGER
GIFT
SHARING

BENEVOLENT*
GENEROUS
OFFERING
MONEY

*Benevolent may be a new word for you. It describes a person who shares what he or she has with others. Listen for it in worship today.

Use the plan below to write a poem about

A GOOD FRIEND

⌣'s name _____

2 words that describe ⌣ _____ _____

3 things you and ⌣
like to do together _____ _____ _____

1 word you want to
say to ⌣ _____

PROPER NINE

(Sunday between July 3 and 9 inclusive)

From a Child's Point of View

Today's texts deal with strength. Children are very interested in acquiring strength and in measuring their strength against that of others. Although they think first of physical strength, even young children understand strength of the mind and persuasive leadership. Dealing with these texts near the Fourth of July leads American adults to ponder the kinds of strength our country values. Only the oldest children, however, are beginning to understand such questions.

Old Testament: II Samuel 5:1-5, 9-10. In this passage, God's promise that David would be king is kept. Unfortunately, compared to previous dramatic stories about David, this story seems anticlimactic and has little to attract the attention of children. For them, it is mainly an opportunity to review David's experiences thus far. The theme is that God kept the promise. David has become king—not because he is stronger or smarter than anyone else—but because God has chosen him to be king.

The fact that David probably was about ten (old enough to be out with the sheep but not yet an official male member of the worshiping community) when he was anointed and thirty when he became king, means that it took God about 20 years to keep the promise. For young David, and for today's children, 20 years is a long time, so children appreciate David's patience as he kept waiting and trusting.

Psalm: 48. Reading Psalm 48 is like singing another country's national anthem. Even though one understands some of the words and references, it does not mean much and is impossible to

sing with the fervor of a patriot. Children reading Psalm 48 encounter so many unfamiliar names, places, and events that their attention spans expire before explanations are completed.

Epistle: II Corinthians 12:2-10. Children cannot follow this passage as it is read, but depend on the preacher to set it in context and present its important message. The context is one with which children are familiar. People (in this case, church leaders) are having an "I'm better than you" argument. Paul's opponents have been describing all the ways God has spoken to them and all the miracles they have performed. Paul's response is that he too has had some spectacular experiences of God's presence, but the most significant was the presence of God with him when he was weakest. Instead of trying to impress others with his strength, Paul told about God's help in dealing with his "thorn." Paul does not rely on his own strength, but trusts God's strength.

Like adults, children enjoy guessing what Paul's thorn might have been and identifying the thorns in their own lives. The passage can be used to explore either God's presence with us when we are coping with our thorns, or Paul's put-down of boasting about our strength.

Gospel: Mark 6:1-13. These two stories describe what children can expect as followers of Jesus. Jesus' family and friends did not understand or believe him. Likewise, when children today live as disciples, their friends and even their families may think they are a little crazy. When Jesus sent out the Twelve to proclaim his message, he did not send them well-equipped, trained knights on a quest, but as poor messengers, ready to speak to whomever would listen, and then move on without any big show when people did not listen. To children bombarded with encouragement to be strong and capable, this says that among Jesus' followers, it is more important to obey God than to be strong. If we obey God, God will do powerful things through us, just the way we are.

Watch Words

Because children do not know the literal meanings of the *Zion* vocabulary in Psalm 48, they are totally lost if it is used symbolically.

The opposite of *strong* in today's texts is not *weak*, but *trusting*. Rather than trust in their own limited *strength*, David and Paul *trusted* God's unlimited *strength*.

Let the Children Sing

"God of Grace and God of Glory" is a prayer of trust in God's strength. Though children learn the meaning of the verses slowly, even the youngest can join in on the repeated chorus, "Grant us wisdom, grant us courage."

The repeated lines at the beginning and end of each verse make "Go Forth for God" a hymn in which children can join the congregation in committing themselves to discipleship like that of the Twelve.

The Liturgical Child

1. Base a Prayer of Confession on our tendency to trust our own strength, rather than to depend on God:

God of the Universe, all of us want to be strong. We are quick to claim, "I did it myself," when we do something good. We dream of doing magnificent deeds. We want to think that we can do anything, if we only work at it. But when we are honest, we admit that the strongest of us are weak. We depend on you for the air we breathe, for life itself. We confess that we get into the most trouble when we ignore you and depend on our own strength to do things our own way. So finally, we must depend on you to forgive us. We ask you to forgive us when we use our strength selfishly or cruelly, to stick with us when we ignore your power, and to stand by us when we find ourselves at the end of our strength.

Assurance of Pardon: Hear the Good News! God's love is powerful, indeed! On the cross, Jesus had the strength to forgive those who killed him and the thief who was hanging beside him. Through Jesus, God also forgives us, and loves us, and gives us the power to live as God's people. Thanks be to God!

2. Base the Charge and Benediction on the commissioning of the Twelve:

As Jesus sent out his twelve disciples, I send you out. These are your instructions: Share God's love with everyone you meet this week. Make friends with those who are lonely. Help those who need you. And stand up for God's loving ways. For this mission, you do not need any fancy equipment or special training. Simply use what you have. It will be enough. It will be enough, because the loving God who is the Strength of the Universe will be with you, and will work through you with power that will surprise and amaze you. So go out in God's name, and go in peace.

Sermon Resources

1. To help worshipers get the feel of the argument that is the context of the Epistle reading, act out one or more similar arguments from today's world:

"On my vacation, I . . . ."
"Well, on *my* vacation, I . . . !"
or
"My dog can . . . ."
"Oh yeah? Well, *my* dog can . . . ."

2. In *Star Wars*, Luke Skywalker slowly learned to obey "the force" and let it work through him. It was not his light saber, but his obedience to "the force" that gave him the power to conquer the dark side. Similarly, Christians do not receive their strength from anything magic, but from obeying God and doing God's will. When we obey God, we are often surprised at what can be accomplished.

If you are focusing on David this summer, collect the children's "Where's David?" pictures from the Worship Worksheets to post on a prominent bulletin board.

Follow the string to find the letters of a word we use in worship today.

Listen for what we say about it. Write your own prayer about it.

You have seen the Where's Waldo books. To make a **Where's David** picture, draw what David did before becoming king.* In each picture draw a crown, but draw David in only one.

* Ideas: David anointed king, David taking care of sheep, David fighting Goliath, David with his friend Jonathon.

PROPER TEN

(Sunday between July 10 and 16 inclusive)

From a Child's Point of View

Old Testament: II Samuel 6:1-5, 12b-19. The story of David bringing the Ark to Jerusalem includes several subplots, each of which makes a comment on God's presence. The core of the story is the description of the great parade led by David. (Children need a brief description of the Ark, its history, and its importance as a symbol of God's presence.) As the parade moved to the new capital city, there was lots of music and everyone sang and danced to honor God. It was an exuberant celebration of God's presence. Most children wish more worship would be like that parade.

Verse 16 begins, but does not conclude, the story of Michal's response to David's behavior. Older children, as they begin to feel the pressure of peers who belittle involvement in church activities, find a good example in David's response in verses 20-22. David was willing to have anyone, even his wife, look down on him in order to express his praise and gratitude to God. We are to do likewise. (It is not necessary to point out David's exposure to get to the message of this story: David did not act dignified, "like a king," but became caught up in the singing and dancing as he celebrated God's presence with all his might.)

Psalm: 24. This is a psalm for children to experience, rather than understand. If it is presented dramatically as a responsive Call to Worship, children will follow the questions and answers, and sense the joyful mood of gathering to worship in God's presence. Though they understand the words of the Good News Bible's translation more easily, they sense the mood of the New Revised Standard translation and may recognize verses that are used frequently in your worship.

Epistle: Ephesians 1:3-14. In a way, the writer of these verses is dancing before God with his pen, just as David danced before God with his feet. Unfortunately for children, the writer uses impossibly complex words and ideas, and praises God's work on the unfamiliar cosmic plane. About the only way to present this message to children is to paraphrase some of the individual blessings of God which the writer recognizes. For example:

- Before our birth, God planned for us to belong to God.
- God loves us so much that God sent Jesus so that we might be forgiven.
- God's plan for the world is that we will all become one family, with Jesus as the leader.
- God is carrying out this plan. It will happen.

Gospel: Mark 6:14-29. At first blush, this is not an appropriate story to tell children. It is, however, possible to explore the sin that brought about the death of John the Baptist without going into detail on the sinful sexuality that ran rampant in the family of Herod. Herod's offer of any gift his daughter asked for is similar to the wishes offered by genies in fairy tales. Children are properly appalled at the mother's use of that gift to have an old enemy murdered. They wish the daughter had been brave and righteous enough not to do the terrible thing her mother suggested. They can imagine how angry and hurt Herod must have been by the way his family tricked him. They are ashamed of Herod's giving in to the fear that his friends would laugh at him if he did not give his daughter what he had publicly promised. And they are indignant that a good person like John should be killed in the vicious feuding of this evil family.

Scholars suggest that Mark told this story to foreshadow the way Jesus would be caught up in the sinful power struggles that would lead to his death. So the children's reaction is on target and leads to discussion of how sin can spread to destroy even the good people and things of life.

Watch Words

The Epistle reading may lead you to speak of *election, predestination,* and *revelation.* Remember that these, as well as many of the theological terms in the text, are big, abstract words which have little meaning for children.

Describe this *Ark,* which was not a boat like Noah's ark.

Let the Children Sing

In Psalm 24, worshipers talk about opening the gates of the Temple. In "Lift Up Your Heads, Ye Mighty Gates," we sing about opening up the doors of our hearts and lives to God. Point out this difference before singing the song.

The Presbyterian hymnal includes a version of Psalm 24 (titled "Psalm 24"), set to a whirling Israeli folktune which captures the feeling of David's dancing before God. It is more effective sung well by a choir than haltingly by the congregation.

Other appropriate hymns of praise include "All Creatures of Our God and King," "Earth and All Stars," and "To God Be the Glory."

The Liturgical Child

1. Psalm 24 reflects bringing the Ark into the sanctuary. It is a conversation between those inside the sanctuary and those approaching it, and therefore is most dramatically presented as a Call to Worship by two groups—two halves of the congregation, the congregation and the choir,

or two choirs (one at the front of the sanctuary and one at the rear). If the last is chosen, it may be followed by a processional hymn, during which banners, candles, crosses, and so forth precede the outer choir. Older children enjoy serving as this outer choir. With encouragement, they read their verses with the exuberance of David dancing before the Ark:

Group 1: 1*a*	Group 1: 5-6
Group 2: 1*b*	Group 2: 7
Group 1: 2*a*	Group 1: 8*a*
Group 2: 2*b*	Group 2: 8*b*(pause)9
Group 1: 3	Group 1: 10*a*
Group 2: 4	Group 2: 10*b*

2. Base a Prayer of Confession on the sins in Herod's family:

Lord God, you teach us right from wrong. But we ignore you. Like Herod's family, we do what we want, greedily taking what we want, no matter what. We are quick to take revenge on those who hurt us. We pay more attention to what our friends think of us than to what we know is right. Even when we know that others are hurt by what we do, we make no changes. Loving God, forgive us. For we pray in Jesus' name. Amen.

Hear the Good News. God *is* loving and forgiving. More than that, God works in us, giving us the power to do what is right. Thanks be to God!

Sermon Resources

1. In the movie *Chariots of Fire,* Olympic runner Eric Liddell said, "God made me fast," and claimed that he could feel God's pleasure when he ran well. For sports-minded children, Eric, running in God's presence, is a powerful parallel to David, dancing before God with all his might.

2. *The Quarreling Book,* by Charlotte Zolotow, describes how sin spreads through a family and into the community, as one person hurts another after being hurt. The pattern is reversed when a dog continues to wag its tail when snarled at by a little boy.

DAVID praised God with all his might.

Draw a picture of a way YOU praise God with all your might.

or

Write a prayer telling why YOU praise God.

_____ praises God!

(your name)

Listen carefully as Mark 6:14-29 is read. It tells about many sins in Herod's family.

Make a hidden word puzzle by adding words about sin to the empty squares. REVENGE, HATE, and MURDER were problems in Herod's family. What sins are problems for others?

R		H	A	T	E
E					
V					
E					
N					
G					
E	M	U	R	D	E	R

Remember, there is no sin so awful that God will not forgive us if we confess and are truly sorry.

PROPER ELEVEN

(Sunday between July 17 and 23 inclusive)

From a Child's Point of View

Old Testament: II Samuel 7:1-14a. For scholars, this is a key Old Testament text which introduces a new theological theme. For children, it is a fascinating story about gifts. Older children, who enjoy catching the pun about "house" when it is explained, hear the text as a story about a contest of gifts: David offered a gift which God refused, and God then countered with a wonderful promise which reminded David of something he needed to remember: He had not become a great king on his own, for God had chosen him and worked through him. God was still God, and David was still human, even if he was king.

Literal thinkers have trouble with talk about where God lives, and they do not understand the significance of living in a tent rather than a temple. Furthermore, few children understand the intricacies of gifts with strings attached well enough to imagine the ways David might have used the gift-temple to "cage" God. So the royal politics of the story make little sense to them.

When the story is paired with the Gospel and Epistle lessons, children can appreciate the surprising way God kept his promise to David. A king who tirelessly healed and taught, and who died on a cross to make peace, was not the kind of king David would have expected.

Psalm: 89:20-37. If children are alerted to the fact that in this psalm God is speaking about David, and are urged to listen for what God does for David, they hear that God can be trusted and keeps promises. They find security in knowing that though God will punish when punishment is deserved, God continues to love and to keep promises.

Epistle: Ephesians 2:11-22. Elementary children define themselves by the classes, teams, clubs, and friendship groups to which they belong. They tend to focus on the exclusive nature of these groups, and quickly point out that only those who meet all the requirements, or have been properly initiated, belong. All others are outsiders and somehow "less." This distrust of those who are not part of "our" group may be extended to those of other racial, ethnic, and national groups.

Because of this, children are fascinated by the ruthless rules by which the Jews kept the Gentiles away, and they need to hear the writer's message that God is working to bring groups together. Just as Jews and Gentiles became friends in Christ, we are to look at the members of all other groups as potential friends in Christ. This work needs to be illustrated with everyday, specific examples.

Gospel: Mark 6:30-34, 53-56. These summary descriptions of Jesus' ministry show him compassionately teaching and healing the huge crowds who followed him. Because they are general rather than specific, they do not attract children's attention.

Watch Words

Speak of *God's promise to David,* rather than of the *Davidic covenant.*

Describe some of the language Jews used to exclude non-Jews—*uncircumcised* (*circumcision* was an operation for Jewish men and boys), *Gen-*

tile, unclean. Compare these words to language used to belittle members of other racial and ethnic groups today.

Avoid *reconciliation* in favor of *made friends with* or *made peace between.*

Let the Children Sing

Sing a Christmas carol in July to celebrate the surprising way God kept the promise to David. "Once in Royal David's City" and "Joy to the World!" are best.

With open hymnals, study "Great Is Thy Faithfulness" during the sermon before singing it. It connects God's faithfulness to David with Christ's gift of peace. Since younger children learn the chorus first, define *mercies* and help them identify God's mercies to David and to them.

If the focus is on Christ's gift of peace, close with "Blest Be the Tie That Binds" or "In Christ There Is No East or West." Hold hands to emphasize the meaning of the hymn.

The Liturgical Child

1. If the focus is on God's promise to David, place a table-top tree or arrangement of greenery decorated with king-type Chrismons (star of David, crown, and so forth) in the chancel. During worship, explain how each ornament reminds us of both David and Jesus.

2. After a worship leader prays for each in a series of specific groups who need Christ's peace today, the congregation responds, "May your peace be with us and work through us, O Christ." For example:

Lord of all peoples, we know that there are refugees living in our town. We can only imagine how hard it must be to feel at home among people who speak a new language, eat different foods, and wear different clothes. Help us find ways to welcome them. (RESPONSE)

Lord of love, we all know people who seem to have no friends. They are teased or ignored. They are the last chosen for any team, and their names never appear on lists for invitations. But we know that your peace is meant for them too. Teach us how to pass that peace to them. (RESPONSE)

3. If your congregation regularly passes the peace, this is a good day to highlight it and explain its meaning. Instruct worshipers to save one handshake or hug for passing Christ's peace to a person not in the sanctuary.

If your service does not include this ritual, instruct worshipers to introduce themselves to at least one person they do not know well as they leave the sanctuary. They might also say, "Go in peace," to each other as they part.

4. Expand on the traditional "Go in peace" benediction:

Go in peace. Christ is working for peace among people on the playing field, in the swimming pool, at the office, at home, and around the world. Your help is needed.

Go in peace. Refuse to shut anyone out or cut any person down. Look for ways to help people get along together better. Love your enemies into friends.

Go in peace. And remember that you do not go alone. Christ goes with you and works through you.

Go in peace, and the peace of Christ that passes all understanding will be with you today and every day. Amen.

Sermon Resources

1. *The Hundred Dresses,* by Eleanor Estes, tells how two older-elementary schoolgirls teased and belittled Wanda Petronski until she left school. But she left behind gifts which made the girls realize what they had done to an outsider.

2. Remind the congregation of the older man who lived next door in *Home Alone.* Children imagined terrible things about him. But as it turned out, he was the one who rescued Kevin and, with his help, was able to make peace with his own estranged family.

3. To explore God's promise to David, build the sermon around the surprising ways God keeps promises. Open the subject by describing a trip to the beach, during which a rainy night spent playing games in the motel room turns out to be the best part of the trip. Then describe what each of the following people expected and received from God's promise to them: Abraham (What kind of nation did he father?); the escaped slaves (What did it mean to be God's people?); David (What kind of king was his great descendent, King Jesus?).

The words in the message below are divided. Half of each word is on each side of the page. Bring the correct halves together to learn the message.

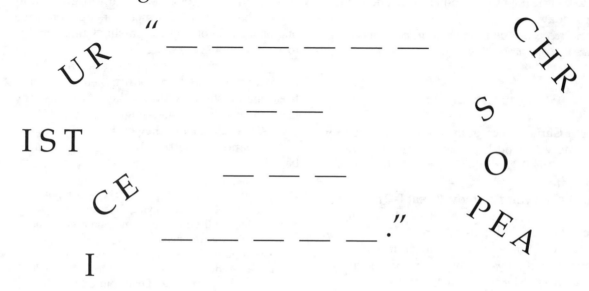

UR   " _ _ _ _ _ _ _   C H R

                  _ _   S

IST   O

CE   _ _ _   P E A

I   _ _ _ _ _ _ . "

See Ephesians 2:14.

People expected God's King to be like David. They were surprised by Jesus. Draw or write one thing Jesus did that surprised them.

PROPER TWELVE

(Sunday between July 24 and 30 inclusive)

From a Child's Point of View

Old Testament: II Samuel 11:1-15. The story of David and Bathsheba is not one most people would choose to tell children. David's key problem, however, was not adultery, but a willingness to break the rules to get what he wanted, and that willingness is something children understand. In early childhood, children assume that the most powerful people (the grown-ups, the teachers, the biggest kids) have the right to make the rules. So they learn from David's story that even the greatest king is subservient to God's rules. Many older children are realizing that rules can be negotiated for the good of the group. This discovery changes their attitude toward rules. As they begin living with negotiated rules, they empathize with David's temptation to ignore those that did not work to his advantage at the moment and are reminded that rules are to be obeyed.

Most children do not understand David's maneuvers in verses 6-13, but they do understand David's murder of Uriah. Therefore, consider reading either the entire chapter or verses 1-5 and 14-15, instead of 1-15. The Good News Bible uses the most "delicate" vocabulary in telling this story.

Psalm: 14. If the psalm is introduced as a poet's response to disobedience like David's, children will catch occasional lines condemning those who break God's rules. A child's paraphrase of "There is no God" is "I will not be caught" or "What I do will not matter."

Epistle: Ephesians 3:14-21. Children will understand little of Paul's message as it is read from any translation. But if the passage is compared to the wishes expressed by families in wedding toasts or on birthday cards, they enjoy exploring Paul's prayer-wishes for Gentile Christians. His wish is that they (and we) will experience and recognize God's great love and will feel God's presence, giving us inner strength.

The images of being rooted in God's love and built on a foundation of God's love need to be illustrated with everyday examples—for instance, a person who knows that God made her and loves her will be disappointed, but will not lose all hope in herself when she loses a championship. Sermons which cite such examples help children build self-esteem, based on the love of God, who created them.

Older children in the middle of sports-oriented summers also benefit from descriptions of the inner strength (rather than the physical strength) that Paul wishes for his friends.

Gospel: John 6:1-21. Most church children are familiar with the feeding of the five thousand. They tend to associate it with Jesus' care of people's needs and take it as an indication of Jesus' willingness to take seriously and use a child's contribution.

When it is pointed out to them, older children understand that John was less like a historian telling us exactly what Jesus did, and more like a person telling us who his best friend is by relating stories about what that friend did and said. They will, however, depend upon the preacher to point out what John is telling us about Jesus in these two stories—that Jesus had great powers (he could feed thousands of people with five loaves and a few fish, and he could walk on water) and that Jesus came to feed or nourish people. The next four Gospel lections tell what it means for Jesus to feed people.

Watch Words

In David's story, *sin* is breaking the rules. His *adultery* was stealing someone else's wife.

In John, *bread* is a code word for what we need to live. Sometimes we call money "bread" because we use it to buy what we need to live. Use *bread* carefully. Children are easily confused when a word is used both literally and symbolically.

Let the Children Sing

"There's a Wideness in God's Mercy" is a good hymn to explore phrase-by-phrase in a sermon about God's great love. Though it includes many unfamiliar words, it also includes some vivid images of the vastness of God's love.

Imagine yourselves among those Jesus fed while singing "I Come with Joy" (whether or not you celebrate communion).

The Liturgical Child

1. Display a basket of small loaves of bread on the chancel table, or hang a banner featuring several loaves of bread and some fish. (The banner might be a summer project for a children's group or class.)

2. To create a Prayer of Confession based on Psalm 14, a worship leader describes a series of ways we rationalize our disobedience. The congregation responds to each one with, "We say it will not matter, but it does. Forgive us." For example:

> Lord, you instruct us to be honest, but we lie when we think we can get away with it. We tell only the part of the truth that makes us look good. And we answer only the questions that are asked. (RESPONSE)
>
> Lord, you instruct us not to steal, but we . . . .

> *Assurance of Pardon:* There is a God. What we do does matter. But God, who insists that we live by the rules, also loves us and forgives us, and gives us the power to try again. Thanks be to God!

3. Before reading the Gospel, invite a crowd of worshipers of all ages, perhaps the front rows of people, to sit with you on the steps. Describe the similar crowd that had gathered around Jesus. Read John 6:1-15 from a Bible held in your lap. Then without announcement, a second worship leader in the lectern (away from the crowd) begins, and reads verses 16-21.

4. Feature intercessory prayer (prayer for others). Describe your congregation's practice of praying for others just before that time in the service. Compare your practice with Paul's prayer for the Gentiles. Consider asking the congregation to identify groups for whom they would like the church to offer prayer-wishes this morning. Then be especially careful to pray with language and sentences simple enough for children to follow.

Sermon Resources

1. Children's explanations of why they disobey rules reflect what David might have thought:

"But the big kids (or name a specific bigger kid) always do it. And I'm in fourth grade now, so—"

"But it's my birthday!" (And I thought the usual rules would not apply on my birthday.)

"But I wanted it *so much!*"

"I knew it was wrong, but I didn't think anyone would mind *just this once!* I won't do it again, I promise."

2. Jesus said he came to feed us. Many professions are, or can be, feeding professions—teaching, medicine, social service. By identifying specific ways these professionals "feed people," children begin to understand what Jesus meant when he said he came to feed people.

3. Corrie ten Boom was a Christian imprisoned by the Nazis for hiding Jews. After the war, during a service at which she spoke about forgiveness, a man she recognized as a cruel prison guard came to shake her hand. She did not want to touch him and felt no forgiveness for him, even though she knew she should. She willed her hand to meet his, but it would not move until she felt a power from beyond her travel from her shoulder down her arm toward the man. With that power, she was able to not just shake his hand, but to really forgive him. She knew that that power was Christ's love.

Listen to the story about Jesus walking on water. Then draw a picture. How do you think Jesus looked? Make the disciples' faces show how they felt when they saw Jesus.

Paul wrote a prayer telling God what he wished for his friends.

Write a prayer telling God what you wish for one of your friends.

Dear God, I pray

for _____

Please _____

Amen

PROPER THIRTEEN

(Sunday between July 31 and August 6 inclusive)

From a Child's Point of View

Old Testament: II Samuel 11:26–12:13a. When it is dramatically presented, children follow the story of Nathan's confrontation of David closely. They are as outraged as David at the actions of a rich man who steals a poor man's lamb. However, they need help in digging through Nathan's symbolic language to identify David as the thief and God's punishment for him: There will be violent fighting instead of peace in his family, and his wives will one day be stolen by another man. This punishment looks fair to children. David will experience all the pain in his family that he has inflicted on the family of Uriah and Bathsheba. With help, older children can understand that David's punishment was a natural result of his behavior. He had led his family into selfish sin, and eventually they all would be hurt by one another.

The Good News Bible offers the easiest translation for children. If its use of *intercourse* in verse 11 is a problem, try The New Jerusalem Bible. The New Revised Standard's heavy use of symbolic language, and its phrasing God's accusation against David in terms of "despising me" rather than "disobeyed my commands" (Good News Bible) or "displeased me" (New Jerusalem Bible) make it a last choice.

Psalm: 51:1-12. Because few children sense their own sin as keenly as the man who composed this psalm sensed his, they need to encounter this psalm first as David's prayer. They can understand why David would feel so guilty about what he had done, and they learn the prayer's meaning for David. As they mature, recognize their own sinfulness, and use parts of the psalm repeatedly

in congregational worship, they will claim it as their own.

The rich imagery of the psalm makes it hard for children to follow. It is probably best to focus attention on verses 1-2 and 10-12, and expect children to catch some of the remaining phrases.

Epistle: Ephesians 4:1-16. This is a rich, complex passage. It may be helpful to focus on only one part of it, to avoid overwhelming children.

Children need to hear specific examples of each of the four abstract qualities urged on Christians. Patience and gentleness are the easiest for them to understand and claim. Humility that puts oneself in a secondary position goes most against the grain of children trying to develop their talents and master their world. Humility is best explored in relation to using one's God-given gifts for the good of the church (see vss. 12-13).

If alerted in advance to listen for them, children enjoy identifying the seven "one" things that hold the church together. Most make immediate sense. "The one hope of your calling," however, needs to be paraphrased as "We all share one goal." With this background, children are ready to identify both the gifts Paul names and the other gifts they see people bringing to their church. (Consider omitting Paul's aside in verses 8-11 to avoid confusing children.)

In exploring verses 14-16, speak of "babies" rather than "children," to preserve Paul's meaning and avoid offending those who have no choice to be anything but children. Paul offers children two important signs of growing up. First, people are growing up when they know right from wrong and cannot be talked into doing what they know is wrong. Second, people are growing up when

132

they do not think about themselves all the time. Instead of demanding that they be the constant center of attention, people who are growing up know how to be a member of a group or team, and are willing to work hard for the group.

Gospel: John 6:24-35. The sixth chapter of John is about the bread of life. Last week's lesson was the story of Jesus, the powerful supplier of food. This week's text describes what the bread of life he brings is *not.* First, the bread of heaven is *not* all the free food you want. Children, who do not worry about providing food, easily interpret this literally and laugh at the misunderstanding of the crowd. They will need help to understand Jesus' real point—that we often are looking for and working for things we think we need to live, but which are not that important. The children are helped most by examples of things people of different ages misguidedly think we must have to live or be happy.

Talk about seals and manna in the wilderness is beyond the understanding of most children.

Watch Words

This is a good opportunity to explain words your congregation uses frequently in confession, but not in everyday conversation. *Transgression* and *iniquity* are old words for *sin. Mercy* and *merciful* are words about God's *forgiving love* and *kindness.* Remember that for most children, *offence* is the team with the ball.

Today, *bread* stands for what we need, or think we need, to live.

Let the Children Sing

Be careful in choosing penitence hymns, most of which are filled with symbolic references to Jesus' blood which make little sense to children. Sing "There's a Wideness in God's Mercy" again, if it was studied during sermon last Sunday.

Sing "Be Thou My Vision," to focus on what really "feeds" us. Save the "bread" hymns for the next two weeks.

Substitute Paul's characteristics of Christians (humble, gentle, patient) in the verses of "Lord, I Want to Be a Christian."

The Liturgical Child

1. Continue to display a basket of bread or a banner featuring loaves and fish in the chancel.

2. While a worship leader reads the confrontation between David and Nathan dramatically, two adults pantomime their interaction. Three additional actors may take the parts of the people of the assembled court, responding to what is happening. Actors should wear either biblical dress or dark slacks and shirts, with a crown for David.

3. In a responsive Prayer of Confession, the congregation responds to the leaders' prayers with, "Create in me a clean heart, O God, and put a new and right spirit within me."

4. If you regularly use parts of Psalm 51 in your prayers of confession, highlight them today, pointing out their connection to David and explaining their meaning.

Sermon Resources

1. Like the crowd that followed Jesus, children are often mistaken about what they "gotta have" to live and be happy: "I gotta have a Nintendo!"; "Everyone *else* has a purple polo shirt. I'll be *no one* unless I have one too!"; "If we don't win this year, I'll die!"; "I just gotta go to . . . . Haven't you seen it on TV? It's AWESOME!"

2. To illustrate the difference in being a "baby" and growing up, point out some truths about babies: (1) Babies pay attention only to what is directly in front of them. Therefore, they are easily persuaded. If you want a baby to stop playing with a toy, you can simply replace it with a different toy. (2) Babies think only of themselves. They see themselves as the center of the world, with everyone and everything arranged around it to meet its needs.

3. Turn the sermon into either a "locker-room pep talk" or a "recruiters speech" about church membership. Describe the church as God's team, focusing on the seven "one" things that hold the church together. Then point out the qualities of good church members and that it is important for them to use all their gifts for the good of the "team." Use the direct language of a coach.

When we disobey God's rules, everything gets upside down backwards and WRONG! Use the decoder to straighten out these words into a good prayer for such times.

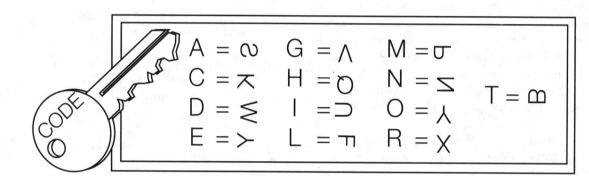

_____ _____ _____ _____ _____ _____ _____ _____ _____ _____ _____ _____ _____ _____ _____ _____ _____ _____

_____ _____ _____ _____ _____ , _____ _____ _____ .

CODE

A = ꙅ	G = ∧	M = ꟼ	
C = ꓘ	H = ◌	N = И	T = ꓭ
D = ꟽ	I = ꟷ	O = ⅄	
E = ⋏	L = ꓶ	R = X	

Paul said God gives everyone at least one gift to use for the good of the church.

Draw a picture or write about one gift God gave you to use for the church.

TO: _your name_
FOR: the church

Proper 13 | © 1993 by Abingdon Press.

PROPER FOURTEEN

(Sunday between August 7 and 13 inclusive)

From a Child's Point of View

Old Testament: II Samuel 18:5-9, 15, 31-33. These verses are too terse to tell the story of Absalom's rebellion meaningfully. But the full story, which fills II Samuel 13-19, is too complex for children. They need to hear your adaptation of this story of a son who could not wait to be king. Its key elements concern Absalom, parading through the streets, offering to take over his father's position as judge, proclaiming himself king, raising an army to fight his father, and finally being caught and killed in battle.

Children are touched by David's love and grief. Teenagers have more sympathy for Absalom (especially if they hear about David's failure to punish Amnon for raping Tamar), and they understand the struggle between father and son. But worshipers of all ages recognize and feel the destructive, painful results of selfish struggles within families that are so evident in this story.

Psalm: 130. Children understand this psalm best as a prayer David may have prayed as he worried about or mourned for Absalom. In that context, they hear both the pain and the trust. The Good News Bible's translation is the easiest for them to understand. The New Jerusalem Bible is second choice.

Epistle: Ephesians 4:25–5:2. When 5:1-2b is read both first and last (omitting the final phrase, "a fragrant offering and sacrifice to God," to avoid confusing children with sacrificial terminology unnecessary for Paul's point), children recognize, in the remaining verses, specific suggestions for ways to live like Christ. They also recognize advice that would have been helpful to David's family and can be helpful to our families today.

Verses 26, 25, and 29 speak of two key concerns to children: Verse 26 assures them that it is OK to be angry, but it is important to handle their anger well. Children often misunderstand adult responses to a child's angry outbursts to mean that being angry is bad. "Good boys and girls do not get angry." The fact is that anger is the appropriate response to many situations. Good boys and girls *do* become angry! But Paul insists that they are not to let their anger make them do things that are wrong—hitting, name calling, and the like. Instead, they are to control their anger and work to solve the problem that caused it. Adults know, and children need to be told, that this is *never* easy!

Verses 25 and 29 highlight the importance of what we say. Elementary children are learning the power of words to both help and hurt. They are also learning to take responsibility for their words. Especially among fifth- and sixth-graders, more conflicts are started by what someone said, or by what someone thought they heard someone say, than by what they do to one another. Paul insists that learning to control what we say is part of growing as a Christian.

Gospel: John 6:35, 41-51. The first misunderstanding in this chapter was that the bread Jesus offered was free food. When Jesus insisted that he was not offering free food, but spiritual food from God, a second misunderstanding erupted. The crowd expected messengers bringing spiritual food from God to be somehow special or different. But Jesus was just another person they had watched grow up among them. Children are interested in the question behind the misunderstanding: "How do you recognize bread (or messages) from God?" Jesus' answer—that God helps us—is only partially satisfying. Children want to know *how* God helps us. They wish for more concrete descriptions than Jesus' statement that God "draws us to" the messages. The preacher may want to identify ways the church traditionally has recognized God's messages—for example, that they are consistent with the record of God's action in the Bible.

Watch Words

Avoid abstract political language such as *coup, intrigue,* and *treason,* in favor of *plot, plan,* and *taking his father's place as king.*

Today, *bread* is God's Word, or messages from God.

Let the Children Sing

"Nobody Knows the Trouble I See" parallels Psalm 130 and is a song David and all those with troubles in their family can sing.

Sing "Lord, I Want to Be a Christian," to respond to the Epistle.

Point out that though "Break Thou the Bread of Life" is often sung as a communion hymn, it is really a hymn about hearing and knowing God's Word. Put several phrases into your own words to illustrate this point before inviting the congregation to sing the hymn.

The Liturgical Child

1. Continue to display bread in the chancel. Today, feature loafs of bread and an open Bible.
2. Invite worshipers to pray for their families. A worship leader offers general prayers aloud, then pauses so that worshipers may pray silently about their particular families. For example:

Lord of life, you have placed each of us in a family. You have given us mothers and fathers, sisters and brothers, aunts, uncles, cousins, nieces and nephews, and grandparents. Some of us

have step-families and people who have become "like family" to us. Hear our prayers, thanking you for all the people who are our family. (PAUSE)

Lord of love, we also must admit that love is not always easy in a family . . . .

3. Create a responsive Prayer of Confession based on Paul's teachings in today's Epistle. A worship leader presents each teaching, following the same format: "Paul told us to . . . , but we . . . ." The congregation responds, "Forgive us, God." For example:

Paul told us to control our anger, but we often let our anger control us. In anger, we say cruel, hurting words which we later regret. In anger, we fight back, even throw punches. In anger, we try to get even with people, rather than try to solve the problems between us. (RESPONSE)

Paul told us to always tell the truth, but we . . . .

4. Ask several children to present the Epistle. Each child reads, or memorizes, one of Paul's instructions. All children repeat Ephesians 5:1-2*b* in unison, both before and after the individual teachings. The sequence is: All: 5:1-2*b*; Reader 1: 4:25; Reader 2: 4:26-27; Reader 3: 4:28; Reader 4: 4:29; Reader 5: 4:30; Reader 6: 4:31; Reader 7: 4:32; and All: 5:1-2*b*.

Sermon Resources

1. Devote the sermon to telling and exploring the story of David and Absalom. Edit out extraneous details and side plots to focus on the key events and the feelings of the main characters. Walter Brueggemann's commentary in *First and Second Samuel* (Interpretation Series [Westminster John Knox, 1990]) offers helpful insights for such storytelling. Trust the story to carry its own messages without preacher-imposed moralizations.

2. *Harriet the Spy,* by Louise Fitzhugh, tells about a sixth-grade girl who kept a notebook of very honest but not very kind comments about everyone and everything she saw. In chapter 10, her friends accidentally find what she had written about them, it takes three chapters to describe their anger, Harriet's anger, and how she finally found a way to apologize. *The Hating Book,* by Charlotte Zolotow, offers a similar story.

Listen to the story of David and his son Absalom. They loved each other but also fought each other.

Draw a picture of one person in your family.

Write your prayer for that person.

God of families, I pray for

_____

_____

_____

_____

_____

Amen.

Below is a list of suggestions for Christians.

Put a ▼ by each one as you hear it read in **Ephesians 4:25–5:2.**

Underline the one that is easiest for you.

(Circle) the one that is hardest for you.

Tell the truth.

Be angry, but do not sin.

Do not steal.

Speak only kind words.

Be forgiving.

What advice can you give others to help them do one that is easy for you?

My Advice is _____

_____

_____

_____

PROPER FIFTEEN

(Sunday between August 14 and 20 inclusive)

From a Child's Point of View

Old Testament: I Kings 2:10-12; 3:3-14. The story of God's offer of a gift to Solomon is like many stories in which a person is granted one or more wishes. Children easily understand what is going on. Younger children, however, need help to get through all of Solomon's rich language to what he is really asking God to give him. God's response is more easily understood. Children appreciate both Solomon's choice of the gift of the wisdom to rule well, and God's response to that selfless choice by giving him extra gifts.

Psalm: 111. This psalm of praise is too general to catch and hold the attention of children. They are more likely to hear and appreciate an occasional phrase. Though it is an acrostic, emphasizing the alphabet base as the psalm is read gets in the way of the message, rather than enhancing it.

Epistle: Ephesians 5:15-20. Paul warns today's children to be wise, and then suggests ways to be wise. The key to wisdom is to know God's will. Children are to live by God's will in two ways: They should use their time well and avoid alcohol (and drugs). Paul insists that they can have more fun and be just as happy by living in the singing Christian community. Children, bored as summer winds down and thinking about what clubs and teams to join when school starts, need to hear the directions about using their time well. They also need strong warnings against any involvement with alcohol and drugs and those who use them.

Gospel: John 6:51-58. Today John's focus is on the bread of communion. The question raised is one that literal-thinking children share: "What does it mean to eat the body of Christ in communion?" The answer is that when we eat the bread, we become part of Christ, and Christ becomes part of us.

Fifth- and sixth-graders are interested in the ancient practice of eating food that has been sacrificed to the gods, in order to become one with the gods. With information about the Jewish practice of eating what was sacrificed at the Temple (especially the Passover lambs), and the meals of the mystery religions which were familiar to John's readers, older children begin to understand what Jesus' words about eating his flesh meant to his first hearers.

All children can follow modern scientific understanding of digestion to reach conclusions similar to those of the first-century readers. Children know that what we eat becomes part of us. (We are what we eat.) So if we eat bread that stands for Jesus, Jesus becomes part of us.

On an emotional level, children also recognize our feelings of closeness to the cook as we eat a specialty: the cookies Grandma sent or Dad's special pancakes. So when we eat the bread of communion, we feel close to Jesus, who left it for us as a special sign of his love.

Watch Words

Today, *bread* is the bread of Communion. Speaking of *bread* both symbolically and literally confuses children, so avoid poetic images—*bread of life* or *bread of heaven*—and speak specifically

138

and only about the physical *bread* we eat in Communion, and what it means for us.

Children use many words to talk about different kinds of *wisdom. Genius, brainy, smart, smart alec* (or *wise guy*), *common sense*, and *good judgment* are part of their vocabulary. The *wisdom* they most crave is the ability to understand what is going on around them and to know what to do in all situations.

Let the Children Sing

Sing about wisdom with "Be Thou My Vision" or "Seek Ye First."

"Become to Us the Living Bread," with all its Alleluias and its focus on eating the bread, is perhaps the best choice for children. Sing "For the Bread Which You Have Broken" or "Here, O My Lord, I See Thee" after explaining their meaning during the sermon. All three deal with what it means to eat the bread, or body, of Christ.

The Liturgical Child

1. Pray for wisdom:

Lord, like Solomon, we pray for wisdom.

We pray for the wisdom that comes with education. We thank you for schools and for teachers, and we ask you to help us learn. Help us to pay attention and to understand new ideas. Give us knowledge of the world and how it works.

We pray for the wisdom to do the right thing. We need your help to know right from wrong and your power to do what is right. Be with us to show us your ways and to help us follow them.

We pray for the wisdom to say the right words. Even when we try to be kind and helpful, we sometimes cannot find the words we need to show our love. Give us wise, helping, disciples' words.

God of Wisdom, it is not just for ourselves that we pray. We pray too for the leaders of our world, for presidents and prime ministers, for governors and legislators. Give them the wisdom to make decisions and pass laws that benefit all people. We pray for business men and women. Give them the wisdom to look beyond what makes money to what makes life better for all of us. We pray for those who serve—sales clerks and bus drivers, phone operators, and waiters. Give them the wisdom to understand, and to treat kindly even those who do not treat them with respect. Amen.

2. Even if you do not normally celebrate Communion on this Sunday, consider doing so if the bread in the Gospel lesson is to be the focus of worship. Celebrating the sacrament helps worshipers of all ages act on what they have heard about this bread in the sermon. If you do not celebrate communion, display bread and a chalice, or communion banners that feature bread.

3. The return to school is an intense time for children. Many will have new clothes and school supplies and will be looking forward to new experiences. Those for whom school was difficult last year hope that this year will be different, but fear it may be more of the same. The hopes and fears are most intense for those who will be going to new schools. Remember all these concerns in the church's prayers on the Sunday before classes begin.

Sermon Resources

1. Especially if children are going back to school in the next week or two, develop an alphabet sermon on wisdom. For each letter of the alphabet, identify and comment on a word that begins with that letter and is related to wisdom for living in today's world as Christians: B is for the Bible, through which we know God's will; D is for drugs wise Christians avoid; and so on.

2. Illustrate the wisdom God gave Solomon by telling how he settled the dispute between two mothers who claimed the same child (I Kings 3:16-28). Children need help to understand how Solomon's "decision" helped him identify the true mother, but are impressed by what Solomon did.

3. In order to clear up any magical thinking about the bread of communion, tell where the bread your church uses is bought and how it is prepared. Then talk about what does make it special.

Find six words about communion bread in this loaf.
Listen for them in our songs, prayers, and sermon.

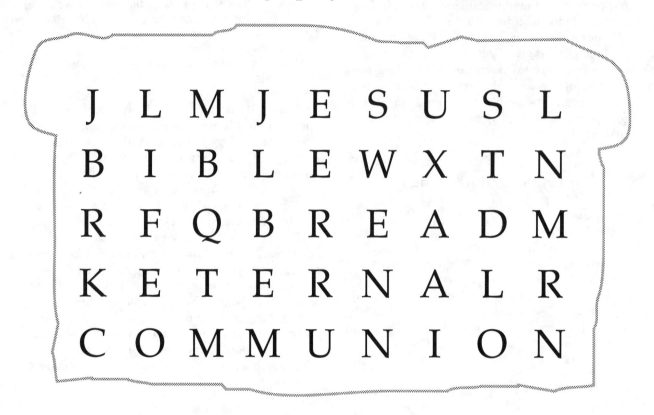

```
J L M J E S U S L
B I B L E W X T N
R F Q B R E A D M
K E T E R N A L R
C O M M U N I O N
```

The words are: bread, Jesus, Bible, communion, life, and eternal.

The vowels (A,E,I,O, and U) are missing in the words below.
Write the correct vowel in each blank to find Paul's advice
to Christians.

B_ C_R_F_L TH_N H_W Y__

L_V_, N_T _S _NW__S_

P___PL_ B_T _S W_S_.

Proper 15 / © 1993 by Abingdon Press.

PROPER SIXTEEN

(Sunday between August 21 and 27 inclusive)

From a Child's Point of View

Old Testament: I Kings 8:(1,6,10-11), 22-30, 41-43. The story of the dedication of the Solomon's Temple leads children to ask three questions: What was Solomon's Temple like? What is special about our sanctuary? What is special about, or what is the function of, any sanctuary?

The parenthetical verses offer only a partial answer to the first question. Children want to hear more about what the building looked like. They are interested in the similarities between Solomon's Temple and their sanctuary—Solomon used the best he had (cedar and gold) and we use our best woods and stone. (If a picture of how the temple may have looked can be found, or a model of the Temple made by an older children's classes is available, display it today.)

This text offers an opportunity to speak about your congregation's understanding of, and attitudes toward, your sanctuary. Children are often confused by adult demands for special behavior in the sanctuary "because this is God's house," and adult insistence that God is everywhere. It helps to explore the related truths that we can pray and worship God anywhere, and that a sanctuary is a place set aside for worshiping God.

Verses 41-43 insist that all people are to be welcome in God's sanctuaries. Both children and adults need to identify people they tend to exclude.

Psalm: 84. Going on a trip to worship in a special sanctuary is a novel idea for most of today's children. They are interested in what it was like to travel with a large group to Jerusalem to celebrate holy days at the Temple. Once they have heard a little about travel realities, they can imagine what it felt like to chant certain lines of Psalm 84 while walking toward Jerusalem. Verses 1 and 10 especially catch their attention.

WARNING: before reading the psalm, point out that the psalmist uses the words *courts* or *courts of God* to describe the Temple.

Epistle: Ephesians 6:10-20. Children in our culture, especially boys, are brought up to compete and fight. Children's cartoons pit characters against each other in ongoing battles. Heroes are those who fight against enormous odds and win. Sports are contests in which other teams are met as "the enemy." To such children, Paul says that for Christians, there is only one really important battle and that is not a battle between people. It is a battle against powers we cannot see, but which do serious damage to individuals, families, and communities. Though Paul does not name those powers, children need to hear *selfishness, greed, cruelty,* and such things named as the unseen powers we must fight. Once the fight is defined, children understand that the fight requires unseen armor, and they see the value of the items on Paul's list.

Gospel: John 6:56-69. All the misunderstandings of the chapter come together in this conversation. Some people left Jesus because they wanted free food, not spiritual food. Others left because they could not believe that God would send spiritual food through a person as plain as Jesus. Still others left because they understood exactly what Jesus was saying and did not want to let God get that close to them. They wanted to run their own lives rather than let God live and work through them. But a few decided to stay. They knew that life would be different and better if God was them every day.

Though children have trouble understanding the content of these decisions, older children, especially those who are approaching confirmation, can hear that we, like the people in this chapter, do have a decision to make. We can follow Jesus and let God's presence and power direct our lives, or we can ignore Jesus and spend our lives on other things. We make this decision in big ways at confirmation. We also make it every day in lots of little ways, when we choose to either listen to or ignore God's voice when it tells us we are special and asks us to love and care for those around us.

Watch Words

Use and clarify "sanctuary" vocabulary. Explain that both *temples* and *sanctuaries* are places set aside for worshiping God. Define such words as *chancel, nave, altar,* or *communion table,* and so forth. Point out the difference between the *sanctuary* (a place) and the *church* (God's people).

Children recognize the pieces of armor more quickly than the Christian equivalents. Presenting Paul's nouns in verbal phrases helps: *knowing* and *telling the truth; knowing* and *doing what is right; telling the good news of God's loving forgiveness; trusting God's power and God's ways* (faith); *counting on God's love, no matter what* (salvation); and *knowing and living by God's Word.*

Let the Children Sing

Though its vocabulary is challenging, consider singing "Christ Is Made the Sure Foundation," and highlighting verses 2-4 in the sermon. "I Come with Joy" features communion, but thanks God for the joys of all congregational worship.

Beware of warrior hymns that sound like calls to fight people instead of unseen powers. "I Need Thee Every Hour," with its repeated phrases for new readers, is closer to the Epistle's message. "Fight the Good Fight," "We Shall Overcome," and "Take My Life, and Let It Be Consecrated" are also good choices.

The Liturgical Child

1. If school begins this week, include back-to-school concerns in the congregation's prayers (see Proper 15).

2. Ask children to join you on the steps to read the psalm. Describe pilgrimages on which whole families traveled to Jerusalem to worship in the Temple, and detail what they saw at the Temple. Then open a Bible on your lap to read the psalm as a song which families may have chanted together as they walked. Conclude by asking the children and congregation to repeat after you, shouting with joy the phrases of verses 1 and 10*a*.

3. Confess our willingness to fight the wrong battles with the wrong armor and weapons:

Lord, we admit that we are too ready to fight the wrong battles. We are ready to fight when we feel we have been unfairly treated. We are ready to fight over name-calling and disagreements about who gets what. But we wait idly when you call us to fight injustice done to others. And we give in, rather than face up to powers like greed and selfishness. Forgive us, and help us to fight your battles. Teach us to rely on your armor and weapons, rather than on fierce words and actions that hurt and destroy. For we pray in the name of Jesus, who wore your armor on the cross and rose again. Amen.

Sermon Resources

1. Tell stories about your sanctuary. Tell when and how it was built, why it was built the way it is, and stories about its use. Tell about the ancestors of families in the current congregation, and any famous people who have worshiped in this sanctuary. If possible, find and share a copy of the dedication ceremony order of worship, and especially the prayers offered at that dedication.

2. If you feel really brave, compare the violent weapons and methods used by the Ninja Turtles with those suggested by Paul.

3. In *The Chronicles of Narnia,* C. S. Lewis describes four children's battles against evil powers in an imaginary land, which they enter through a wardrobe. With little help, children realize that it was not the White Witch who got Edmund into trouble, but greed for the candies she offered him.

Draw a picture of the inside of your sanctuary.

Listen to the prayer Solomon prayed for people who worshiped at the Temple. Write your prayer for people who worship in your sanctuary.

Cross out every third letter to find Paul's message.

B E S Q T R O A N

G I M N T H A E

L O M R D .

Q: What kind of strength do you think God wants for you?

A:

PROPER SEVENTEEN

(Sunday between August 28 and September 3 inclusive)

From a Child's Point of View

Old Testament: Song of Solomon 2:8-13. The Song of Solomon is a collection of love poems. Children are surprised to find them in the Bible and tend to giggle when they are read. But they learn from them that God is interested in love between men and women and blesses that love. If it is pointed out, they also see this as one example of God's involvement in all parts of our lives.

Though some older children can grasp the symbolic way Jews and Christians have traditionally understood these poems to speak of God's relationship to individuals and/or to God's people, they find it rather contrived and prefer to take the poems at face value.

Psalm: 45:1-2, 6-9. This psalm is a wedding song composed by a loyal member of the court for the king on his wedding day. The poet rejoices with the king and reminds the king that his power is a trust from God. Children follow what is said fairly easily, but find little of significance in it. The format, however, provides an interesting invitation for them to write their own prayer-psalms for friends and family members at special times, such as birthdays or the beginning of a new school year.

Epistle: James 1:17-27. This passage includes a series of loosely related wise sayings which overwhelm children with their variety and complexity. Two points make the most sense to them. First, we are to be quick to listen and learn, and slow to speak and act (especially in anger). Active children hear this point frequently from parents and teachers as school starts, and they do not par-ticularly welcome it. Second, we are to act on what we hear.

Children know about using mirrors, but need help to get James' point. Compare a person who fixes the messy hair or washes the dirty face seen in a mirror with one who ignores what is seen. When it is specifically pointed out, children can see the similarities between ignoring the changes in our appearance suggested by mirrors and ignoring the changes in the our behavior suggested by the Bible.

Gospel: Mark 7:1-8, 14-15, 21-23. While active children rebel at James' insistence that we be quick to listen and slow to act (especially in anger), they respond positively to Jesus' refusal to be upset about how clean a person is. On a literal level, they are delighted to hear that God is not concerned about how dirty our exterior is, but with whether we say kind words and do loving, obedient deeds. With a little adult help, they can move from talk about what makes a person "clean" to what makes a person "good."

Teachers, coaches, and other kids define a "good" person in different ways. Comparing some of those definitions helps children understand how the Pharisees made their mistake and clears the way for talking about God's definition of what makes a person "good."

Potential Misunderstanding: In Jesus' day, people had not yet learned about germs that enter our bodies on dirty food and hands. Today we know that though dirty hands and food will not make us "bad," they can carry the germs that make us sick. Jesus did not say that we need not wash our hands before we eat!

Watch Words

When Jews talked about what made a person *clean*, they actually were talking about what made a person *good*. Children hear similar talk today. A Scout learns to be *clean* in thought, word, and deed. People who are drug free or have no criminal record are declared *clean*. Similarly, children know about *dirty* words, books, and so on.

Let the Children Sing

Thank God for all the gifts, especially the gifts of human love, with "For the Beauty of the Earth."

Choose a hymn from the wedding or marriage section of your hymnal. It will probably be unfamiliar, but children will benefit by knowing that just as the Bible includes the love poems of the Song of Solomon, the hymnal includes some hymns about human love.

If the focus is on clean hearts, dedicate your hearts to God with "Lord, I Want to Be a Christian (in my heart)," and your whole body with "Take My Life, and Let It Be Consecrated."

The Liturgical Child

1. See Proper 15 for prayer suggestions for the Sunday before school begins. On the Sunday after school begins, pray for new teachers (both those who are interesting and those who are frightening or boring), for new friends and old friends, for exciting new studies and scary ones, and for the things we already love and hate about riding the bus, eating lunch, and playing on the playground.

2. Ask a young woman to present the Song of Songs lesson from memory, while standing in a lectern and pretending to look out a window. Then ask a man to take the role of the court poet, to present Psalm 45, also from memory. For full dramatic impact, place an ornate chair in the chancel area and instruct the congregation to imagine the king sitting there with his court, awaiting the arrival of his bride. (The New Jerusalem Bible offers clear translations of both these poems.)

3. Create a responsive prayer of petition about how we live. The congregations response is, "Create in us clean hearts, O God." For example:

When we feel that we are being treated unfairly and feel anger rising in us, (RESPONSE)

When we see others being treated unfairly and are tempted to ignore it or to be thankful that it is their problem, not ours, (RESPONSE)

Sermon Resources

1. Build a sermon on Christian views of romance and marriage. Illustrate today's Old Testament poems by telling the stories of biblical couples such as Abraham and Sarah, Ruth and Boaz, Aquila and Priscilla.

2. Make a variety of statements about what "good" people are like and what they do: "Good" people wear clean clothes and keep their shoelaces tied. "Good" people always say, "Yes, ma'am" and "Yes, sir." "Good" people like hamburgers and would have to be forced to eat raw fish. Explore and debunk those statements, then make correct statements about what "good" people do.

3. In *Words By Heart* by Ouida Sebestyen, Lena, an African American girl whose family has moved to Kansas after the Civil War, must begin to live by the Bible verses she has memorized to win a school contest and impress everybody with her "magic mind."

4. Remember to use the Worship Worksheets as conversation starters as children leave the sanctuary. See if they completed the puzzle. Quickly read their psalm and comment on it.

James gave us good advice in James 1:22. To find that advice, match the numbered letters in the example with the numbers below.

"19 4   9 17 4 6 10   17 5
___ ___ ___

13 14 4   11 17 6 9 ,   2 8 9
___ ___ ___ , ___ ___ ___

8 17 13   1 4 6 4 18 16
___ ___ ___

14 4 2 6 4 6 10 . "
___ ___ ___

For example:

MAKE FRIENDS WITH EVERYONE.
1 3 2 4   6 12 8 9 10 11   12 13 14 15 4   16 17 8   4 19

ALWAYS BE FAIR.
2 18 11 16 10 6   5 7   4 13 2 12

Psalm 45 is a prayer for a king on his wedding day. Listen as it is read. Then write a prayer psalm for yourself as a new school year begins.

Psalm #_____ (your grade)

(for _____ (your name) as school starts)

Give God thanks for _____

Remember that _____

May God help you when _____

PROPER EIGHTEEN

(Sunday between September 4 and 10 inclusive)

From a Child's Point of View

Old Testament: Proverbs 22:1-2, 8-9, 22-23. Though children may know several proverbs, they often do not recognize the term *proverb* or know what a proverb is. Pointing out familiar proverbs, such as "A penny saved is a penny earned" is a good introduction.

Today's proverbs deal loosely with riches and poverty. The Good News Bible offers clear translations that make sense to children. Few of the ideas in these proverbs are new to them, but they come to life when illustrated with everyday examples of the truths they state.

In verse 9, be sure to point out that the blessings one receives when one shares food with the poor are not special rewards, but the experiences one has in the process of sharing food.

Psalm: 125. The first two verses offer images of dependability that children enjoy. Because they think literally, they hear in verse 1 that a good person is physically stuck in one place just as a mountain is. Help them grasp the poetic meaning of "cannot be moved" by comparing a person who is your friend today but says mean things about you tomorrow, is honest today but cheats tomorrow and generally cannot be depended upon, with a person who is always your friend and always honest.

Verse 2 tells us that God is as likely to move away from the people as the mountains around Jerusalem are likely to move away from Jerusalem. Clarify the point by paraphrasing it in terms of the geography of your region—God will not leave God's people, any more than the James River will go around Richmond instead of through it's center.

Verses 3-5 are a prayer children readily offer, because it expresses their longing that everyone should receive what they deserve, and it admits, unlike some of the proverbs, that sometimes those who sin are not punished, but rewarded. Again today, The Good News Bible offers the clearest translation of this psalm for children.

Epistle: James 2:1-10 (11-13), 14-17. Because children think specifically and concretely, they can speak of treating "the poor" well and then make fun of the poorly dressed kid in their class, not recognizing the inconsistency. James' story of the two people who come to worship is helpful because it identifies a poor person in terms they understand. To continue what the story begins, offer other descriptions—kids who bring funny lunches or get free lunch, kids whose books are always a mess because they don't have a backpack to carry them in, and so forth. Such specifics help children recognize "the poor," and therefore enable them to treat "the poor" among them well.

Consider omitting verses 11-13, which are beyond the understanding of children.

Gospel: Mark 7:24-37. Everything about the story of the Syrophoenician woman confuses children. The conversation takes place in poetic vocabulary they cannot understand. And though they do not understand what is said, they are bewildered by what they sense is Jesus' unkind treatment of this woman. Mark's point is lost to them. The most helpful introduction is to point out that though it sounds as if Jesus is being

147

unkind, he was really being more kind than anyone there expected. Explain Jesus' kindness, but do not expect many children to understand. Instead, know that, before tuning out, they will have designated this story as "difficult to understand" rather than "disturbing."

The healing of the deaf-mute is more interesting and child accessible. All the details give the story a reality that other healing stories lack. Older children appreciate Jesus intimate touching of a person whom many considered "dirty" or "gross."

Watch Words

The *Syrophoenician woman* lived in Tyre, which was a *Phoenician* port city in *Syria*. That means she was a *Gentile. Gentiles* were people who were not Jewish, and Jewish people thought they were not as good as Jews.

Speaking of *the poor* gives the children the idea that *the poor* are easily identifiable and definable, and can be treated as a group. Speaking of people who do not have enough money for food or clothes, or who cannot afford a decent place to live, identifies *the poor* simply as people with specific needs and problems.

Let the Children Sing

Explain the first two verses of "Help Us Accept Each Other" before singing them. Children will miss the meaning of the last two verses.

The phrases repeated at the beginning and end of each verse of "Go Forth for God" invite young readers to sing at least those phrases.

Celebrate the healings with "Jesus' Hands Were Kind Hands," sung by the congregation or by a children's class or choir.

The Liturgical Child

1. Introduce the topic of today's proverbs, then ask several children to read or recite one each.

2. Highlight the two healing stories in the Gospel reading by having them read by different readers, or by pointing out the change of story as you read. Use your hands to illustrate how Jesus healed the deaf-mute man.

3. Before the offering, describe some of the ways your church uses money to help the poor. As you dedicate the offering, pray that it brings real relief to people in need.

4. Base a Prayer of Confession on our tendency to treat others as inferior:

Loving God, we admit that we often think we are better than others and therefore treat people very badly. We look down on and tease people whose clothes look strange to us. We feel sorry for and ignore people who live in houses that are shabbier than ours. We boast about our grades in front of those whose grades are worse, and we describe our accomplishments in detail to people whom we know could not do what we have done. We are even willing to make others look worse than they are, so that we can look better than we are. Forgive us. Teach us to accept one another as we are and to treat all people as brothers and sisters in your family. We pray in the name of Jesus, who made friends with and taught and healed all who came to him. Amen.

5. See Proper 17 for prayer suggestions for the week after school starts.

Sermon Resources

1. There is a frequently told story about a great preacher who was to preach at a certain church. The crowd that gathered that Sunday included many community leaders who seldom attended church, all dressed in their best. As time for the service arrived, the ushers became nervous because the preacher had not appeared.

They were also bothered by a poorly clothed barefoot man who waited quietly to be seated. After debating about asking him to leave, they decided to seat him in the very back corner. Those seated in the area shifted away as he sat down.

Then at pause in the music, the man quietly walked up the center aisle to the lectern and opened the Bible to today's text in James. As he read, people realized that he was the great preacher. (If you use this story, invite children to draw pictures of the man and what happened.)

2. Natalie Babbitt's *The Devil's Other Storybook* contains the short story "Boating," which tells of three sisters who spent eternity circling hell in a very cramped boat, because they felt they were too good for the other people there.

Listen to today's proverbs. Then write our own proverb about how to treat people. For example, "To have a friend, be a friend."

Turn your proverb into a cross-stitch picture. Form the letters of each word with X's. Shade in the squares. Make the letters 5 spaces tall and 3 spaces wide.

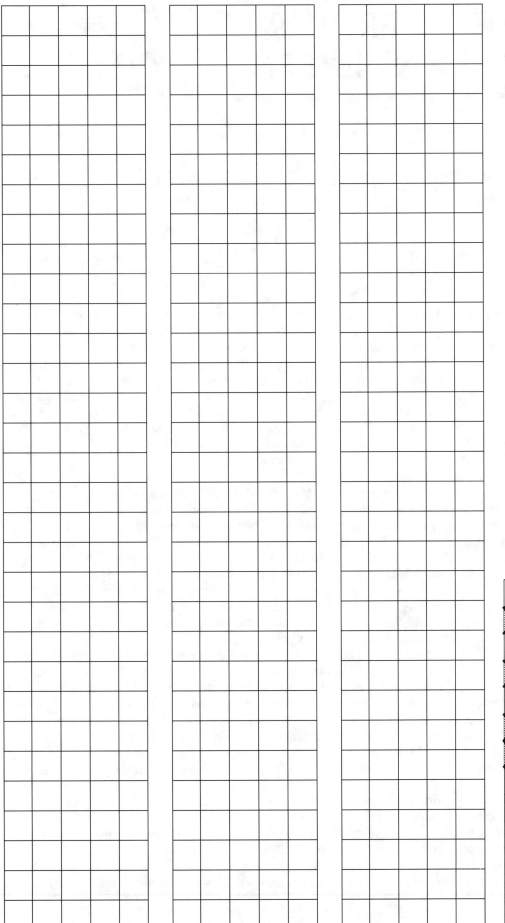

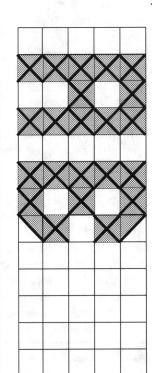

PROPER NINETEEN

(Sunday between September 11 and 17 inclusive)

From a Child's Point of View

Old Testament: Proverbs 1:20-33; Psalm: 19 or Wisdom of Solomon 7:26–8:1. Too often, Wisdom, when personified, sounds as if it is either a fourth person of the Trinity or some kind of angel. Most children simply tune it out as incomprehensible adult talk. But because they have been exposed to Indian lore, or "wisdom," children can make sense of the "wisdom of God" as being the ideas and values that come from God. This makes Psalm 19 the easiest of today's wisdom lections for children. Older children enjoy identifying the synonyms for "wisdom" in verses 7-9 and noting what the psalmist says about each one.

The abstract language in the Wisdom of Solomon makes it the least child-accessible of the three.

At the beginning of a new year of teams and clubs, children benefit from comparing the wisdom of the coach, the wisdom of the teacher, and the wisdom of God.

Epistle: James 3:1-12. Children understand and enjoy James's images about our tongues. As the autumn fire-prevention season arrives, they are aware that a small match can start a large fire, and from experience, they know that one mean word can start a fiery fight between friends. At an early age, children learn what it is to regret what they have said but be unable to undo its damage. The images of the bit in the horse's mouth and the rudder of the sailboat may be less familiar and therefore harder to explain to children. Finally, children chuckle knowingly at the mental picture of a circus lion tamer making tigers and lions and tongues do their assigned tricks. Laughing at this ridiculous image leaves a mental picture that reminds them to control their tongues.

"Tongue problems" that cause trouble among children include saying mean words that hurt others, telling lies to make themselves look good or others look bad, telling secrets they promised to keep private, and (among younger children) sticking out their tongues to show their distain.

Gospel: Mark 8:27-38. Children empathize with Peter in this question-and-answer session. Like him, they have answered a question almost correctly, and then made a mistake which the teacher seemed to think was more important than the part that was right. Peter knew the right answer to the question about who Jesus is—the Christ. He just did not understand what it meant to be the Christ or to be a follower of the Christ.

Like Peter, children need help in understanding and following Christ. Because they do not yet have a clear understanding of what "self" is, they cannot understand what self-denial means. For them, Jesus' call is to give up "what I think would be wonderful for me" or "what I want to do," in order to do "what is good for someone else." Examples help, so speak of such things as giving up a movie with your friends in order to baby-sit with your younger sister so your parents can go out. When the examples come from their own experience, children begin to realize that the happiness that comes from such giving is better than the happiness that comes from getting or doing what they want. This realization is a solid foundation upon which they can build their understanding of and response to Jesus' call.

Watch Words

Wisdom consists of all of God's ideas about how the world should be and how we should treat one another.

For children, a *cross* is the wooden form on which Jesus was killed. Calls to *take up your cross* are interpreted as calls to die in that same way. So, speak instead of doing what God commands, even when it is not to your advantage, and of giving up what is rightfully yours to take care of others.

Remember that it is not our *tongues,* but our *words* that get us into trouble.

Most children think *Christ* must be Jesus' last name. There is value in explaining what Peter and others meant when they said that Jesus was "the Christ."

Let the Children Sing

"God's Law Is Perfect and Gives Light" sets Psalm 19:7-14 to music in simple phrases that older-elementary readers can follow. Its repeated chorus, "Grant us wisdom, grant us courage," makes "God of Grace and God of Glory" another good wisdom hymn.

Avoid hymns in which "cross" is used as a symbol for self-sacrificing love. Hymns such as "Must Jesus Bear the Cross Alone" or "Beneath the Cross of Jesus" are interpreted literally and therefore easily misunderstood.

This is the first of six Gospel lessons on discipleship. Consider repeating one less-familiar discipleship hymn each week. With repeated use, children can learn "Christ of the Upward Way" or "Take Thou Our Minds, Dear Lord," if the words are highlighted in other parts of worship. "Lord, I Want to Be a Christian," "I Sing a Song of the Saints of God," and "Take My Life and Let It Be Consecrated" are the discipleship hymns children sing most readily.

The Liturgical Child

1. Have a man read Proverbs 1:20-21 (the introductory verses) before a woman, in the role of Wisdom, reads verses 23-33. Though children do not understand what or who wisdom is, they will catch occasional phrases in what she says.

2. Create a responsive prayer, asking either for wisdom in several areas of life, or for help in using our tongues well. The congregational response for either is from Psalm 19:14: "May the words of my mouth and the meditations of my heart be acceptable to you, O Lord." For example:

> God of Wisdom, be with us when we want too much. When we watch interesting commercials and see wonderful things for sale in stores, give us the wisdom to know the difference between what we want and what we need. When we see what others have and want it for ourselves, remind us that jealousy always leads to trouble. (RESPONSE)

3. Invite worshipers to affirm their faith with Peter by responding, "He is the Christ!" to each of a series of statements about what Jesus did and who Jesus is:

> Jesus was born in a barn because there was no room available in the inn. The innkeeper and most of the people in Bethlehem that night thought he was nobody, but we say, (RESPONSE)
>
> Jesus made friends with everyone. He ate dinner with Zaccheus, the cheating tax-collector. He healed foreigners. He touched lepers. Lots of people said he was a troublemaker, but we say, (RESPONSE)
>
> Jesus was a teacher. Crowds of people gathered on hillsides to hear him speak about God's love. The teachers in the Temple said he was wrong about God's love, but we say, (RESPONSE)
>
> Jesus said, "Love your enemies," "Give to those in need," and "Those who lose their life for my sake will save it." Most people thought he was crazy, but we say, (RESPONSE)
>
> Jesus was arrested, tried, and sentenced to die on a cross. The political and religious leaders thought they were rid of him, but he rose, and he lives. We know that . . . (RESPONSE)
>
> When Jesus said, "If anyone wants to come with me, he must forget himself, carry his cross, and follow me," most people went home. But we stay, and we say, (RESPONSE)

4. See Proper 17 for prayer suggestions for the Sunday after school starts.

Sermon Resources

1. Proverbs tells us what Wisdom cries out in the marketplace. Create speeches that Wisdom might give at school (do your homework and learn what is required, so that you will be able to get along in the world and do God's work effectively); at home (treat people at home with the same consideration you give people at work and at school); and at church (learn God's ways, and then follow them—as a church and as individual Christians).

2. Jiminy Cricket, the little voice that constantly reminded Pinocchio about right and wrong, may come closest to personifying Wisdom for children. Older children connect both Jiminy Cricket and Wisdom with our consciences.

Shade the spaces with dots in them to find an important word.

Circle each picture when you hear the word there:

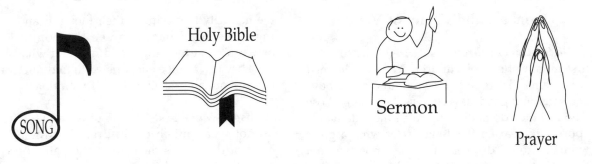

SONG

Holy Bible

Sermon

Prayer

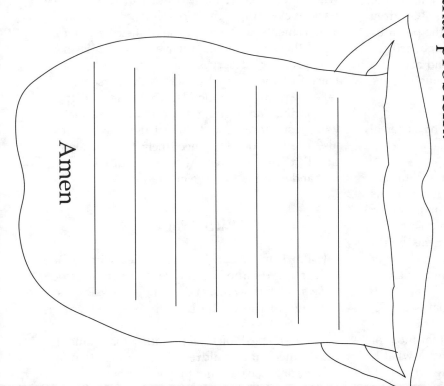

Amen

Write a prayer telling God about that problem.

Below are several problems caused by tongues. Circle one that causes trouble among your friends.

bragging

LIES

mean words

telling secrets

name calling

PROPER TWENTY

(Sunday between September 18 and 24 inclusive)

From a Child's Point of View

Old Testament: Proverbs 31:10-31. During the first month of school, children are overwhelmed with demands to be good students, good boys and girls, and good class citizens. Especially those who feel they do not live up to all these demands appreciate hearing this long list of what a good woman should do. Learning that most women find this list as exasperating as the children find all the demands they face, is liberating for them.

Once freed from the volume of the demands, children are ready to identify the qualities for which all Christian women, men, and children should work. They gain more from the poem by using its alphabet format as a springboard for starting lists of Christian qualities and activities for themselves than by exploring the qualities the poet assigns to women.

Psalm: 1. See the Seventh Sunday of Easter in this book for commentary on Psalm 1.

Epistle: James 3:13–4:3, 7-8a. The general abstract vocabulary and sophisticated logic of this passage quickly lose children, who can, however, understand the basics of the two main points.

They can compare the wisdom of this world with that of God. They recognize the "wisdom" of this world in the the bossy, unpleasant behavior of the "know-it-all" or "smart alec." They also recognize the wisdom of behavior that is gentle, fair, caring, and kind.

For children, the second point is that most of our mean actions start with jealous, want-what-I-can't-get thoughts and feelings. Though they lack the maturity to discipline their thoughts and feelings, they can begin to see the connection between what they think and feel, and what they do. They can also be encouraged to find safe ways to work out angry feelings and frustrations.

Gospel: Mark 9:30-37. The passion predictions do not mean much to children. For them, the heart of this text is the conversation about greatness. Children, like the disciples, argue about who is the greatest. They argue about whose team is the greatest, whose clothes are the best, even whose pets are the most wonderful. They compare everything—their trophies, grades, and achievements, and even those of their hero/ines. In all these arguments, their expectation is that "the greatest" deserves "the best." Jesus' insistence that the greatest person is the person who takes care of everyone else challenges all this comparing and arguing. Children know exactly what Jesus means, and they struggle with idea just as adults do. They need help to understand the difference between wanting to *do* our very best and wanting to *be* the greatest.

Watch Words

Psalm 1, in all translations, is filled with unfamiliar words about good and evil: *scornful, scoffers, mockers, cynics,* and even *righteous.* Put the message of the psalm into simpler everyday terms.

Children speak of *jealousy,* rather than James's *envy.* Since most children think of *ambition* as *working toward a goal,* and they understand both as

154

desirable, they are confused when James calls *ambition* into question. Speak of *selfish ambition*, instead of just *ambition*, to help them grasp the problem.

Let the Children Sing

Sing "Be Thou My Vision," if it is familiar to children. See Proper 19 for a list of discipleship hymns for this series of Gospel lessons.

"Lord, Make Us Servants of Your Peace" paraphrases the prayer of Saint Francis in words older-elementary children can read and sets it to a simple tune.

The Liturgical Child

1. See the Seventh Sunday of Easter, The Liturgical Child, for a way to highlight Psalm 1 with a floral illustration (No. 1), and a way to read the psalm (No. 2).

2. Emphasize the acrostic format of Proverbs 31:10-32 by asking one person to call out the letters of the Hebrew alphabet and a second person to read the appropriate verse. Consider using an older child as the first reader. (The New Jerusalem Bible prints the appropriate Hebrew letter by each verse.)

3. Invite people to pray with their hands, and with eyes open, so that they can follow the movements of the prayer leader. Direct them to clench their fists as each dangerous thought or feeling is mentioned, then let their hands fall open, releasing all the tension, each time you pray, "Help us to let go . . . ."

Lord of all of our lives, we need your help with thoughts and feelings that can lead us into trouble.

Loving God, when we see others who are better looking than we are, who are smarter than we are, who seem to have more friends than we do, we feel jealous. We want to be like them, and even better than they are. It is easy to let our jealousy turn into hate and meanness. Help us to let go of our jealous thoughts, and work with us to turn them into admiration of your good gifts to others.

Giving God, we confess that we are greedy people. We want every good thing we see. We want designer clothes; picture-perfect houses; every toy and gadget we see on TV; fabulous trips to tropical islands, snowy mountains, and amusement parks; and more. Help us to let go of all our wants. Open our hands, so that instead of reaching out to grab selfishly, we can reach out to make friends.

God, we often do not feel like being cooperative. We want to do what we want to do, when we want to do it, and the way we want to to it. We want to tell others what to do and have them do it. We want to have our own way. Help us to let go of our bossy wishes. Teach us that getting our own selfish way often brings more unhappiness than happiness.

Forgiving God, we admit that we do not forgive easily. We hold our hurt, angry feelings close. We remember every wrong done to us. And we long to get even. Help us to let go of our hurt and anger. Be with us, so that we can learn from you how to forgive and forget.

We pray in the name of Jesus, who reached out his hands to welcome people, opened up his hands to heal people, and finally stetched out his hands to be killed on a cross, to forgive us all. Amen.

Sermon Resources

1. Create an alphabet sermon to identify, for each letter, one characteristic or activity of a good Christian in your community. Comment briefly on each of the 26 characteristics and activities you identify. Children need not understand all of them, but will enjoy marking your progress through the alphabet and appreciate hearing you describe a few activities in which they participate and that the characteristics are applied to both children and adults. Possibilities: B is for Bible student; D is for "doing the Word" (especially if you have preached on that), and so on.

2. In *The Pain and the Great One* by Judy Blume, an eight-year-old girl describes all the unfair advantages of her six-year-old brother, "The Pain." And he describes all the unfair advantages that she, "The Great One," has. The two monologues include hints that the two really need each other and that part of their problem is the fear that their parents love the other more. The entire book can be read aloud in five minutes. Or, sections of it can be cited to illustrate points about "greatness" competitions.

Each of the words below thinks it is **SO GREAT** that it has added another letter to itself. Cross out the extra letter in each word to find a message that all people need to hear.

WHOEVERS WHANTS TON BET

FIERST MOUST BED...

SERVEANT GOF TALL.

Mark 9:35

Listen to the description of a good wife in Proverbs 31. Now write about yourself. Write a word that begins with each letter and that you hope describes you and what you do. Listen for ideas in our readings, songs, and prayers.

A — Christian?
B
C
D
E
F
G
H
I — Kind?
J
K
L
M
N
O
P
Q
R
S — Soccer Star?
T
U
V
W
X
Y
Z

How many did you get?

This is HARD!

PROPER TWENTY-ONE

(Sunday between September 25 and October 1 inclusive)

From a Child's Point of View

Old Testament: Esther 7:1-6, 9-10, 9:20-22. Esther and Mordecai were two courageous people. Theirs is a story most children enjoy, but few have heard. Unfortunately, today's lection tells only the heart of it. Most worshipers of all ages need to hear the whole story, in order to make sense of the banquet conversation and the death described in chapter 7.

The picture of personal courage presented here counters the violent courage presented in most children's cartoons. Esther and Mordecai each do what they can in their situation. They have no magic gifts and do no physically incredible feats. Mordecai, though a captive in a foreign land, refuses to bow to foreign dignitaries as if they were gods, because he knows that only God deserves his worship. Esther, though she knows that the previous queen was banished for ignoring court etiquette, appears in court without an invitation in order to save her people. Their courage calls on children to act bravely in their own daily lives.

Psalm: 124. Psalm 124 is one of the pilgrim psalms sung by groups of travelers as they walked toward Jerusalem to worship in the Temple. The first verse indicates that this psalm was lined out by a leader. The psalm itself is a series of poetic images which describe how God saves us. Children understand the images more by experiencing the upbeat mood of the psalm as it is read dramatically, than by examining their meaning.

Epistle: James 5:13-20. James's call to prayer tells us that we can and should share with God all our needs, feelings, hopes, and fears. Prayer is not just saying the right words in the right way at the right time. It is sharing honestly, simply talking with God about what is important now. Children, who are developing their own prayer lives, appreciate James's point but need specific suggestions about praying in this way.

"Help me" prayers are among the earliest uncoached childhood prayers. Because children often do not receive what they pray for, they have trouble with James's unstated message that people will. Those whose prayers for ponies, good grades, and healing for sick loved ones have not been answered as they wished, want to know why prayer worked for Elijah, but not for them. James offers no answer, but it is to be hoped that preachers who focus on prayer will. In most instances, children are satisfied by the truth that God loves us too much to give us everything we think we want and need. But it is important to acknowledge that we sometimes do not understand why God does not give us what we have prayed for—especially when we pray for healing.

Gospel: Mark 9:38-50. This text offers a series of points about being a disciple. Some of them speak more clearly than others to children.

Older-elementary children become aware of the different Christian denominations as they visit other churches with friends and relatives. While they are learning about the similarities and differences, they need to hear their congregation express Mark's attitude that these different groups are not threatening, but interesting, and that rather than fearing or fighting one another, all of us can do God's work together.

Verse 42 insists that if we lead others into sinful activities, we are responsible for what happens to them. For children, this means that they are responsible if they encourage younger children to do what they themselves know is wrong. If they have led the way, they cannot claim that they are innocent and the younger child is responsible for his or her own actions.

Literal thinkers respond to the demands of verses 43-48 with graphic mental pictures of severed limbs. It is, therefore, important to focus clearly on Mark's point—that we are to be serious disciples, not merely occasional ones.

Verses 49-50 are more easily understood by illustration rather than by explanation. Today they can be well illustrated by the stories of Esther and Mordecai, whose discipleship was tested and who proved themselves "salty," or worthwhile servants of God.

Watch Words

Redefine *courage* to fit the courage of Esther and Mordecai, rather than that of the Ninja Turtles.

Connect the word *disciple* with the *discipline* required to succeed in sports or performing arts, rather than with parental *discipline*. The former *discipline* is self-chosen and admired by children.

Prayer is sharing with God the things that are important to us.

Let the Children Sing

Continue the discipleship hymns begun with Proper 19. "I Sing a Song of the Saints of God" is particularly appropriate for Mordecai and Esther. Further celebrate their courage by singing "We Shall Overcome," the hymn sung for courage by people working for social justice.

Though they miss many of the words in the verses, children, when encouraged, can join in the repeated prayer, "Grant Us Wisdom, Grant Us Courage," in "God of Grace and God of Glory."

Children understand some of the ideas about prayer in "What a Friend We Have in Jesus." A children's class or choir might present "Kum Ba Yah" as an anthem.

The Liturgical Child

1. Pray for courage like that of Esther and Mordecai at school, on school buses, in offices, while hanging out with friends, and so forth.

2. Introduce the historical context of Psalm 124, then preserve its format by lining out the psalm with the congregation. Instruct the congregation to repeat your dramatic emphases, as well as your words. If you have already read Esther, invite worshipers to imagine themselves among the Jews, celebrating the first Purim with this psalm.

3. To encourage personal prayer, make today's major prayer an outline, with pauses in which individuals can offer their own silent prayers on the subject. For example:

> God, each of us has some kind of family. Sometimes our families make us happy. At other times, they drive us a little nuts. Hear each of us as we pray for the members of our families. (PAUSE)

Sermon Resources

1. Devote the sermon to reading or telling the entire story of Esther. Because children become lost in the details of the biblical account, tell the story in your own words or read from a Bible storybook. *The Children's Bible in 365 Stories,* by Mary Batchelor, presents the story in good storytelling style, which both children and adults find appropriate and enjoyable in the sanctuary. It is available in secular as well as religious bookstores.

2. If the sermon is on courage, *Sounder,* by William Armstrong, details the courage of a young black boy searching for his father, who has been imprisoned for stealing food for his hungry family. *Ramona the Brave,* by Beverly Cleary, describes the more everyday bravery of a first-grader who deals with a difficult teacher and other problems at school and at home.

3. If you focus on prayer, provide several specific suggestions for prayer that both children and adults can try. A "breath" prayer is a short prayer that can be prayed throughout the day. It consists of two short phrases said in one breath—while breathing in, and while breathing out. For example: (while breathing in) "When I feel all alone"; (while breathing out) "Lord, be with me," or "When I'm mad enough to punch, Lord, help me to be kind." Many disciples use the same breath prayer for a day or a week.

Listen to the story of Esther as it is read.
Draw a picture of a scene in that story.

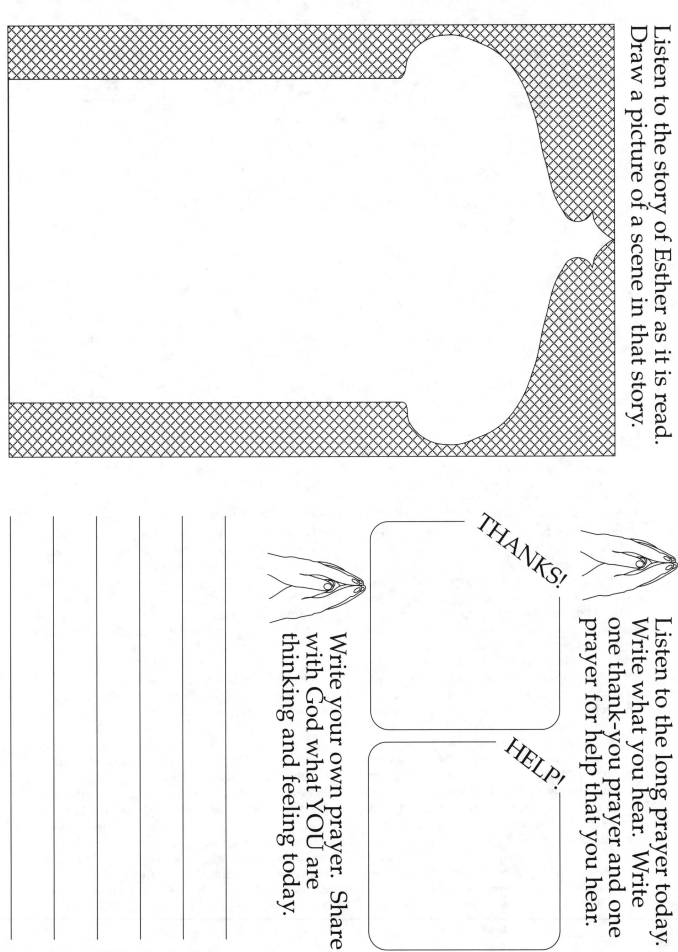

Listen to the long prayer today.
Write what you hear. Write
one thank-you prayer and one
prayer for help that you hear.

THANKS!

HELP!

Write your own prayer. Share
with God what YOU are
thinking and feeling today.

PROPER TWENTY-TWO

(Sunday between October 2 and 8 inclusive)

From a Child's Point of View

Old Testament: Job 1:1, 2:1-10. Because children hear stories from the Bible literally, they must be told clearly that Job was not a real person—that the story about Job was made up to tell people something important about God. Without this information, children hear that God is capable of toying with people just to see what they will do in terrible situations, and they worry that God might do the same with them. They are also frightened to hear that God might allow children to be killed to test their parents, and they need to be reassured that God does not do such things.

Job's response to adversity in verse 2:10 requires more experienced understanding than children possess. Basically, Job says that it is easy to love God and to say thank-you prayers when we have everything we need, but we are to love God even when we do not have everything we need. Preadolescents, for whom a relationship or friendship with God is becoming important, learn from Job that we are not to use God to get what we want. Our conversations with God should include more than "Please, give me," and "Thank you." We are not nice to our best friends just to get what we want. We love them no matter what, and our relationship with God should be like that with our friends. (The Good News Bible's translation of 2:10 is the translation that makes most sense to children.)

Psalm: 26. If this psalm is introduced as a psalm Job could have prayed and read from the Good News Bible, children catch some phrases about how the poet lives and some of the phrases that praise God.

Epistle: Hebrews 1:1-4, 2:5-12. Children are baffled by this passage as it is read. But with help, they respond well to its definition of Christ, which focuses on what he does rather than what kind of being he is. However, they depend on the preacher to translate this list of activities into more familiar terms:

- Christ worked with God to create the world.
- Christ continually cares for the whole universe.
- Christ lived among us as Jesus of Nazareth and accepted being crucified.
- Christ is just like God. When we learn what Jesus Christ is like, we learn what God is like.
- Christ forgives us.
- Just as Christ was at the beginning with God, Christ will be at the end of the world with God.

On Worldwide Communion Sunday, Christ is the host of the sacramental meal to which the whole world is invited.

Gospel: Mark 10:2-16. In a culture that endorses serial marriage, children need to hear the church's insistence that God intends marriage to be a lifelong commitment. Such commitments need to be described and held up as the Christian ideal. Children need to listen in on adult-oriented sermons that suggest practical ways to make and maintain such marriages. In the process, they will begin to lay the foundations for their own marriages. On the other hand, children also need to hear that just as God forgives us when we are greedy or lie or steal, God also forgives us (and our parents) when we (or they) fail to make marriages last a lifetime. Divorce is sad and sinful, but forgivable.

Jesus' blessing of the children is familiar to most church children and taken by them to mean simply that Jesus liked children and took them seriously. Adults may tell children to "grow up" and be more like adults. But Jesus tells the adults to be like children.

Watch Words

The *devil* and *Satan* are clearly tied to evil in the minds of children. Older children are interested in the different role taken by *Satan* in the story of Job. The *adversary* who comes closest to paralleling *Satan* is the sparring partner with whom a wrestler or boxer develops power and skill.

Christ is a somewhat confusing word for many children. They tend to think of it as being Jesus' last name. Introduce it as a title that belongs only to Jesus. Tell what the *Christ* does. Be consistent in using *Jesus Christ, Jesus the Christ,* or some other form.

Beware of the abstract language in Hebrews.

Let the Children Sing

Praise the God of family love with "For the Beauty of the Earth." If its examples of the work needed to make a marriage last a lifetime are highlighted during the sermon, "When Love Is Found" can be sung by children. Celebrate Jesus' love of children with "Jesus Loves Me" (see esp. the second verse).

"Come Christians, Join to Sing," with its Alleluias, and "When Morning Gilds the Skies," with its repeated phrase "May Jesus Christ be praised," invite children to praise Christ.

The Liturgical Child

1. Have youth or adult actors pantomime Job's story as it is read (consider reading Job 1:1–2:10). God and Satan could wear white turtleneck shirts and stand together at one side, while the other actors wear dark turtlenecks and work at the center of the chancel.

2. To turn the section of the Apostles Creed about Jesus into a responsive affirmation, a worship leader pauses after each phrase, as the congregation responds: "We believe Jesus is the Christ."

3. If you focus on the meaning of the title "Christ," welcome worshipers to the communion table at which Jesus Christ is host. Present it as Christ's feast, or party table, to which everyone in the world is invited. See Proper 21 in Year C of this series for more general suggestions on ways to celebrate Worldwide Communion with children.

4. Follow Jesus' example of blessing the children by praying for the children of your congregation. Pray for their families, give thanks for specific ways their classes, choirs, and so on contribute to the life of the congregation, and mention the joys and problems at school and on sports teams. In smaller congregations, pray for each child by name.

Sermon Resources

1. Most children have heard of the saying, The Devil Made Me Do It, or have seen it on T-shirts and bumper stickers. They understand that it is an attempt to wiggle out of responsibility. Job could have cursed God and said, "The Devil made me do it," but he didn't. The devil or Satan may test us, but only we can decide how to respond. Job knew the truth that children are learning—that only we can make ourselves do or not do anything. Like Job, we are responsible for what we say and do, even in the most difficult situations.

2. If you focus on Christian marriage:

• Let couples indicate by a show of hands, or by standing, how long they have been married. For example: "Will all who have been married between 10 and 20 years stand where you are." In an informal congregation, determine who has been married longest and who is the most recently wed.

• Read and discuss the marriage vows used in your congregation. Put the vows into your own words. Cite everyday examples of the ways these vows how they are kept.

• Compare the work required to live by your congregation's wedding vows with the unrealistic ending of many fairy tales: "And they lived happily ever after."

3. Match what the writer of Hebrews said about Christ with the symbols for Christ displayed on the paraments, in the windows, or other places in your sanctuary. Point out and explain the meaning of different crosses and other symbols. The final and most important symbol on Worldwide Communion Sunday is the presence of the loaf and cup on the communion table.

There are many pictures of Jesus with children. In some, he holds children quietly on his lap. In others, he plays games and laughs. Draw a picture of one thing you think Jesus did with children.

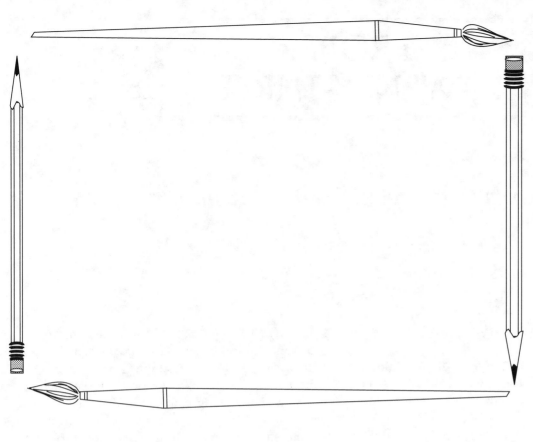

Jesus is the Christ

Listen when Hebrews is read. Then fit each thing Christ did onto one letter in the word Christ.

C _ _ _ _

H _ _ _ _ _

R _ _ _

I _ _ _

S _ _ _ _

T _ _ _ _ _

forgives

loves

teaches

heals

dies

creates

PROPER TWENTY-THREE

(Sunday between October 9 and 15 inclusive)

From a Child's Point of View

Old Testament: Job 23:1-9, 16-17. As children learn to accept responsibility for their actions and for the results of their actions, they often mistakenly conclude that they are responsible when any bad things happen to people or pets they love. They fear that God is punishing them when someone or something they love is hurt or dies. The result is crushing guilt. Job's insistence—that he does not deserve what has happened to him—can be used to help children identify the difference between natural results of our bad actions and the fact that sad things *do* happen to good people.

Job's speech is also an indication that it is OK to feel angry with God and far away from God. When children are helped to understand Job's angry loneliness as he missed his family and nursed his hurting body, they empathize. They then find permission for their own angry, lonely feelings—after all, Job and his feelings were printed in the Bible!

Children will, however, gather neither of these important messages from the reading of the text. They depend on the preacher to set Job's speech in context and paraphrase its content.

Psalm: 22:1-15. This is another prayer that Job might have prayed. When children are told that Jesus also prayed this prayer aloud while he was dying on the cross, it reenforces the messages found in the Job passage. (The Good News Bible's presentation of the psalm's poetic images is the easiest version for children to understand.)

Epistle: Hebrews 4:12-16. This passage makes sense only to readers who know the Jewish sacrificial system and can decode the poetic images. Children are lost in it. Alert older children often draw the frightening conclusion that God is a severe judge, from whom we are protected by the more understanding Jesus. (Using the text as a foil to Job's sense of isolation only increases the likelihood of such misunderstanding.) Because the core ideas of this Epistle text are better expressed in other places, it is advisable to skip it in favor of the Old Testament or Gospel readings.

Gospel: Mark 10:17-31. When they hear the story read dramatically, children understand it quickly and are as concerned as adults about its point. They are relieved by Jesus' recognition that it is hard to be a disciple, a fact children often feel that adults fail to appreciate. They know from experience that doing disciples' work, such as being kind to those who are mean to you, really is about as impossible as putting a camel through the eye of a needle.

Few younger children see themselves as wealthy. But fifth- and sixth-graders are beginning to recognize their relative wealth among their friends, in their community, and even worldwide. These older children need to hear that having money enables us to pay more attention to what we wear, what toys we want, where we can go, and what we can do. Money makes it so much easier for us to pay attention to what *we* want that we forget to be disciples.

164

Watch Words

In a day when few people sew at home, many children do not know that the *eye of a needle* is the hole in the needle that the thread goes through. (Illustrate *threading a needle,* using a large darning needle and some yarn.)

The Word that is like a sharp sword and also is equated with God, together with the *great high priest, mercy,* and *grace,* make the Hebrews passage unintelligible to children.

In describing Job's feelings, avoid such words as *alienation, isolation,* and *existential despair* in favor of *loneliness, hopelessness,* and the feeling of being *lost* or *forgotten.*

Let the Children Sing

The powerful feeling in the spiritual "Nobody Knows the Trouble I See," when sung dramatically by a choir or soloist, may best match the feelings of Job and Jesus. The mood of the hymn "Be Still, My Soul" also communicates with young readers, even before they begin singing the repeated phrase. "Kum Ba Yah" is a hymn about God's presence that many children know.

Continue singing the discipleship hymns from Proper 19.

The Liturgical Child

1. Briefly review Job's story and the accusations of his friends, then assume Job's role to present today's lection. At the very least, read it with the passion Job expresses. Use your hands, posture, and facial expressions to emphasize these feelings. For maximum impact, present the passage from memory. (Remember that even children who do not understand all the words can still understand Job's feelings.)

2. Read the story of the rich young man, taking the parts of various people. Face slightly one way when reading the rich young man's lines, the other way when reading Jesus' words. Speak directly to the congregation when delivering Jesus' words to his disciples. Use your hands and facial expressions to show how people reacted to what was said.

3. Invite worshipers to write or draw on slips of paper, or in the eye of the needle on their Worship Worksheet, one disciple's promise for this week, to place with their offering in the plate as it is passed. Dedicate both the promises and the money with prayer.

4. Offer bidding prayers for disciples, being sure to include child disciples. For example:

We pray for Christians who work for your justice: For children who insist on fair play on the playground; for students who refuse to cheat; for business men and women who will not take unfair advantage, to make bigger profits; for those who write letters to the editor and to public officials, to demand just laws. Each of us offers our prayers for disciples who thread needles for justice. (PAUSE) Strong God of Justice, give your disciples the courage we need to stand up for your justice.

We pray for Christians who care for the mistreated: . . .

5. Ask groups of two or more children to form arches just inside each sanctuary door as the worshipers leave. Instruct them to say to each worshiper who passes through their arch, "Go in peace. God loves you." The spoken benediction is as follows:

As you leave, you will find that children's arms have formed an arch that is rather like the eye of a needle. Listen for their encouragement as you thread through their needle to enter a week of discipleship. And as you do, remember that what is impossible with human power is possible with God. So go in peace, in love, in strength, and in joy. Thread those disciples' needles! Serve God, who loves you more than you can imagine and who can work through you to do mighty deeds. Amen.

Sermon Resources

1. To explore why bad things happen, compare two stories about responsibility. In the first, a boy leaves a gate open after he has been warned to keep it closed. His dog gets out and is hit by a car. In the second, a boy is at school when his dog digs under a fence, gets out, and is hit by a car. The boy sadly remembers that he chose to watch TV rather than play with his dog the night before and concludes that God is punishing him for his unkindness.

2. If Job's list of complaints leads you to make a list of today's complaints, be sure to include a variety of children's complaints: rain on game day; the kid who gets straight A's (or is a star athlete) without trying, while you work hard to get C's (or come in last); illnesses and handicaps that limit what you can do; your parents getting a divorce; someone you love dying; and so forth.

Listen carefully when Job 23 is read.
Circle the words that describe Job's feelings.

Happy

ANGRy

sad

lonely

funny

HA HA HA HA HA HA HA HA HA

Draw a picture or write about a time when you felt like Job. Tell God about how you felt.

Listen to the sermon about **threading a needle.**
In the eye of the needle below, draw a picture of yourself doing hard disciple's work.
(Idea! Draw yourself being kind to a person who is mean to you.)

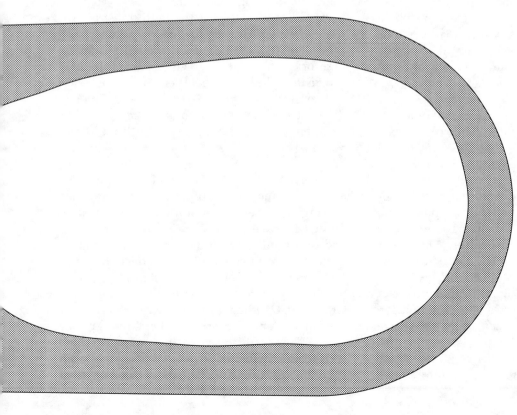

PROPER TWENTY-FOUR

(Sunday between October 16 and 22 inclusive)

From a Child's Point of View

Old Testament: Job 38:1-7 (34-41). The summary of God's answer to Job is that God is "more" than Job can even imagine. For children, that is not a very satisfactory answer to Job's questions. It is rather like what adults say when they tell children they must do something because "I say so and I am the mother and you are the little girl." But it does invite children to explore their unanswerable questions about God:

• What was there before God?
• How can God be everywhere at the same time?
• How can God know everything that everyone in the world is thinking and doing all the time?
• How could God make the world out of nothing?

The answer to all these questions and others, is that God is bigger and "more" than we can imagine. The response is to celebrate God's power and "moreness."

Psalm: 104:1-9, 24, 35c. The first four verses describe God's "moreness" with poetic images that children appreciate. The remaining verses describe God's power as the Creator. When older children are told about "the deep" and the psalmist's ideas about how the world was created, they particularly enjoy the mental picture of the receding waters in verses 5-9. The language and verb tenses of The New Jerusalem Bible make it easiest for children to follow.

Epistle: Hebrews 5:1-10. To explain to Jewish readers who Jesus is and why Jesus is important, the writer of Hebrews compared Jesus to something very familiar to Jews, a high priest. Because they knew high priests and their work, those readers immediately caught what the writer was saying about Jesus. But today's readers, especially children, must start by learning about high priests. Even then, it is hard for them to catch the writer's point, because the priest's job of killing an animal to say we are sorry for our sins does not "make sense" today. Still, fifth- and sixth-graders, who are interested in the different ways people understand and do things, are interested in this comparison. They are helped if the high priest is presented as a go-between for the people and God. When the details of the three ways Jesus and a high priest are alike are then examined, Jesus is shown to be the best go-between imaginable.

(Next week's Epistle details the ways Jesus is different from any human priest. The texts could be combined to explore Jesus' priesthood in one Sunday.)

Gospel: Mark 10:35-45. Though adults may be appalled at the request of James and John about seating, children understand and empathize. Those who have had to share a piano bench at the end of a family-reunion dinner table, or have been sent to eat in the kitchen, feel the importance of where one sits. They want to sit in a "big" chair near the guest of honor (especially if it is Grandma). Children also know that the other ten were not offended by the brothers' request, but angry. They were angry that the two had gotten their request in first.

Because children are often told what to do, they

long for the day when they can make their own decisions. In frustration, they long for the tables to be turned, so that they can give the instructions. It is that wish that makes them bossy with one another, and it is to this that Jesus speaks. Jesus insists that he is not impressed by those who sit in the best places or give orders; instead, he is impressed by those who go about quietly, taking care of the needs of others.

Watch Words

This is a good opportunity to focus on the big words that describe the ways God is more than we can understand—*immortal, omniscient, omnipresent, holy,* and so forth. Define them and use them repeatedly. Celebrate them!

The deep does not refer to the waters of deep oceans. It was the water that covered the entire earth before the continents were formed.

Do not use priestly or sacrificial language without explaining it.

Let the Children Sing

The vocabulary of "I Sing the (Al)mighty Power of God" makes it one of the easiest creation hymns for children. "God of the Sparrow" may be best sung by a children's choir or class. The impossibly big words in "Immortal, Invisible, God Only Wise" normally deter children but can be attempted today to invite them to sing about God's greatness. Before singing, point out some of the big words and briefly tell what they say about God.

Continue singing discipleship hymns noted in Proper 19. Though children do not understand many of the words of "Are Ye Able?" they enjoy the format and can sing the "Lord, we are able" answer sincerely.

The Liturgical Child

1. Use Psalm 104:1-4 as a Call to Worship. The congregation responds in unison, "Bless the Lord, O my soul!" and then sings a hymn praising God.

2. Because they are familiar with the feelings involved, children can easily pantomime today's Gospel lesson as it is read by a worship leader. Biblical costumes would help them to assume their roles.

3. A Prayer of Confession about being servants:

When we read Jesus' call to be unselfish servants, God, we are embarrassed. We are embarrassed because we know how hard we work to get our own way; we know how much we want to be first in every line; we know how greedily we grab for the most of everything; and we admit that we dream of winning every game, every prize, every award. Even when we try to follow your example, we find that we think first about ourselves and what we want and need. Forgive us, and remake us into people who can love and serve others. For we pray in Jesus' name. Amen.

Assurance of Pardon: Jesus did not give up on James or John, or any of the other self-centered disciples. Instead, he kept loving them and forgiving them and teaching them. He worked in them and through them, to start the church. And he will do the same with us!

Sermon Resources

1. Children face today's Gospel teaching most directly when older children are left "in charge of" younger children or siblings. The older ones struggle with the tension between making the younger ones do what the older ones want them to do, and helping them do what they want to do. Younger ones clearly refer to this passage in demanding "their rights."

2. The classic *Charlotte's Web* by E. B. White offers several examples of gentle, loving service. Wilbur, the runt of the litter of pigs, is saved from early death by Fern, who refuses to let her father kill him, and then nurses him to health until he becomes a championship pig. Wilbur is saved later from becoming Christmas ham by a spider named Charlotte, who weaves complimentary words about Wilbur into her web above his pen. After Charlotte saves Wilbur, she dies giving birth to her young, who continue to be Wilbur's friends.

3. Describe several "used-to thinks" about God. For example:

Christians used to think that the world was flat and that God lived up above it. Now we think that the earth is a very small round planet in a vast universe, and God moves everywhere throughout the universe.

OR:

I used to think that if God spoke to me, it

would be with words my ears would hear. Now I have found that God communicates with me in many ways, such as through things I see and words that other people say or write.

"Used-to-thinks" emphasize the truth that we never know all there is to know about God, so they encourage worshipers of all ages to keep revising their understandings about God.

Psalm 104 says,

"The earth is full of your creatures."

Draw one animal God made and write a verse about it.

God dressed penguins in fancy suits, then sent them out to slide on the ice.

These letters and words do not understand!

I'm # 1

OUT OF MY WAY

We're first!

The last letter in each word below has pushed its way to the front of that word, and the last word in the message has shoved itself to be first. Put the letters and words in the right places. What did Jesus say?

LAL RWHOEVE SWISHE

OT EB TFIRS TMUS

EB ESLAV FO.

Jesus said,

"— — — — — —

— — — — —

— — — — ."

Mark 10: 44

Proper 24 | © 1993 by Abingdon Press.

PROPER TWENTY-FIVE

(Sunday between October 23 and 29 inclusive)

From a Child's Point of View

Old Testament: Job 42:1-6, 10-17. The writer's literary ploys make this text difficult to follow. The free translation of The Good News Bible presents its gist in the most understandable language.

Job learned that he did not know, and would never know, everything. Some questions, like why God lets terrible things happen to good people, are unanswerable. Children tend to assume (and adults often reenforce that assumption) that there are answers to every question and that adults know them all. Children also assume that if they work hard enough, they eventually will know all the answers too. Job's story is an opportunity to introduce unanswerable questions and the possibility of living comfortably with them because we can trust God, who does know the answers.

As Halloween approaches, children focus on mysterious, scary stories and phenomena. Older children test their abilities to face fears in dealing with the unexplainable. This week before Halloween, Job insists that though there are things we cannot explain, we do not need to be afraid. God understands them all and is in full control.

Psalm: 34:1-8, 19-22. This psalm makes most sense when read in context. It is a prayer David offered after his escape from Abimelech, and one that Job might have prayed as his trials ended. The language of the New Revised Standard Version reflects these contexts most clearly and is easiest for children.

As they listen, children catch individual phrases about God's dependable care. Hearing the verses literally, alert children who have broken their own bones wonder whether verse 20 is a mistake, or perhaps an indication that they are not among the righteous.

Epistle: Hebrews 7:23-28. Last week's Epistle reading highlighted the ways Jesus is like a high priest. This week, the focus is on the ways Jesus is better than any human high priest.

Children place more value on Jesus' permanence than on his perfection. Dependability is important to them. Epecially those who must regularly find new "best friends forever" when they move, and those who move from household to household within their extended families, crave a relationship with God and Jesus that lasts "forever and ever, no matter what."

Gospel: Mark 10:46-52. Without help, children hear this simply as another healing story that demonstrates Jesus' power. They can be helped to find more meaning in it by specifically comparing James and John with Bartimaeus. James and John were insiders, friends who had been with Jesus for some time, and so should have understood what Jesus had been teaching and doing. Bartimaeus was an outsider, a blind beggar along the road. No one expected him to understand anything. Mark's surprise is that it is Bartimaeus who knows what to ask for, and he who responds by becoming a follower of Jesus. With such explanations, older children enjoy Mark's subtle point that James and John were really the "blind" ones who could not "see" what Jesus had been telling and showing them, while Bartimaeus was the one who could "see" clearly.

Watch Words

Mystery is a good word for things we do not understand. Begin with Halloween mysteries (maybe a local ghost story or spooky legend) and mystery stories (many adults and children know the Hardy Boys and the Nancy Drew series), then go on to describe the mysteries of real life.

Be careful about priestly vocabulary. To many children, a *priest* is a Roman Catholic minister, and a *sacrifice* is giving up something you want. The *sacrifice out* in baseball is closer to the Old Testament sacrifice.

Before using *blind* metaphorically, compare what James and John failed to *see* with what the physically blind Bartimaeus could see.

Let the Children Sing

Though its obsolete vocabulary is a problem, "A Mighty Fortress Is Our God" can be sung as a Halloween hymn, and also in honor of Job. Verses 2 and 3 are the most meaningful ones to paraphrase for, and sing with, children at Halloween.

Highlight their references to vision before singing "Amazing Grace" or "Be Thou My Vision" (if they are sung frequently in your congregation).

Sing of Christ, our High Priest, with "What a Friend We Have in Jesus" and "Come, Christians, Join to Sing" (lots of Alleluias for young readers). Identify Jesus as the one "begotten of the Father," and point out the "forever" images before singing "Of the Father's Love Begotten." The first verse is the most understandable for children, but the "evermores" in the other verses can be sung by all.

The Liturgical Child

1. To set Psalm 34 in context, tell briefly how David and his followers celebrated his escape from Abimelech. Then ask several prepared children to take the role of his followers, calling out the letters of the Hebrew alphabet as the worship leader reads the appropriate verses. (The New Jerusalem Bible prints the Hebrew letter before each verse.)

2. To set up the comparison of James and John with Bartimaeus, have both stories read and pan-tomimed by children. Jesus could stand in the middle of the chancel, with James, John and other disciples (perhaps played by the same children who pantomimed their story last week) on one side, and Bartimaeus on the other. Instruct "Jesus," in asking the repeated question to each side, to use the same movements and to read the question with the same emphasis and tone.

4. Build prayers of confession or petition around the ideas of blindness and vision. Instruct worshipers to pray by closing their eyes each time they hear "We close our eyes . . . ," and open them each time they hear "Open our eyes . . . ." For example:

Lord, we close our eyes to people who are not like us. We do not even see those whose clothes or skin or manners are different. We ignore them on the playground, in the grocery store, and at the office. We never meet them or make friends with them.

Open our eyes, so that we may see those who are different. Help us get to know each other, so that we can enjoy and learn from our differences and work together to solve our problems.

5. Remember the upcoming celebration of Halloween in the church's prayers. Praise God, whose power is greater than that of any monster or ghost. Pray that we continue to act like God's loving children, no matter what costume we wear.

Sermon Resources

1. Cite the questions in the folk song "Tell Me Why," as examples of questions to which there are no exact answers. ("Tell me why the stars do shine, . . . the ivy twines, . . . the sky's so blue," and so on.)

2. Describe how several people saw and "were blind to" an elderly woman traveling on an airplane. The stewardess saw a person who needed help getting to her seat and would need more help in an emergency. The teenager seated next to her saw an "old fuddy duddy" and put on his headset. The man seated across the aisle saw her wallet bulging with pictures, and hid in his newspaper so he wouldn't have to hear about her grandchildren. The people who met her at the airport recognized her and said, "Welcome to our city, madam. It is an honor to have an artist like you visit us."

Write the name below of each hymn you sing today.

_____
_____
_____
_____
_____
_____

Draw a * by the one you like most.

Draw a ! by those that praise God.

Draw a P by those that are sung prayers.

Draw a picture to illustrate one hymn or part of one hymn.

Copy words you illustrated here.

_____
_____
_____
_____

PROPER TWENTY-SIX

(Sunday between October 30 and November 5 inclusive)

From a Child's Point of View

Old Testament: Ruth 1:1-18. Underlying this story are the social realities for single women without a man for support, and laws about leviratic marriage. Older children, teenagers, and adults are interested in detailed explanations of these realities, but younger children get lost in the explanations. The only essential information for listeners of any age is that at the time of this story, women who did not live with their fathers or husbands had very hard lives, and Jewish people did not want foreigners living among them. Consider reading verses 19-22 to clarify the situation of Ruth and Naomi when they returned to Bethlehem. (*The Children's Bible in 365 Stories* offers helpful ideas for presenting the cultural details simply.)

The focus of this part of the story is on Ruth's difficult, loving decision. Had she, like Orpah, returned to her father's house, she would be staying in her hometown and would have a chance to marry again. If she went with Naomi, she would be a very poor foreigner in a country where foreigners were hated. But Naomi was older now, and needed her. So Ruth decided to go with her.

Children struggle between their desire to do only what they want and the responsibility they are beginning to feel for other members of their families. Ruth provides them with a model, someone who did more than was required, or than was even requested, to take care of a member of her family.

Psalm: 146. Children will hear and under-stand occasional phrases about God's help and care in this psalm when it is read with expression.

Epistle: Hebrews 9:11-14. Hebrews was written for Jews who had personal experience with the animal sacrifices at the Temple. For today's children, who have no such experience, the text raises confusing questions about why the loving God needs blood (either that of animals or of Jesus) to be able or ready to love us. There are no answers that satisfy literal thinkers. Until their mental abilities develop enough to enable them to hear the text from the point of view of the original readers, and to understand what it meant to them, children are baffled. Though younger children may use the sacrifice language of their elders, they cannot explain its meaning in their own words until early adolescence.

Gospel: Mark 12:28-34. The two great Commandments are familiar to most church children. They have studied them in church school and enjoy encountering them in the sanctuary. They are most helped by everyday examples of people who are following the commands. We express our love for God by singing for God, by using well the gifts God has given us, and by telling God what we are doing (just as we would for any friend). We express our love for others in the way we treat our friends, the people we meet but do not know well (grocery-store cashiers, people riding on the same bus), and even the people with whom we do not get along. Ruth's decision to go with Naomi is an fine example of keeping the Second Commandment.

Watch Words

Do not assume that children know that *widows* are women whose husbands have died. In a small congregation, the preacher may name some widows the children know and compare their situations to that of Ruth and Naomi.

Adult Christians use *blood* vocabulary symbolically. Children hear it literally, and the results are confusing. Avoid making statements about the *blood of Christ* that make it sound like a special substance that was offered to God.

Let the Children Sing

Choose story hymns about the blood of Christ in which blood is used literally (e.g., "Deep Were His Wounds and Red" or "The Old Rugged Cross"), rather than hymns in which it is used symbolically (e.g., "Nothing But the Blood" or "There Is a Fountain Filled with Blood").

"Love, Love, Love, That's What It's All About" is included in many church school repertoires. Ask a children's class or choir to sing it as an anthem.

Choose hymns that reflect the two great Commandments: Sing of our love for God with "For the Beauty of the Earth"; sing about loving neighbors with "Help Us Accept Each Other."

The Liturgical Child

1. Because Ruth is a story about two strong women, suggest that women read the Old Testament Lessons today and next Sunday.

2. If the focus is on Ruth, invite worshipers to pray about their families.

Call to Prayer: Families come in all shapes and sizes—big, small, and all sizes in between. They may live in one house or be spread all around the world. Families change over the years as people are born, marry, and die. Ruth and Naomi, a mother-in-law and daughter-in-law were one family. Let us pray for our families.

Prayer: We begin our prayers by thanking you, O God, for families. We thank you for all about them that is good. We thank you for the people in our families who love and care for us. (PAUSE) And we thank you for those we love and care for.

(PAUSE) We thank you for the good times we have with our families. (PAUSE) And we thank you for the times our families have stood by us when we needed them. (PAUSE)

But we must admit that our families are not always loving. Hear us as each of us tells you about those in our family with whom we are having trouble. (PAUSE) Hear the ways we have hurt one another. (PAUSE) Forgive us when we think only of ourselves, when we work only for what we want and need, paying no attention to what others want and need. Forgive us, and help us to be as loving as Ruth. (PAUSE)

Because we love them, we pray for those in our families. We share with you what we wish for and worry about, for each one of them. (PAUSE) We know there are some things we need to work on as a family. Help us do the work that is needed. (PAUSE) Most of all, we ask you to be with us. Guide our families and protect us, in Jesus name. Amen.

3. Proper 25 in Year A of this series includes a responsive Prayer of Confession and Assurance of Pardon, based on the two great Commandments.

Sermon Resources

Work through a sequence of comments about blood:

A. Blood is fascinating. Talk about Halloween costumes covered with "blood" and haunted houses in which catsup "blood" spews from victims' mouths. Note that some people faint at the sight of blood.

B. Blood keeps us alive. We can go for three days without water, for seven days without food, but without blood, we die immediately. Describe the biological function of blood and the meaning of the Red Cross call to "Give the gift of life."

C. Blood is often used to prove the closest relationships. Describe Native American blood-brother ceremonies. (Also note the AIDS danger today, to warn children against entering blood-brother pacts with their friends.) Briefly tell about the time Moses splashed blood on the people to show that they accepted the Ten Commandments. Finally, retell the last supper story, when Jesus offered the disciples wine, with the words, "This is my blood . . . ," and talk about what it means to drink the grape juice or wine at communion.

Draw a picture of each person in your family. Show in your drawing at least one thing they like to do.

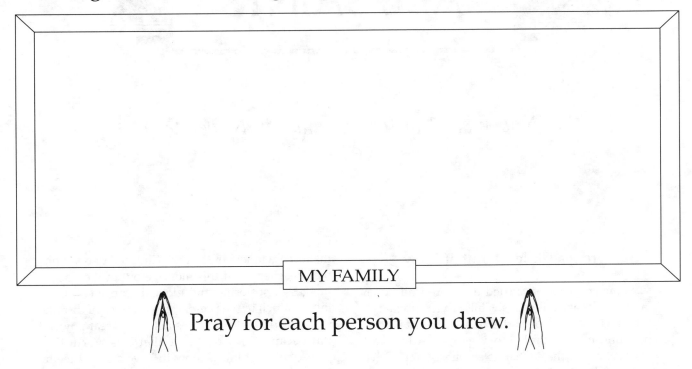

MY FAMILY

 Pray for each person you drew.

Jesus was asked to pick the most important of hundreds of rules. Use these nine clues to find his choice.

1 = heart	4 = soul	7 = with all your
2 = mind	5 = strength	8 = your
3 = neighbor	6 = the Lord your God	9 = you shall love

Jesus said,

9 6 7 1 and 7 4 and 7 2 and 7 5.

9 8 3 as 8 self.

"

_____

_____

."

_____

Proper 26 | © 1993 by Abingdon Press.

ALL SAINTS

(November 1 or first Sunday in November)

From a Child's Point of View

Some churches have tried to ignore Halloween and emphasize All Saints. Children are invited to dress as "saints" for parties that focus on Christian heroes and Bible-story games. Adults, of course, prefer the All Saints emphasis on positive role models to the Halloween emphasis on gore and evil powers. Children, however, want and need both holy days and so have resisted this move. They need to revel in God's power over the worst evils we can imagine *and* they need to celebrate Christian heroes and heroines. So recognize Halloween on the Sunday before, and celebrate All Saints the Sunday after Halloween.

The All Saints readings for Years A and C focus on the saints. Today's readings focus more on the power and promises of the God of the saints. It is interesting to note that in the Middle Ages, churches celebrated both All Hallowed Eve and All Saints Day.

Old Testament: Wisdom of Solomon 3:1-9 or Isaiah 25:6-9. Both these passages are filled with poetic images that are difficult for children to interpret. If you celebrate communion today, choose Isaiah's description of the messianic meal. God promises that one day, all the saints of all time will be gathered for a great feast. All the pains and troubles of life will be ended. Most children miss the burial images in verse 7, but grasp the promise of no more tears in verse 8, because tears are a common experience for them. A meal with no tears is worth waiting for!

The Wisdom of Solomon promises that though the saints may take a beating now, God will make them the winners in the end. Children depend on the preacher to lift this message out of the poetic images of suffering and glory. Because children live so much in the present, the promise of distant relief for present pain does not have great power. But because they do know that it is worth the pain of getting braces now to have straight teeth later, they can begin to understand the acceptance of suffering now, with the promise that a better day is coming.

On the Sunday after Halloween, Isaiah also promises that no matter what terrible punishment evil powers may inflict, in the end, God's power will prove greater, and the victims will be relieved.

Psalm: 24. This is a psalm for children to experience, rather than study. They best understand both its exuberance and its definition of who is among the saints when it is reenacted in worship.

The psalm does insist that though all are welcome, there are requirements for being among the saints. If we want to claim the promises of God to the saints, we must live like saints.

Epistle: Revelation 21:1-6a. The poetic images of a "city dressed as a bride coming down from heaven" and "water from the fountain of life" are too much for children. But the message to the saints from "the one who sits on the throne" is simple: A time is coming when God will live among the saints and take such care of them that there will be no more tears, and every need will be met.

Gospel: John 11:32-44. On All Saints, the story

of Lazarus is proof that God is more powerful than anything—even death. Like Martha, children think dead is dead. They are amused by, but understand, Martha's concern that if they unseal the tomb after four days, "there will be a stench" (it will stink!). They are touched that Jesus cared enough about his friends that he wept with them, even though he knew that Lazarus was not gone forever. And after all the Halloween ghost stories, children are comforted by the proof that not even death can separate saints from God's care.

Watch Words

A *saint* is not just a person declared to be a *saint* by the Roman Catholic Church, nor is it a person who is impossibly good (no child wants to be this kind of "saint"!). A *saint* is any person who is one of God's people.

Let the Children Sing

"I Sing a Song of the Saints of God" is the best All Saints song for children. Before singing "For All the Saints," associate it with God's All Saints promises, and urge even nonreaders to join in on the Alleluias.

If the Call to Worship features Psalm 24, sing "Lift Up Your Heads, Ye Mighty Gates" as the opening hymn.

If "I Want to Be Ready" is sung responsively between a soloist and the congregation (see *The United Methodist Hymnal*), children can sing along with the congregation. Meaning is added when worshipers are reminded of what the promises of God meant to the saints who first sang the song in slavery.

If you celebrate communion, read through the verses of "For the Bread Which You Have Broken" and connect them to the texts before singing the hymn.

The Liturgical Child

1. Display paraments and banners with the Alpha and Omega letters. Refer to them in exploring Jesus' promise to be at both the beginning and the end.

2. Begin worship with Psalm 24, shouted respon-sively between a choir at the front of the sanctuary (probably the adult choir) and a children's choir or class at the back. See Proper 10 for a script. Then during an opening hymn, have children process with banners of saints. Display the banners around the sanctuary during the service. At the end of the service, the children could lead the recessional with the banners, enabling the congregation to follow the saints into the world.

Assign classes (in a larger congregation) or children (in a smaller one) saints for whom to make large banners. Include biblical characters, figures from church history, even models from your own congregation. Each banner begins with an outline of the body of a child, on which appropriate clothes and props can be drawn. The saint's name can be printed on the banner in large letters. To make your own banner stands, tape the top of the banner to a yardstick and attach the yardstick to the clip at the end of a mop handle. Such banners will stand in a tall juice can filled with sand.

3. Point out that during communion, we often think about Jesus' death and are sad, but communion is also a time to think about the promised feast and be happy. Then keep the mood of the sacrament celebrative. Speak with happy confidence, rather than somber importance. As background music, choose familiar, upbeat hymns about God's power.

Sermon Resources

1. To explore God's promise about tears, list things that make us cry. Babies cry when they are wet, hungry, lonely, and hurt.

Young children cry less frequently than babies: when they are hurt (but they can be brave about small hurts); when they become really angry (throw a temper tantrum); and when they see something sad.

Teenagers are more likely to cry because of hurt feelings. Grown-ups cry when sad things happen to them or to people they love. We all tend to cry at funerals, and when good friends move away.

Some people cry at movies. And some people even cry when they are very, very happy (but theirs are not the tears we are thinking about today).

2. Tell stories of familiar suffering saints such as Martin Luther King, Jr., who refused to give up

when there were threats against his life. He said that he could go on because he had "been to the mountain," referring to the mountain in Isaiah.

3. Encourage children to add their drawings of the saints they want to be like to a display board, previously titled "Saints," located in the narthex or a nearby hallway.

See All Saints in Years A and C of this series for further suggestions.

Listen as **Revelation 21** is read.
THE ONE WHO SITS ON THE
THRONE makes several promises

1 is that God will one
day live with the saints.

Another is that there will
be no more

S E R

A N T

D E A T H

Draw a saint you want to be like.

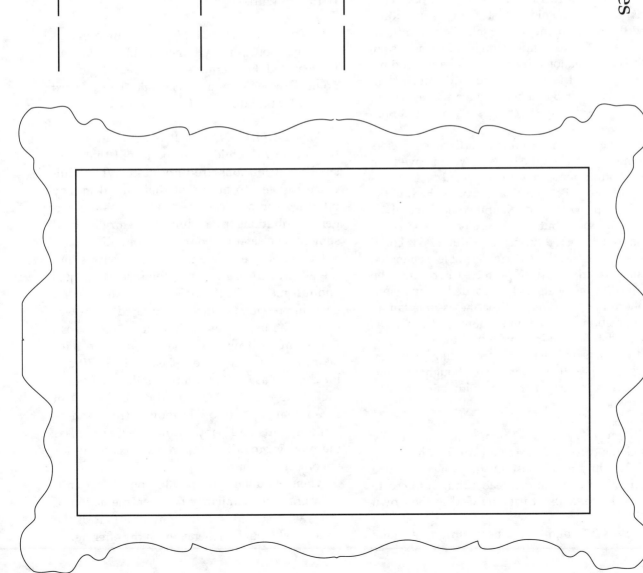

PROPER TWENTY-SEVEN

(Sunday between November 6 and 12 inclusive)

From a Child's Point of View

Old Testament: Ruth 3:1-5; 4:13-17. Both children and adults enjoy the story of Naomi, Ruth, and Boaz. It is an interesting tale about admirable people who acted with courage and kindness in everyday situations. It even has a happy ending. It is a story that begs to be told, more than preached upon. So, rather than read today's summary texts, pick up the entire story from last Sunday.

Out of concern for others, all three characters do more than is required. Ruth would have been better off at home, but accompanied Naomi to a difficult life in Bethlehem and worked hard in the fields to provide food. Naomi could have given up in self-pity, but she carefully worked out a plan to find a good husband for Ruth. Boaz could have ignored Ruth as an undesirable, somewhat distant relative, but he protected her when she worked in his fields and responded compassionately to her brave request that he assume family responsibility for her and Naomi. Their actions are models for children and adults today.

To understand the court proceedings, children need only hear that any man who bought the land that Ruth inherited from her husband had to marry her.

Psalm: 127. Verses 1-2 remind us that we rely on God's trust and care in all we do. The examples of building a house or guarding a city are straightforward and can lead children to create parallel verses about trusting God in their own activities.

Verses 3-5 might have been sung by Obed's family at his birth. Unfortunately, boys today may use these verses to prove their claimed superiority over girls.

Epistle: Hebrews 9:24-28. After four previous readings about priestly things, children's interest is exhausted. Furthermore, the content, logic, and point of these verses are too subtle. This is a text to read for the adults.

Gospel: Mark 12:38-44. It is tempting to use this story with children to point out that their small contributions are important. While children do need to hear that their small money offerings and services are as valued as the bigger contributions from adults, this story is about something else. It is about giving our all.

The difference between the proud scribes and the generous widow is that the scribes put just enough money in the offering box to make a good impression (all they really cared about was getting the best of everything for themselves), while the widow gave everything she had, because she truly wanted to help. It is as difficult for children as it is for adults to follow the example of the widow. Among other things, it can mean sharing "my own" money (received as birthday gifts and baby-sitting fees), as well as the money provided by parents specifically for the offering at church.

When the details are pointed out, older children grasp the similarity between the action of Ruth, who stayed with Naomi, and that of the widow, who put both her coins in the offering.

Watch Words

Gleaning is not a familiar activity for even farm children today. If your church is active in a Second Harvest ministry, explain how it *gleans* leftover food from food producers, grocery stores, and restaurants to feed hungry people.

Modern translations do not use *mite*, but the church has traditionally spoken of the *widow's mite*. If you use the term, define it.

WARNING: The small boxes in which children collect coins for special offerings, once called *mite boxes*, now are often called *coin banks* or *coin boxes*.

Scribes are simply church leaders.

Let the Children Sing

In honor of Ruth, Naomi, Boaz, and the generous widow, use "I Sing a Song of the Saints of God." To recall the truth about God's care, which each of them knew, sing "Lord of Our Growing Years." Note which verse goes with which character and urge singers to find the verse that fits them. Though they cannot follow the verses, even beginning readers can join in on the repeated chorus of "Great Is Thy Faithfulness."

"Be Thou My Vision," with its emphasis on what is most important, and "Take My Life and Let It Be Consecrated," with its offer of all parts of our bodies, are good ways to offer ourselves completely to God.

The Liturgical Child

1. Display a large standing arrangement of wheat or other brown grasses, instead of flowers. Leave several stalks lying on the table (waiting to be gleaned). Refer to this display to explain gleaning.

2. If you read most of Ruth, keep listeners' attention and emphasize the story by having it read in good storyteller style by one male and one female reader:

1:22*b*–2:23: Male reader describes the meeting of Boaz and Ruth.

3:1-18: Female reader tells Naomi's plan.

4:1-12: Male reader describes Boaz in court.

4:13-22: Female reader tells the outcome.

3. From the lectern, begin reading the Gospel in proud tones. After verse 40, move to stand near the offering plates. Gesture toward the plates as you read verses 41-42 in a normal tone. Face the congregation directly to read Jesus' words to the disciples in 43-44.

4. Offer a prayer about giving:

Lord, we dream of doing brave deeds and giving generous gifts. But we seldom do the deeds or give the gifts. We are too easily frightened by what might happen. We are afraid we might be hurt, we are afraid we may have to work too hard, we are afraid we might fail, we are even afraid of what other people will think. Forgive us for giving in to our selfish fears. Help us, instead, to see more clearly what we might be able to do, and give us the courage to help others by trying to do the difficult things. Make us into your strong, loving people. We ask it in Jesus' name. Amen.

Assurance of Pardon: God understands our fears. Jesus prayed that he not be crucified. Like us, he did not want to be hurt. But Jesus loved us and knew what we needed, so he faced crucifixion. Just so, God can give us the courage and power to do the loving deeds that frighten us and that we fear will hurt us. Thanks be to God!

Sermon Resources

1. Devote the sermon to retelling, with commentary, the story of Ruth and Boaz. *The Children's Bible in 365 Stories* presents the story clearly and suggests simple ways to explain the cultural context. A male/female team could preach a dialog sermon in first person, assuming the roles of Boaz and Ruth (perhaps near the end of their long lives together) to retell and comment on the story.

2. The most familiar examples of young people who give everything in order to do what is most important to them are the young athletes who are preparing for sporting competitions like the Olympics. To practice their sport they give up participating in all other clubs and activities. They may even go to special schools or move away from their families to live with the very best coaches.

3. *Last Week When I Was Rich,* by Judith Viorst, tells how a boy spent the $2.00 his grandparents had given him, but ended up with nothing he really wanted. Sloppy stewards of all ages recog-

nize themselves in this humorous tale and can compare this boy with the widow who gave everything she had for what was most important to her.

If you use the Gospel half of the Worship Worksheet, enlarge it to a full page to provide room to work.

The psalm writer tells how God's care is needed for a strong house and a safe city. Read the poet's verses. Then make up your own verses to tell how you need God's care in your life.

If the Lord does not build the house, the work of the builders is useless.

If the Lord does not protect the city, it does no good for the watchmen to stand guard.

If _____

_____ ,

_____ .

If _____

_____ ,

_____ .

IDEAS! Write about God's care for your schoolwork. Or make up a verse about playing on a team or learning how to play a musical instrument.

Listen carefully as Mark 12: 38-44 is read. Then:
- Draw a proud scribe and the widow giving their offerings.
- Write words around them that describe each one.

Use 2 of the words in your own prayer _____

PROPER TWENTY-EIGHT

(Sunday between November 13 and 19 inclusive)

From a Child's Point of View

Old Testament: I Samuel 1:4-20. The story of Samuel's birth suggests several interesting areas for exploration. First, children are pleased that God took the side of the pestered person. Since most children, at one time or another, feel as pestered and unhappy as Hannah, they are relieved to know that God cares for such people and works to help them. Just as God did not choose the wife with many children to be Samuel's mother, God might choose the less-than-straight-A student or the non-star athlete for special work.

Similarly, they find security in hearing that God can and does act to right what look like hopeless situations. Just as God surprised Hannah, God can surprise us!

Finally, it brings up the always interesting subject of birthdays. Hearing the story of Samuel's birth invites children to hear stories of other births and the truth that God is involved in planning for and guiding each one. If it is the Sunday before Thanksgiving, the story may lead to thanking the God who creates us as we are, sets us in unique families, and watches over us.

WARNING: Hannah's answered prayer leads some children to ask why God has not answered their prayers—especially when they have prayed as earnestly as Hannah did about situations as critical as hers.

Old Testament: I Samuel 2:1-10. If children hear in advance that this is a prayer Hannah prayed when Samuel was born, and they hear it read with great feeling, they will catch the meaning of occasional lines.

Epistle: Hebrews 10:11-14 (15-18), 19-25. This lection summarizes the series of readings on Christ as the high priest. To understand it, the reader needs to have understood the previous points about the perfection and finality of Christ's sacrifice, and the function of Christ's blood. Children who have heard these points have lost interest in the whole idea. Those who have not heard them in previous weeks are quickly overwhelmed by explanations of the whole idea on a single Sunday.

Verses 22-25 are more child-accessible. They are a call to gather under the leadership of Christ, our High Priest, to worship, to care for one another, and to encourage one another to be good disciples. Children respond well when this call is illustrated with examples of specific things they can do to answer the call. The Good News Bible offers an easier translation for children.

Gospel: Mark 13:1-8. In their history classes, older children are learning the stories of the rise and fall of nations, and in the process, they often read about people who lived through periods of great change. They therefore are beginning to grasp that some events, which at the time may have seemed like the end of the world, in the long run proved to be only small changes. With this knowledge, they can accept Jesus' insistence that nothing—not even the Temple, or Jerusalem—lasts forever. Only God is forever.

Older children need to hear Jesus' warning about people who claim that they know when the end of the world is coming, or those who say that they are leading God's people toward the final day. Because they will inevitably hear such claims, they need to be told clearly, and in advance, by the leaders of their church, to ignore them.

This text can be paired with Hannah's song, to emphasize the wisdom of trusting only God's love and power.

Watch Words

Speak of God's *loving care,* rather than God's *providence.*

Do not let Jesus' talk of the end of time lead you to speak about the *apocalypse* or *millennium* without explaining the terms.

See previous weeks for notes about *high-priest* terms.

Let the Children Sing

If the focus is on God's providence, highlight the verses about family love in "For the Beauty of the Earth," and enjoy the repeated phrases in "God Be with You Till We Meet Again" and "God Will Take Care of You."

If the focus is on the Gospel, "Hymn of Promise" offers simple words about everyday things like seeds and butterflies.

The Liturgical Child

1. Read the story of Samuel's birth from *The Children's Bible in 365 Stories,* rather than from a Bible translation. While one would not want to make a habit of reading the free translations of storybooks instead of the Bible itself, this particular story is so winsomely told that it helps both children and adults appreciate what happened more fully than does the Scripture.

2. Have a young mother take the role of Hannah, to read Hannah's song with all the feeling tha Hannah expressed.

3. Invite the children to join you as you sit on the steps. Describe how Americans from other parts of the country feel when they visit Washington, D.C., for the first time. Point out that the disciples felt the same way when they saw the Temple in Jerusalem. Just as the tourists are proud and often feel that a country that could build such buildings and monuments will last forever, the disciples felt that the Temple and Jerusalem would last forever. With this background, open the Bible on your lap and read about the conversation between Jesus and his disciples as they looked at the Temple. You may want to conclude with some summary remarks, such as "Nothing but God lasts forever."

4. In the chancel, prominently display a birthday cake with one candle on it. At the end of the service, give each worshiper a cupcake with one candle. (Perhaps an older-children's class could be ready to pass them out.) Suggest that as the cupcakes are eaten, people recall the stories of their birth and give thanks to God for all the ways God cares for them.

5. Offer a responsive prayer to God. A worship leader cites a variety of seemingly hopeless situations, in which God surprises us with powerful, loving care (e.g., an enemy becomes a friend at the end of the Cold War; we find that we can do something we were frightened to try). To each, one the congregation responds:

"There is no Holy One like the Lord!
There is no Rock like our God!"

Sermon Resources

1. Tell the birth dates, and perhaps the stories of the births, of the youngest and oldest members of the congregation.

2. Tell stories of other special births from the Bible: Abraham and Sarah, who thought they were too old to have a baby; Naomi and Ruth, who expected to live out their lives as poor widows until Ruth married Boaz and Obed was born; Zechariah, who was so surprised when he learned that Elizabeth would have a son that God struck him mute until John was born; and so forth. Also recall the "normal" births (such as that of Moses) of people whom God loved and used to raise up God's involvement in all births.

3. Tell stories about leaders who announced that the end of time was coming soon and convinced people to give them all their money. The false leaders promised that the money would be used to save others and that the givers would be rewarded in the new world. While children and adults tend to laugh when they hear some of these, the stories prepare them to evaluate new claims.

Listen as **Hebrews** 10 is read.

Draw a picture of your church building in the △. Then draw or write about one way your church does the activities in Hebrews.

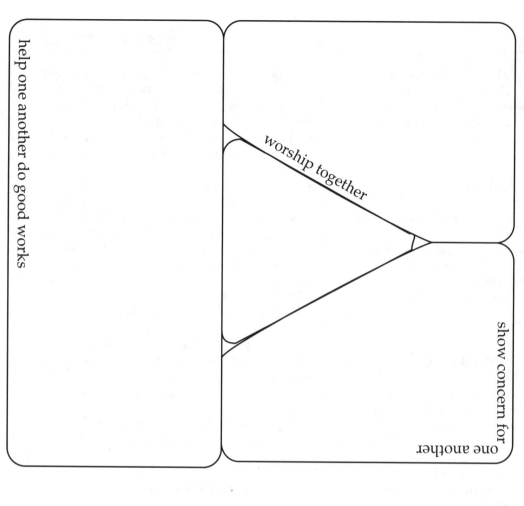

worship together

show concern for one another

help one another do good works

Listen as Hannah's story is read in I Samuel. Hannah talks to God twice.

1. She prays for God's help.
2. Then she sings a prayer of thanks for what God does.

In your worship bulletin, circle all the prayers and songs.

Mark each one with either an **H** for a prayer for help, or **T** for a thank-you prayer.

Write your own prayer for today. Will it have an H, a T, or both?

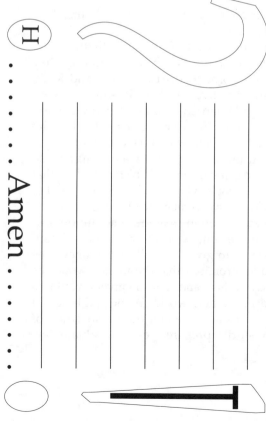

H . . . .

. . . . . . Amen . . . .

PROPER TWENTY-NINE
CHRIST THE KING

(Sunday between November 20 and 26 inclusive)

From a Child's Point of View

Gospel: John 18:33-37. The Gospel lesson announces that Jesus is King, but a very different kind of king from most earthly kings.

Many earthly kings rule all the people who live in an area they have conquered. Their subjects must obey or move away. King Jesus does not force his rule on anyone. He is the ruler of all people everywhere who listen for the truth. His subjects are not forced into his kingdom, but choose to enter it.

The subjects of many earthly kings listen obediently to whatever the king says. They understand that whatever the king says must be obeyed just because the king says it. Subjects of King Jesus have listened to what Jesus says and decided to obey him because they think he is right.

Old Testament: II Samuel 23:1-7. In the context of the day's other lections, David's last words describe good and bad kings, thus offering a comparison to Jesus. David insists that a king (or president) who rules justly and according to God's will is as welcome as the sun that rises on a cloudless day, or that shines on the grass after a soft rain. An evil king is as welcome as sticker bushes that have thorns so sharp they can be handled only with tools and that are burned when they are found. David knows that good kings make such a difference that he says he will die happy with God's promise that his descendants will be good kings and (Christians would add) that God's special king would come from his family. The Good News Bible offers the best translation for children.

Psalm: 132:1-12 (13-18). An understanding of this psalm requires knowledge of David's life, the Davidic covenant, and Zion theology. Few adults and fewer children have such knowledge, and offering detailed explanations in the context of worship on Christ the King Sunday is counterproductive. If you do read this psalm to illustrate David's kingship, use the Good News Bible's translation.

Epistle: Revelation 1:4b-8. John wrote Revelation to be read by groups of Christians hiding out together. It was meant to be read aloud for encouragement and inspiration, rather than studied for detailed information. Because all the poetic images were readily understood by listeners, they provided great dramatic punch. Today, understanding the images in detail requires scholarly study. But when the text is read dramatically, even children grasp its basic point—that Christ is Lord of all. So, instead of dissecting the passage in the sermon, use it in liturgy today to celebrate Christ's kingship.

Watch Words

See the note in Year C of this series about objections to using "King" language to describe Jesus.

Speak of *King Jesus.* Enjoy royal vocabulary familiar to most children—*royal, majesty, rule, decree, obey, subjects.* Avoid or introduce terms such as *reign, monarchy, sovereignty,* and *omnipotent* (especially if you feature the *Hallelujah Chorus*).

Let the Children Sing

"He Is King of Kings" is probably the Christ-the-King hymn children sing with most zest. It may be sung as a congregational hymn or as an anthem, perhaps with a children's choir singing the chorus and an adult singing the verses.

"Come, Christians, Join to Sing," "Rejoice, the Lord Is King," and "When Morning Gilds the Skies" have repeated phrases that make them easy for nonreaders. While the vocabulary of "All Hail the Power of Jesus' Name" makes it impossible for even advanced-elementary readers, the repeated "and crown him Lord of all" can be sung by everyone.

Sing "Joy to the World" to welcome Christ, who is King all through the year. Though they cannot read the difficult words, young readers recognize this carol and enjoy singing it in a different season. (If you sing it today, be sure to also include it at Christmas, and remind worshipers then about singing it today.)

The Liturgical Child

1. Use Revelation 1:4b-8 as the Call to Worship, with three adult worship leaders reciting the verses loudly and dramatically, from three separate places at the front of the sanctuary:

4b-6: Stand behind the communion table. If there is a chalice on the table, lift it high with both hands on verses 5b and 6, making those verses almost a toast.
7: Stand to one side, perhaps in the lectern. Take the role of the messenger.
8: Stand to the other side, perhaps in the pulpit.
ALL: "Let us worship God!"

2. Emphasize the conversation in the Gospel either by turning in different directions and assuming appropriate postures, attitudes, and tones for Pilate and for Jesus, or by turning it into a readers' theater, with narrator, Jesus, and Pilate. Plan ahead for ways to express key phrases vocally and with gestures and facial expressions. Verses 34 and 35 require particular attention.

3. *Prayer of Confession:* Jesus, we claim that you are King, but we are not loyal subjects. We want to get ahead, wear fine clothes, play the sports we enjoy—these are the real kings of our lives! Forgive us.

Lord, we claim that you are King, but we do not obey you. We ignore the rules you have given us, and we follow our own selfish desires. Forgive us.

Christ, we claim that you are King, but we do not serve you, and we do not follow your call to serve others who need our help. Instead, we greedily serve ourselves and our own wants. Forgive us.

Forgive us, and remake us into loyal subjects who do your will so completely that everyone around us will recognize you, working through us. We pray in Jesus' name. Amen.

Assurance of Pardon: Christ did not come to us to be a high and mighty king who looked down on us. Christ did not come to judge us. Christ came to love us and to forgive us and to give us the power to do better. Christ the King is the loving Lord who saves us. Thanks be to God! Amen.

4. Feature the "Hallelujah Chorus" from *The Messiah*, with all its references to the rule of Christ. Before it is sung, compare our feelings when we sing it at Christmastime with our feelings at Easter. Suggest the meaning of singing it on Christ the King Sunday. Print the brief text in the bulletin, and urge children to listen for repeated phrases about Christ the King.

5. See Proper 29 in Years A and C in this series for suggestions about using the section of the Apostles Creed on Christ and the royal phrases in the Lord's Prayer.

Sermon Resources

1. Display one banner for each season of the church year. Use them to review the meaning of the different seasons. Point to different symbols on each one, recalling all the ways we know and worship Jesus. (Consider having the banners carried in and set in place by older children during the opening hymn.)

2. Children's literature offers both good and bad kings to use as examples. Compare the emperor in *The Emperor's New Clothes*, who demanded that all his subjects admire his nonexistent clothes, with Jesus, who is King of truth. Or describe King Arthur, more like the good king that David wanted for his people, who claimed that "right makes might"—not "might makes right."

Use the King's decoder to find a greeting for King Jesus.

Listen for it in Revelation 1: 4-8.

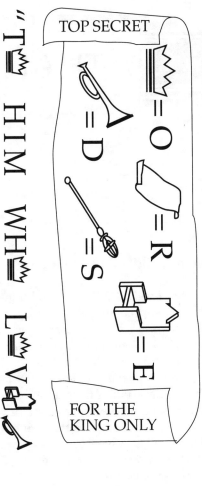

TOP SECRET

◇ = O ◇ = R

◇ = D

♛ = S

◇ = E

FOR THE KING ONLY

"T♛ HIM WH♛ L♛V ◇

"

AN ◇ F ◇ ◇ ◇ U

____

B ◇ ____

GL♛ ◇ Y ____

F ♛ ◇ ◇ V ◇ ◇ !" ____

Copy each of these words that describe a king . . .

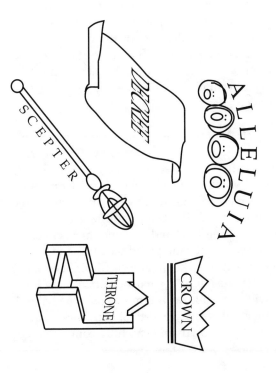

A L L E L U I A

DECREE

SCEPTER

CROWN

THRONE

. . . near the parts of worship in which you hear them today:

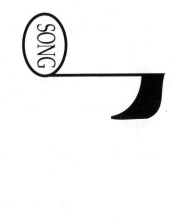

SONG

Proper 29 | © 1993 by Abingdon Press.

THANKSGIVING

From a Child's Point of View

Old Testament: Joel 2:21-27. Before children can understand and appreciate Joel's words, they need to recall the miseries of a locust plague. Suburban American children may have experience with cicadae or gypsy moths. With help, they grasp the difference in the problems such pests cause us and the devastation they cause in areas where people depend on their own farms or gardens for food and live in houses that are not so bug-tight. Many children have read descriptions of insect destruction in stories of the early West, such as *Little House on the Prairie.*

The promise that "you shall know that I am in your midst and . . . am your God" offers an opportunity to alert children to recognize the giver as well as the gift. Children whose needs for food and clothing are met assume this as part of life. Children whose parents have not taught them to recognize the love of the giver that lies behind birthday and Christmas gifts may pay attention only to the gifts. At Thanksgiving, Joel calls us to recognize the Giver—not just name our God-given gifts.

Gospel: Matthew 6:25-33. Worrying is the opposite of showing trust in God. The worries Jesus describes are based on our fears that we will not have what we need. The fearful worries of children tend to take somewhat different twists than those of adults. While adults are worried about providing food and clothing, most children are worried about eating food they like and wearing clothes that make them look all right to their friends. While adults are worried about how long they will live, children are more concerned about how they will grow. Basketball enthusiasts count every inch of growth and carefully compare their growth with that of their friends. Young gymnasts and dancers, on the other hand, worry about growing too big. And all want to grow up to be attractive.

To the children's worries, Jesus says that just as God plans for the birds and plants to grow up right, God plans for each of us to do the same. We are not to worry, but to know that growing short or tall or plain or beautiful is part of God's good plan. The challenge is to find out why God is making us the way we are.

Epistle: I Timothy 2:1-7. Paul offers one more bit of information about God's loving care. God loves everyone. Part of God's plan is that everyone should know God's love and be part of God's loving family. Jesus came for this purpose. Paul is carrying out Jesus' purpose by being a missionary to the Gentiles (telling them about God's love). When Paul's pointed inclusion of even the government officials who were persecuting the Christians is pointed out, children will get Paul's point. If Timothy and his Christian friends were to love and pray for people who were trying to kill them, then surely we are to love and pray for the people (both the individuals and nations) who give us trouble.

Psalm: 126. The transition after verse 3 from the celebration of God's restoration to prayer for restoration makes this a difficult psalm for children to follow. If it is read with great feeling, however, young listeners do catch a few short phrases about God's care.

Watch Words

When speaking of God's *loving care,* avoid long Thanksgiving words like *providence.* Also, remember that, to most children, a *blessing* is mealtime prayer.

Children use the word *worry* rather than *anxious*.

Choose harvest words carefully when speaking to urban children. *Sow, reap, sheaves,* and so forth may be new terms.

Let the Children Sing

Joel called on soil, wild animals, and the children of Zion to join in praising God. Call on still others to join the praise by singing "All Creatures of Our God and King." "All Things Bright and Beautiful" and "I Sing the (Al)mighty Power of God" also highlight God's good plan for nature.

Remember that we no longer can count on public-school teachers to explain the obsolete vocabulary of such traditional Thanksgiving hymns as "Come, Ye Thankful People, Come" or "We Gather Together to Ask the Lord's Blessing." So unless children are learning these hymns in choir or church-school classes, they will be unfamiliar and unsingable. Choose instead "For the Beauty of the Earth," which is both familiar and easy to sing, or "We Plow the Fields and Scatter," which is less familiar but quite singable and uses harvest vocabulary literally.

The Liturgical Child

1. Display two banners—one titled "Look at the Birds"; the other, "Consider the Lilies." They may be simple, of colored chart paper on which children have arranged and glued selected pictures of a variety of birds and flowers. Or they may be adult designs, with birds and flowers cut from a rich variety of fabrics and stitched into place. Children may work with adults on either kind. The banners could be in place at the beginning of the service, or brought in during the processional or Gospel reading.

2. To set Joel's words in context, tell briefly about the great invasion of grasshoppers in this country. Invite worshipers to imagine what it was like as the insects ate everything green in the fields, vegetable gardens, and even flower gar-

dens. Tell about the farmers who tried desperately, without success, to save their crops. Describe the sound of millions of hoppers, munching and flying day and night, and the frustration of finding them everywhere—in your clothes, in your bed, even in your flour bin. Then read the Old Testament Lesson.

3. See Proper 20, Year C, for two prayers based on I Timothy 2:1-7. The first is a prayer trip around the world; the second, a bidding prayer of petitions.

4. In the church's prayer, include children's excitement about trips to visit distant family and friends. Also pray for the patience we need to cope with less-than-desirable seating plans for meals, uncomfortable sleeping arrangements, and crowded back seats on long rides.

Sermon Resources

1. *Ramona the Brave,* by Beverly Cleary, describes the anxieties that beset Ramona during first grade (which also beset other children during other years): a teacher who seems not to like her; sleeping alone in a bedroom of her own; and the fear that her parents love her sister more than they love her. In *The Pain and the Great One,* by Judy Blume, a brother and sister take turns describing each other's worst traits and activities. At the root of their problems is the fear of each of them that they are not getting their share of the goodies because one is not loved as much as the other. Use these incidents as sermon illustrations, or let them remind you of children's worries as you prepare to preach.

2. To illustrate the value of recognizing the giver behind the gift, tell real stories, or remind worshipers of funny commercials in which a family member (usually Mom) becomes sick or goes on a trip, leaving the family to realize how much he or she gives—the food we like, clean clothes, knowing when we need to be where, bedtime stories, and hugs.

Enlarge the world-drawing half of the Worship Worksheet to give children more space to work. Display their drawings on a bulletin board.

Draw a picture of the world God made. Draw in it things you hear mentioned in our Thanksgiving songs, prayers, and readings.

Follow the three letter trails to find three words we use in worship today. In each one omit the letter that is repeated.

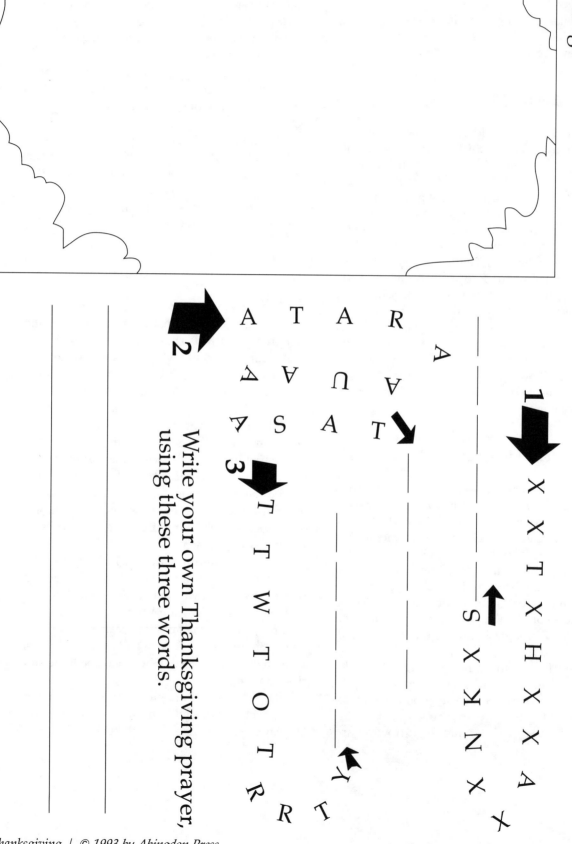

Write your own Thanksgiving prayer, using these three words.

SCRIPTURE INDEX

This index is provided especially for those who do not use the lectionary every week. The page numbers are those on which the commentary for each text appears. Read all the suggestions for the Sunday a text is featured to find the related worship suggestions.

TABLE OF LITURGICAL DATES

Advent Through Epiphany

	1999–2000 B	2000–01 C	2001-02 A	2002–03 B	2003–04 C	2004–05 A	2005–06 B	2006–07 C
Advent 1	Nov. 28	Dec. 3	Dec. 2	Dec. 1	Nov. 30	Nov. 28	Nov. 27	Dec. 3
Advent 2	Dec. 5	Dec. 10	Dec. 9	Dec. 8	Dec. 7	Dec. 5	Dec. 4	Dec. 10
Advent 3	Dec. 12	Dec. 17	Dec. 16	Dec. 15	Dec. 14	Dec. 12	Dec. 11	Dec. 17
Advent 4	Dec. 19	Dec. 24	Dec. 23	Dec. 22	Dec. 21	Dec. 19	Dec. 18	Dec. 24
Christmas 1	Dec. 26	Dec. 31	Dec. 30	Dec. 29	Dec. 28	Dec. 26	Jan. 1	Dec. 31
Christmas 2	Jan. 2	———	Jan. 6	Jan. 5	Jan. 4	Jan. 2	———	———
Epiphany 1	Jan. 9	Jan. 7	Jan. 13	Jan. 12	Jan. 11	Jan. 9	Jan. 8	Jan. 7
Epiphany 2	Jan. 16	Jan. 14	Jan. 20	Jan. 19	Jan. 18	Jan. 16	Jan. 15	Jan. 14
Epiphany 3	Jan. 23	Jan. 21	Jan. 27	Jan. 26	Jan. 25	Jan. 23	Jan. 22	Jan. 21
Epiphany 4	Jan. 30	Jan. 28	Feb. 3	Feb. 2	Feb. 1	Jan. 30	Jan. 29	Jan. 28
Epiphany 5	Feb. 6	Feb. 4	———	Feb. 9	Feb. 8	———	Feb. 5	Feb. 4
Epiphany 6	Feb. 13	Feb. 11	———	Feb. 16	Feb. 15	———	Feb. 12	Feb. 11
Epiphany 7	Feb. 20	Feb. 18	———	Feb. 23	———	———	Feb. 19	———
Epiphany 8	Feb. 27	———	———	———	———	———	———	———
Last Sunday	Mar. 5	Feb. 25	Feb. 10	Mar. 2	Feb. 22	Feb. 6	Feb. 26	Feb. 18

Ash Wednesday Through the Day of Pentecost

	2000 B	2001 C	2002 A	2003 B	2004 C	2005 A	2006 B
Ash Wed.	Mar. 8	Feb. 28	Feb. 13	Mar. 5	Feb. 25	Feb. 9	Mar. 1
Lent 1	Mar. 12	Mar. 4	Feb. 17	Mar. 9	Feb. 29	Feb. 13	Mar. 5
Lent 2	Mar. 19	Mar. 11	Feb. 24	Mar. 16	Mar. 7	Feb. 20	Mar. 12
Lent 3	Mar. 26	Mar. 18	Mar. 3	Mar. 23	Mar. 14	Feb. 27	Mar. 19
Lent 4	Apr. 2	Mar. 25	Mar. 10	Mar. 30	Mar. 21	Mar. 6	Mar. 26
Lent 5	Apr. 9	Apr. 1	Mar. 17	Apr. 6	Mar. 28	Mar. 13	Apr. 2
Passion Sun.	Apr. 16	Apr. 8	Mar. 24	Apr. 13	Apr. 4	Mar. 20	Apr. 9
Holy Thur.	Apr. 20	Apr. 12	Mar. 28	Apr. 17	Apr. 8	Mar. 24	Apr. 13
Good Fri.	Apr. 21	Apr. 13	Mar. 29	Apr. 18	Apr. 9	Mar. 25	Apr. 14
Easter Day	Apr. 23	Apr. 15	Mar. 31	Apr. 20	Apr. 11	Mar. 27	Apr. 16
Easter 2	Apr. 30	Apr. 22	Apr. 7	Apr. 27	Apr. 18	Apr. 3	Apr. 23
Easter 3	May 7	Apr. 29	Apr. 14	May 4	Apr. 25	Apr. 10	Apr. 30
Easter 4	May 14	May 6	Apr. 21	May 11	May 2	Apr. 17	May 7
Easter 5	May 21	May 13	Apr. 28	May 18	May 9	Apr. 24	May 14
Easter 6	May 28	May 20	May 5	May 25	May 16	May 1	May 21
Ascension Day	June 1	May 24	May 9	May 29	May 20	May 5	May 25
Easter 7	June 4	May 27	May 12	June 1	May 23	May 8	May 28
Pentecost	June 11	June 3	May 19	June 8	May 30	May 15	June 4

Trinity Sunday Through Christ the King

	2000 B	2001 C	2002 A	2003 B	2004 C	2005 A	2006 B	2007 C
Trinity	June 18	June 10	May 26	June 15	June 6	May 22	June 11	May 27
Proper 4	———	———	June 2	———	———	May 29	———	June 3
Proper 5	———	———	June 9	———	———	June 5	———	June 10
Proper 6	———	June 17	June 16	———	June 13	June 12	June 18	June 17
Proper 7	June 25	June 24	June 23	June 22	June 20	June 19	June 25	June 24
Proper 8	July 2	July 1	June 30	June 29	June 27	June 26	July 2	July 1
Proper 9	July 9	July 8	July 7	July 6	July 4	July 3	July 9	July 8
Proper 10	July 16	July 15	July 14	July 13	July 11	July 10	July 16	July 15
Proper 11	July 23	July 22	July 21	July 20	July 18	July 17	July 23	July 22
Proper 12	July 30	July 29	July 28	July 27	July 25	July 24	July 30	July 29
Proper 13	Aug. 6	Aug. 5	Aug. 4	Aug. 3	Aug. 1	July 31	Aug. 6	Aug. 5
Proper 14	Aug. 13	Aug. 12	Aug. 11	Aug. 10	Aug. 8	Aug. 7	Aug. 13	Aug. 12
Proper 15	Aug. 20	Aug. 19	Aug. 18	Aug. 17	Aug. 15	Aug. 14	Aug. 20	Aug. 19
Proper 16	Aug. 27	Aug. 26	Aug. 25	Aug. 24	Aug. 22	Aug. 21	Aug. 27	Aug. 26
Proper 17	Sept. 3	Sept. 2	———	Aug. 31	Aug. 29	Aug. 28	Sept. 3	———
Proper 18	Sept. 10	Sept. 9	Sept. 8	Sept. 7	Sept. 5	Sept. 4	Sept. 10	
Proper 19	Sept. 17	Sept. 16	Sept. 15	Sept. 14	Sept. 12	Sept. 11	Sept. 17	
Proper 20	Sept. 24	Sept. 23	Sept. 22	Sept. 21	Sept. 19	Sept. 18	Sept. 24	
Proper 21	Oct. 1	Sept. 30	Sept. 29	Sept. 28	Sept. 26	Sept. 25	Oct. 1	
Proper 22	Oct. 8	Oct. 7	Oct. 6	Oct. 5	Oct. 3	Oct. 2	Oct. 8	
Proper 23	Oct. 15	Oct. 14	Oct. 13	Oct. 12	Oct. 10	Oct. 9	Oct. 15	
Proper 24	Oct. 22	Oct. 21	Oct. 20	Oct. 19	Oct. 17	Oct. 16	Oct. 22	
Proper 25	Oct. 29	Oct. 28	Oct. 27	Oct. 26	Oct. 24	Oct. 23	Oct. 29	
Proper 26	Nov. 5	Nov. 4	Nov. 3	Nov. 2	Oct. 31	Oct. 30	Nov. 5	
Proper 27	Nov. 12	Nov. 11	Nov. 10	Nov. 9	Nov. 7	Nov. 6	Nov. 12	
Proper 28	Nov. 19	Nov. 18	Nov. 17	Nov. 16	Nov. 14	Nov. 13	Nov. 19	
Proper 29 (Christ the King)	Nov. 26	Nov. 25	Nov. 24	Nov. 23	Nov. 21	Nov. 20	Nov. 26	